# The Myth of the Democratic Peacekeeper

# The Myth of the Democratic Peacekeeper

*Civil-Military Relations and the United Nations*

ARTURO C. SOTOMAYOR

Johns Hopkins University Press

BALTIMORE

Johns Hopkins University Press
2715 North Charles Street
Baltimore, Maryland 21218-4363
www.press.jhu.edu

Library of Congress Cataloging-in-Publication Data

Sotomayor, Arturo C.
    The myth of the democratic peacekeeper : civil-military relations
and the United Nations / Arturo C. Sotomayor.
        pages cm
    Includes bibliographical references and index.
    ISBN-13: 978-1-4214-1213-9 (paperback : alk. paper)
    ISBN-13: 978-1-4214-1214-6 (electronic)
    ISBN-10: 1-4214-1213-6 (paperback : alk. paper)
    ISBN-10: 1-4214-1214-4 (electronic)
  1. United Nations—Peacekeeping forces. 2. Civil-military
relations. 3. Peace building—International cooperation.
4. Democratization—International cooperation. I. Title.
    JZ6374.S67 2014
    322'.5091724—dc23        2013016637

A catalog record for this book is available from the British Library.

*Special discounts are available for bulk purchases of this book. For more
information, please contact Special Sales at 410-516-6936 or
specialsales@press.jhu.edu.*

Johns Hopkins University Press uses environmentally friendly book
materials, including recycled text paper that is composed of at least
30 percent post-consumer waste, whenever possible.

*To my family—Elsa, Aure, and Paola—for their unconditional support*

*To my intellectual mentors—Dick Betts and Page Fortna—for their savvy advice*

*and*

*To all my students—at the Centro de Investigación y Docencia Económicas in Mexico City and the Naval Postgraduate School in Monterey—for the many life lessons I have learned from them throughout my teaching career*

# Contents

# Figures and Tables

# Acknowledgments

As I began to assemble a list of individuals who contributed to this book, I realized that I had acquired a very large intellectual debt. I am most indebted personally and intellectually to my academic mentors Richard K. Betts and Virginia Page Fortna. Their superb academic guidance and inspirational teaching filtered my interpretations and understanding of the military, security studies, and peacekeeping. While I will never be able to replicate their academic success and excellent scholarship, I will always look to them for inspiration. Thank you for always encouraging me to aim high.

Like so many other book projects, this one started as a doctoral dissertation at Columbia University and then evolved into a massive, ten-decade-long research engagement. For those intellectually challenging years in New York City, I thank all my professors in Columbia's political science department who influenced my thinking and graciously provided feedback and intellectual encouragement in one way or another. They include Douglas Chalmers, Robert Jervis, Kenneth W. Waltz, and especially Alfred Stepan and Kim Marten.

Numerous individuals read portions of this book in its various iterations and provided constructive criticism. If this book sheds light on the complexity of UN peacekeeping operations and civil-military relations in South America, it is due in part to the many friends, colleagues, and teachers who helped me at various stages. For suggestions on earlier drafts, I wish to thank Naaz Barma, Alex J. Bellamy, Dawn Brancati, Tom Bruneau, Ludovico Feoli, Guadalupe González, Wendy Hunter, Maiah Jaskoski, Kai Kenkel, Kristina Mani, Danilo Marcondes de Souza Neto, David Mares, Covadonga Meseguer, Lara Nettlefield, David Pion-Berlin, Douglas Porch, Maria Rasmussen, Lorena Ruano, Harold Trinkunas, Paul D. Williams, and David Yost. Likewise, I wish to acknowledge Milena Ang Colla, Adriana Crespo, Sergio Galaz, and Valentín Pereda for their research assistance in gathering data and creating graphs and charts.

In this book, I have tried to follow many of the social science qualitative research methods and insights taught at the Consortium on Qualitative Research Methods at Arizona State University (now headquartered at Syracuse University). In particular, I wish to thank Andrew Bennett, David Collier, Colin Elman, James Mahoney, and Etel Solingen for the many insightful recommendations they provided during the year I attended the consortium.

The generosity of several institutions supported fieldwork for the book. I am especially grateful to the Institute for the Study of World Politics, the Saltzman Institute of War and Peace Studies and the Institute of Latin American Studies at Columbia University, the Academic Council on the United Nations System, and the Naval Postgraduate School Research Initiation Program. In 2008, the Center for Inter-American Policy and Research at Tulane University provided me with an office, access to an excellent library, and an intellectually stimulating environment in which to refine my ideas about Latin America's participation in peace operations. In recent years, I have been fortunate to be a member of the National Security Affairs Department at the Naval Postgraduate School, surrounded by colleagues who have given me valuable advice for this project. For this I am deeply grateful.

I have also been extremely fortunate to be supported by a small cohort of friends who have been far smarter and wiser than I. They provided me with a positive outlook, endless patience, and decisive encouragement, giving me multiple cheers during my low days and smiles during my high days. They have become my second family and made the process of writing this book far more pleasant. I am especially thankful to Richard Heffernan, Richard Ingunza, Ekaterina Papagianni, Clarissa Portal de la Cruz, Mariella Rivadeneyra, Alina Rocha, Erika Ruiz, Alex Segura, and Jean Strejan. I have made multiple friends throughout my field trips to South America and Haiti. I thank those who offered me room, board, food, assistance, and enlightening conversations, including Norberto Beltrán, the Delgado family, Rut Diamint, Samuel Remy, and Brian Woolworth. My Bikram Yoga practice has been instrumental in helping me deal with stress and multiple back injuries. Thank you Cindy, Em, and Will for all those sweaty sessions on the mat, where I left behind nearly all of my physical grievances and mental ghosts.

Throughout these years, I have developed a special appreciation for the military profession and for peacekeepers. The peace soldiers I interviewed widened my understanding of peacekeeping by sharing their vast field knowledge on war and peace. The countless blue helmets who agreed to be interviewed cannot be mentioned here by name, but I greatly appreciated their willingness to put up with my endless inquiries. The ideas developed in this book do not necessarily reflect the views of any of the officers or soldiers I interviewed in this project. While I am critical of the effects that peacekeeping has often exercised on soldiers, organizations, and civil-military relations, this book should not be read as a mere criticism of UN blue helmets.

For the book's publication, I thank the editors and staff at Johns Hopkins University Press. In particular, Suzanne Flinchbaugh's editorial guidance, professionalism, and expediency were immensely encouraging. I am also indebted to an anonymous reviewer, whose incisive feedback improved the manuscript. Freelance editors Anna Faber and Janis Higginbotham did a wonderful job of skillfully polishing my prose. Ashleigh McKown shepherded the book through the copyediting process, carefully proofread every chapter, caught many mistakes, and improved my manuscript still further.

I also wish to acknowledge the publishers who granted me permission to use sections and portions of articles and chapters in which I tested preliminary versions of my argument, notably, "Why Some States Participate in UN Peace Missions while Others Do Not," *Security Studies* 19 (1): 160–95, 2010; "Peacekeeping Effects in South America: Common Experiences and Divergent Effects on Civil-Military Relations," *International Peacekeeping* 17 (5): 629–43, 2010, used with permission from Taylor and Francis; chapter 14, "Uruguay," in *Providing Peacekeepers: The Politics, Challenges, and Future of United Nations Peacekeeping Contributions*, edited by Alex J. Bellamy and Paul D. Williams, 2013, portions of which were used by permission from Oxford University Press (FP no. A23750FP, OUP Ref. R28286/mbc); and chapter 2, "Democratization and Commitment to Peace: South America's Motivations to Contribute to Peace Operations," in *South American and Peace Operations*, edited by Kai Michael Kenkel, 2013, sections of which were used by permission from Routledge. This book certainly has shortcomings; those are exclusively of my own doing. The views expressed do not represent those of my employer, supporting organizations, publishers, reviewers, or colleagues.

Finally, as always, there is my adopted and nuclear family; in part, I dedicate this book to them. My students at CIDE and the Naval Postgraduate School are now part of my extended family. Like children of my own, I have seen them grow, mature, and excel academically. In the process, they have contributed to make me a better teacher and human being. And then, of course, I have my unconditional cheerleaders: my mom (Elsa), my auntie (Aure), and my sister (Paola). I spent way too many years away from them, but they have always been close to my heart. My clan has always rooted for me, even when my self-confidence and alter ego were notoriously absent and gloomy. They provided love, made enormous sacrifices just for me, and educated me in so many vital ways. I dedicate this book to them.

# Abbreviations and Acronyms

| | |
|---|---|
| BRABATT | Brazil's Peacekeeping Battalion |
| CAECOPAZ | Argentina's Joint Peace Operations Training Center |
| CARI | Consejo Argentino para las Relaciones Internacionales (Argentine Council on Foreign Relations) |
| CIMIC | Civil-military activities |
| DRC | Democratic Republic of Congo |
| GNP | gross national product |
| ICRC | International Committee of the Red Cross |
| IDP | international displaced persons |
| MINURSO | UN Mission for the Referendum in Western Sahara |
| MINUSTAH | UN Stabilization Mission in Haiti |
| MONUC | UN Mission in the Democratic Republic of the Congo |
| MONUSCO | UN Organization Stabilization Mission in the Democratic Republic of Congo |
| NATO | North Atlantic Treaty Organization |
| NGO | nongovernmental organization |
| OAS | Organization of American States |
| ONUCA | UN Observer Group in Central America |
| ONUMOZ | UN Operation in Mozambique |
| ONUSAL | UN Observer Mission in El Salvador |
| RENAMO | Mozambican National Resistance Movement |
| SINOMAPA | Uruguay's National System for the Support of Peacekeeping Operations |
| UN | United Nations |
| UNAMIR | UN Assistance Mission for Rwanda |

| | |
|---|---|
| UNAVEM | UN Angola Verification Mission |
| UNCRO | UN Confidence Restoration Operation in Croatia |
| UNDPKO | UN Department of Peacekeeping Operations |
| UNFICYP | UN Peacekeeping Force in Cyprus |
| UNGA | UN General Assembly |
| UNGOMAP | UN Good Offices Mission in Afghanistan |
| UNIKOM | UN Iraq-Kuwait Observation Mission |
| UNIMOG | UN Iran-Iraq Military Observer Group |
| UNITA | National Union for the Total Independence of Angola |
| UNMIH | UN Mission in Haiti |
| UNMISET | UN Mission of Support in East Timor |
| UNMOGIP | UN Military Observer Group in India-Pakistan |
| UNMOP | UN Mission of Observers in Prevlaka |
| UNOMIL | UN Observation Mission in Liberia |
| UNOMSIL | UN Observer Mission in Sierra Leone |
| UNPROFOR | UN Protection Force in the Former Yugoslavia |
| UNTAC | UN Transition Authority to Cambodia |
| UNTAES | UN Transitional Authority in Eastern Slovenia |
| UNTAET | UN Transitional Administration in East Timor |
| URUMAR | Uruguay's Maritime Peacekeeping Unit |

# The Myth of the Democratic Peacekeeper

# Introduction

*Myths and Realities of Peacekeepers in Democratic Transition*

Because of the large spike in post–Cold War peace missions, interest in United Nations peacekeeping operations has reached new heights. For most of the Cold War era, there were never more than five UN peacekeeping missions operating at any one time. By the end of 2011, however, fifteen operations were in place concurrently throughout the world. According to the UN Department of Peacekeeping Operations (UNDPKO), the number of deployed "blue helmets" increased from thirty in 1947 to twenty thousand in 1961 to more than ninety-eight thousand by 2011 (UNDPKO 2010a, 2011). Not only has there been a dramatic increase in the demand for peacekeepers, there has also been a radical change in the number and quality of the blue helmets supplied by troop-lending countries. The so-called middle powers—Canada, Sweden, and Norway—no longer provide the bulk of peacekeeping contingents. Instead, most of the top fifteen UN troop contributors are newcomers, with almost two-thirds coming from the developing world, and the majority of these countries are still democratizing themselves.

Despite these overt trends, little attention has been paid to evaluating why states choose to participate in peacekeeping operations and what the consequences of their involvement might be. This book addresses these issues by focusing on how participation in UN peacekeeping operations affects military institutions, especially in states that are still undergoing democratization processes. In particular, it examines states experiencing the immediate aftermath of a regime change, such as a transition to democracy, which is considered to be of interest as the militaries of such states may confront serious challenges to their traditional institutional identities. A growing conventional wisdom in international relations and civil-military studies also argues that peacekeeping engagement may help ease some of these problems by providing the armed forces with externally oriented roles that are more compatible with democratic practices.

The belief that participating in UN peace operations is an unexpectedly beneficial way for states to reform their militaries has become extremely popular worldwide. In 2000, both the *Economist* (2000, 24–26) and the *Washington Post* (Farah 2000, A23) reported that President Bill Clinton's democratization policy toward Nigeria included training and equipping Nigerian officers to be peacekeepers throughout Africa. According to U.S. and Nigerian officials, the training program would "help Nigeria's effort to reform its armed forces," which had been discredited "by long periods of corrupt military rule" (Farah 2000, A23). A decade later, the *Economist* (2010a, 52) further reported that Brazil was using its out-of-country peacekeeping contributions to help "modernize" its army, which had changed surprisingly little since the military dictatorship of 1964–85. Implicit in both of these representative examples is the assumption that peacekeeping "encourages democratization of the military mindset" (*Economist* 2010a, 52), and that it provides soldiers with an international outlook and new ideas about conflict prevention. And yet, despite these claims touting the institutional benefits of engaging soldiers in UN peacekeeping operations, there has been little systematic research on the effects of peacekeeping participation on uniformed personnel.

There are three gaps in our current understanding of how engagement in UN peace operations affects the military. First, little is known about whether or how peacekeeping actually helps democratizing states to reform their militaries. The studies available usually focus on single, positive cases and on anecdotal experiences. They neglect negative cases in which peacekeeping has had either no impact or a negative one. Given the increasing engagement in UN affairs by transitioning states, one would expect that their civilian leaders would have somehow substantially increased or strengthened their authority over the military. That is untrue, unfortunately. There are plenty of cases in which the military has embraced peacekeeping as a new mission, but has also failed to change its institutional practices or the way it relates to civilian authority. In terms of the second gap, our understanding of how peacekeeping affects soldiers from transitioning countries is imperfect. We know little about the conditions in which peacekeeping contributes—or does not contribute—to the reform of armed forces after a transition to democracy. Finally, we do not well understand the perspectives of democratizing states themselves, which tend to be undeveloped and poor and yet now provide the largest troop contributions to the UN system.[1]

## The Argument

In this book, I aim to rectify these three major shortcomings by drawing upon literature regarding international socialization theory and civil-military relations in an attempt to answer three specific questions. (1) Does peacekeeping reform military organizations? (2) Can peacekeeping socialize soldiers to become more liberalized and civilianized? (3) Does peacekeeping improve defense and foreign policy integration?

In addition to understanding how peacekeeping efforts impact participating armed forces, it is necessary to establish whether the effects experienced are the same in all cases—whether the effect is linear and universal or varies in accordance with the case in question. This naturally requires an explanation of the variations in outcomes in order to discover and evaluate whether the relationship between peacekeeping and military reform is spurious. Most liberal theories of international relations contend that states that engage with each other and become members of similar international organizations tend to generate convergence effects; that is, they tend to adopt similar policies and to assume similar practices as they continue to interact. Martin and Simmons (1998, 753) argue that "environmental institutions should lead to convergence of environmental indicators, such as carbon dioxide emissions. Human-rights institutions acting as substitutes should lead members to adopt increasingly similar human-rights practices." In contrast to these approaches, I analyze how international socialization *within* a single institutional framework—the UN in this case—can sometimes lead to divergences in state practices, thereby magnifying preexisting differences, or overriding them. In other words, participation in UN peacekeeping operations can have divergent effects.

I make three general arguments about the divergent impact UN peacekeeping operations have on their practitioners, particularly those from recently and still democratizing states. To answer whether peacekeeping reforms military organizations, I focus on training and mission orientation as a means of measuring military organizational changes. If peacekeeping does affect military organizations, then it should be possible to detect a transformation in the military's overall orientation and training. Armed forces should adopt and embrace more externally oriented missions when they perform peacekeeping, and their training should also reflect a doctrinal orientation. Military missions matter because they have a greater political dimension, particularly because they deal with the relationship of the military with the state. Missions are specifically assigned to military forces, and while these forces may be responsible for a wide range of tasks (from territorial and sovereign defense to antinarcotics, counterterrorism, and antiguerilla tactics as well as intelligence gathering and peacekeeping), certain missions—individually and collectively—tend to define the military's fundamental role within a nation.[2] For these reasons, mission orientation and training offer fertile ground to assess the potentially divergent effects of peacekeeping participation.

I argue that peacekeeping has multiple, varying, and divergent effects on mission orientation and training. The armed forces may embrace peacekeeping as a mission and train their soldiers accordingly, but doing so does not necessarily make soldiers more outward oriented nor change their inward-looking doctrines (which often focus on antinarcotics, counterterrorism, and antiguerilla tactics, as well as intelligence gathering). Following the insights of organizational theories, I contend that military organizations often evade and resist changes that might disrupt normal routines, operations, and standard procedures.[3] Developing new missions is not easy, so when peacekeeping is first introduced, the military will tend to rely on its previous repertoire of missions as a point of reference. It will perform peacekeeping according to its preferred way of doing things. If policing was the military's dominant, preexisting mission, then peacekeeping will most likely be a policing mission, with little or no implications for orientation and training. The armed forces will train their staff to behave in particular ways: "Those socialized and promoted by the organization to do things in a particular way will, in their turn, apply the same criteria to their subordinates" (Posen 1984, 44).

Military organizations will only occasionally sponsor change and reform. If peacekeeping is to be consequential for military reform, then civilian intervention is required. In analyzing orientation and training for peacekeeping, this volume pays close attention to the role of civilian decision makers and their interaction with the military. Democratization can be treated as a critical juncture, where civilian leaders can maximize their leverage to press for increased measures of accountability and control over the armed forces (Trinkunas 2005, 4). Since elected leaders often make the decision to participate in a peace operation, the chances of exerting changes in the military likely depend on the leaders themselves. Peacekeeping effects yield better results on military reform when decision makers and civilian leaders seize the opportunity and use peace operations as means to induce change within the military—initiating, managing, and then using peacekeeping policies to effectively modify military missions, training, and doctrine.

Conversely, military organizational reform will fail when civilian leaders assume a laissez-faire approach, deferring issues on peacekeeping to their military commanders and leaving key decisions regarding organization, training, and even doctrine in the hands of the armed forces themselves. In other words, the key difference in explaining the varying and divergent effects of peace operations is whether decision makers act as active or as passive managers of peacekeeping policies.[4]

Regarding the second question—whether peacekeeping can socialize soldiers to become more liberalized and civilianized—this volume argues that the main causal mechanism through which peacekeeping can exercise a positive, reform-oriented effect on militaries in transition democracies is through socialization, a process by which actors acquire new identities that lead them to pursue new values and interests. This occurs primarily through regular and sustained interactions of military personnel with broader social contexts, structures, and agents such as the UN. However, there is an important caveat to this argument: the extent to which peacekeeping activities socialize participating militaries from democratizing states will depend on the type of mission being performed, as well as the agents with whom the soldiers interact and socialize during their deployment. Peacekeeping missions are not pure, after all. They can include monitoring, state building, policing, and peace enforcement functions, each of which involves potentially diverse forms of social interaction or socializing effects. Given these variable factors, it is important to remember that participation in peacekeeping operations has its most salutary effects when soldiers are socialized to perform tasks that do not resemble the missions they have traditionally performed at home. This usually means participating in peace enforcement operations, where military force helps implement a UN mandate or resolution. In addition, it means performing monitoring duties, where peacekeepers oversee an agreed-upon truce immediately after a civil war or military conflict. Military socialization invariably occurs in peace enforcement and observation missions. Such missions are forms of professional enticement and are therefore catalysts of sociopolitical reform. The soldier who operates in these contexts must become sufficiently flexible to respond to unexpected outcomes, which means that she must develop skills to effectively implement an international mandate. Since the target militaries in this study often do not teach these skills at home, or do so in an imperfect or haphazard way, participation in peace enforcement and observation missions represents potential steps toward downstream institutional reform. Moves to reform these military services enable mission participants to operate with other seconded forces (interoperability), to give and receive logistical and language training, hone their communications skills, and to develop a greater aptitude for general command. Peacekeeping operations–inspired professionalization can function as a mechanism through which poorly democratized militaries redefine themselves, and therefore improve their capacity for self-organization in order to best serve the state.

In contrast, peacekeeping operations that stress state building and policing (also known as peacebuilding missions) do not provide comparable benefits, primarily because they require soldiers to concentrate on ensuring internal security. Since our subject militaries have already been trained and socialized to complete such missions, they hardly qualify as catalysts for institutional reform. Instead, the missions only reinforce old patterns of behavior, and a military's traditional self-perception.

In addition to describing specific type of missions being performed, I argue that the possibility of guiding a military away from undemocratic practices depends on whether participating forces are exposed to armies with healthy traditions of democratic civilian control. The more interaction between democratizing and already democratized soldiers, the more likely that socialization will serve as a form of emulation and persuasion. In other words, the types of agents with whom soldiers socialize in the field are also relevant. Structure and agency matter in determining reform outcomes. Different types of peace missions and interactions likely have divergent effects, both positive and negative, among the peacekeepers studied.

Finally, regarding the third question—whether peacekeeping improves defense and foreign policy integration—this study contends that participation in UN peacekeeping operations does not necessarily lead to greater integration of foreign and defense policies in participating states. Conventional wisdom maintains that participating in peacekeeping operations automatically improves civil-military relations within a state, and that the improvement is attributable to the increased permeability that occurs between civil and military structures, especially when soldiers perform civilian tasks and interact with diplomats and nongovernmental organizations (NGOs) in different fields. In due course, the argument continues, uniformed personnel break free from their national parochialism and become increasingly democratized, liberalized, and civilianized (Moskos, Williams, and Segal 2000; Norden 1995; Palá 1998). To test this perceived process of acculturation, *The Myth of the Democratic Peacekeeper* traces the historical involvement of three countries in peace operations during the post–Cold War era and finds that most military contingents were simply left to their own devices; that is, they performed their peacekeeping functions with only minimal civilian or diplomatic oversight of their decision-making or operational processes. This willingness to respect institutional autonomy, naturally enough, then led to *less* civil-military integration, not more. It is only when foreign ministries assume an active role in their UN contingent's decision-making processes that peacekeeping deployments can be expected to yield higher levels of integration between a nation-state's defense and foreign policies.

To clarify the above dynamic further, this book applies various insights from principal-agent theory to peacekeeping (Feaver 2003), approaching peacekeeping as a form of delegation whereby the armed forces perform different foreign policy tasks and responsibilities. Within this context, a peacekeeper becomes a de facto foreign representative of his native country and the UN. But the only way to ensure that delegated tasks will be performed properly—without the military shirking its responsibilities, or against the desires of civilian principals—is to establish intrusive monitoring mechanisms. Parliaments and other domestic institutions traditionally have the responsibility of developing and applying the monitoring mechanisms needed to screen their military's action. When conducting a mission abroad under the UN flag, however, it is typically the foreign policy establishment that becomes the preferred oversight mechanism for monitoring the military.

Active intervention by the ministry of foreign affairs in the decision-making and operational processes of the military contingent can sometimes establish a positive process for more general military reform. It introduces a mechanism whereby diplomats work as police patrols and fire alarms for the deployed military; that is, they audit decisions and investigate any irregularities. In addition, if diplomats actively monitor their peacekeepers, the probability of integrating defense and foreign affairs policies grows significantly, with enhanced prospects for improved civil-military relations. And yet, as I will analyze in the following chapters, foreign policy monitoring is not easy to accomplish, especially in democratizing countries where the foreign ministry may lack the policy leeway it needs and the actual capacity to rival the military establishment.

## Research Design

Regrettably, survey instruments measuring attitudes toward peacekeeping deployments have never been administered in Latin America, particularly to determine what participating soldiers think about and learn from peacekeeping operations. To analyze the effects of these operations on transitional military institutions, I employ an intraregional, historical, qualitative-oriented approach and apply it to a controlled comparison between the peacekeeping experiences of Argentina, Brazil, and Uruguay. The selection of these particular cases is not arbitrary. A focused comparison offers four methodological advantages with which to improve our understanding of how peacekeeping affects military institutions in democratizing states.

First, the sample of cases includes countries and institutions outside of Europe, where a favorable regional and domestic context overdetermines international socialization trends. The surplus of regional institutions in Europe—including the North Atlantic Treaty Organization (NATO) and the European Union—and the existence of consolidated democracies both lead to a level of policy and interest convergence that overdetermines the effect of peacekeeping. In fact, most available studies on the socialization of transitional militaries have focused on eastern and southern European experiences; little is known about how the process operates on a broader, international scale (Agüero 1995; Checkel 2007). Under such circumstances, it is difficult to estimate whether an effect occurred because of peacekeeping or because of other intervening variables, to include regional organizations and a favorable regional sociopolitical environment. In contrast, we cannot classify South American experiences as relatively easy or as the "most likely" cases of transnational military socialization, since neither area is as highly institutionalized nor fully democratized as Western Europe. In other words, the regional context does not overdetermine the international socialization process itself.

Second, a focused comparison allows for the dismissal of problems pertaining to structural determinism, primarily because the results point to most likely cases within the sample. To support this approach, I follow Eckstein's (1975) methodology of theory testing by choosing the most likely case to which the conventional theory could be applied, but whose outcome is the absolute opposite of the theory's claims. The failure of a theory to explain a most likely case obviously undermines our confidence in the theory itself, which is why it should serve as an important theory-testing case. For instance, Uruguay should be the most likely candidate to experience military reform because it ranks among the UN's top ten troop contributors and is the world's largest per-capita supplier of military peacekeepers. Given the high levels of peacekeeping exposure and participation, it should be possible to see substantial and perhaps positive socializing effects in Uruguay's military institutions. And yet, this book will show, not only has military reform been sluggish, but foreign and defense policy making has remained distinctly segregated. Also, although Brazil has been a major peacekeeping contributor, it has consistently deployed less than 10% of its overall force to UN peacekeeping missions, which is smaller than that of Argentina and Uruguay. Given these disparities, the socializing effects on Brazilian peacekeepers should be less than on nationals of the other countries in our sample, although the integration of Brazilian foreign and defense policies is actually higher than in Uruguay. Finally, for reasons stated below, Argentina is much like Brazil. It, too, should be a "least likely" case for peacekeeping-inspired socialization. It has the smallest armed forces of the three nations examined here and has an obvious diplomatic deficit, given its territorial and diplomatic disputes with most countries in the region and beyond. Much like Brazil, however, it is precisely in Argentina that the socializing effects of peacekeeping appear to be strongest when compared with other similar cases. Again, by providing focused comparisons between non-European states, this study avoids structural determinism and accommodates counterintuitive truths.

Third, by choosing countries located in the same geopolitical region, such as the Southern Cone of South America, I can hold important suspected variables constant—such as culture, geography, or geopolitics—while analyzing the effects on the hypothesized variables. Argentina, Brazil, and Uruguay face similar external threat conditions, so one cannot claim that varying levels of military reform are due to differences in their external or systemic environments.

Fourth, all the South American cases have similar background conditions but show different outcomes, thus approximating a "most similar" case study research design. All three nations had authoritarian regimes in the 1970s and early 1980s, their military institutions had similar national security doctrines and were accused of human rights violations in the past, and all three countries transitioned to democracy in the early 1980s. Similarly, for the most part, they deployed peacekeepers in the early 1990s and have historically comparable levels of peacekeeping participation. South America is an appropriate region in which to analyze peacekeeping issues; its member states have been actively involved in UN peace missions in the two decades since their general move toward democracy. The region's engagement in peace operations began in earnest with Argentina's involvement in UN enforcement missions in the early 1990s, followed by Uruguay's engagement in 1994 and Brazil's subsequent involvement in the late 1990s. Not only have South American countries since increased their troop contributions, they have also been more heavily involved in joint peace operations. To date, almost half of the troops comprising the UN peace operation in Haiti come from South America.[5] Given the above common experiences, the South American countries in our sample represent likely cases for policy convergence. They should, theoretically speaking, adopt increasingly similar reforms in their militaries as well as in their civil-military practices. Yet, as I explain later, the true pattern observed in South America suggests that increased interaction in peace operations has magnified—rather than reduced—their politico-military differences. In other words, the peacekeeping experience has begotten diverging effects; some of our sample countries have been able to reform their armed forces after their peacekeeping experiences while others have not. Consequently, there is extensive variation in the dependent variable across the case studies, which leads to numerous observations over time.

Having just described the four methodological advantages to using an intraregional, historical, qualitative research design, it is important to note that I also use process tracing as a research method to identify the causal chains of how peacekeeping works. In particular, I emphasize turning points, the sequencing of events, and different peacekeeping trajectories. I look at an aspect of military reform, see when it was implemented, and analyze whether it was introduced after a peacekeeping deployment. I also examine critical junctures, such as the initial decision to deploy troops abroad. I then assess whether that event foreclosed certain paths in military reform. If participation in peacekeeping does generate effects, then the timing and sequence of military reforms should follow the peacekeeping trajectories, as well. More generally, I use process tracing to determine whether similar or different peacekeeping paths caused the military reforms in each of the identified case studies.[6] Finally, I focus on several levels of analysis, looking at military-organizational, institutional or bureaucratic, and individual effects.

For this project, I conducted field research in Argentina, Brazil, Uruguay, and at UN Headquarters in New York City between 2001 and 2010. My research enabled me to assess the different peacekeeping trajectories of each of the involved countries over an extended period of time. As mentioned above, time sequences, trajectories, and horizons are particularly relevant for this study, because they enable me to focus not only on short-term events (one deployment), but also on so-called longue durée, or long-term, trends by analyzing how peacekeeping has affected countries during two decades of democratization.[7] I also visited Haiti in 2010, witnessing how the UN implements a peacekeeping operation in the field, while examining the work performed by South American contingents in the area. During these trips, I was able to conduct interviews with over two hundred political and military leaders, NGO representatives, scholars, diplomats, and frontline peacekeepers. I also consulted peacekeeping articles and reports written by peacekeepers and published in military journals. Additional sources of data include conferences, lectures, and documents that were either staged or written by military officers, especially those with peacekeeping experience. Finally, I use UN official records to evaluate the type of military and civilian tasks that the UN Security Council assigned to the blue helmets, testing my arguments and identifying general trends by analyzing where the peacekeepers deployed, what type of missions they performed, and with whom they socialized most.

## Scope and Definitions

This book focuses exclusively on the effects of peacekeeping operations under the UN flag, authorized by the Security Council and performed after 1990. The UN does not have a monopoly on the operation and doctrine of peace missions. To some extent peacekeeping has become a decentralized activity, with other regional and global organizations now performing various forms of peace operations. In recent years the UN has teamed up with various regional organizations, including the Organization of American States (OAS) in the Western Hemisphere, to conduct peacekeeping operations.[8] Some countries have even undertaken ad hoc independent peacekeeping missions.[9] Despite these trends, however, peacekeeping has become a multilateral policy often associated with the UN system. The term "blue helmet" is commonly used to describe a peacekeeper, who most of the time wears a helmet and badge with the UN logo. Focusing only on UN peacekeeping operations in the post–Cold War period helps ensure that this study accounts for the evolving nature of peacekeeping in a more systematic way. Whereas regional organizations have occasionally conducted certain types of peacekeeping operations throughout its sixty-year history, the UN has carried out a broad spectrum of operations, especially since the end of Soviet-American bipolarity. Lindley (2006, 51) rightfully argues that "the UN is the most prominent present-day security regime and its most visible function is peacekeeping." By focusing on the most global form of multilateral peacekeeping, the study can account for some of the regional biases described above, as the UN has universal membership, worldwide reach, and a diverse range of international peacekeepers. We can expect that peacekeepers from South America will have similar UN peacekeeping experiences to those of blue helmets from other regions. Likewise, by centering on the post-1990 period, it is easier to gauge variability in outcomes by holding constant two additional suspected variables—the demise and collapse of the Soviet Bloc and the wave of democratization that emerged in South America.

In this book, I use the concept of peacekeeping to describe the "deployment of international personnel to help maintain peace and security in the aftermath of war" (Fortna 2008, 5). Because I am interested in the effect of peacekeeping on military reform, this study concentrates on operations performed exclusively by military personnel, even though police and civilian components might also be involved.

A working definition of peacekeeping is certainly necessary, but there are different types of peacekeeping. As I mentioned previously, peace missions are not pure—they involve a mixture of military and civilian activities in which the armed forces are expected to perform preventive diplomacy, peacemaking, peacekeeping, peacebuilding, and peace enforcement.[10] For the purposes of clarity and parsimony, this study focuses on observational, multidimensional, and peace enforcement operations.

In observational or monitoring operations, the peace-preserving soldier serves as a military observer for a twelve-month rotation period. She usually (although not always) deploys individually, separate from a contingent or troop, and performs monitoring tasks in a specific site. Some scholars refer to these missions as first-generation peacekeeping operations that "provide transparency and raise the costs of defecting from and the benefits of abiding by the agreement through the threat of exposure, the potential of resistance of the peacekeeping force, and the legitimacy of UN mandates" (Doyle 2001, 532). The peacekeepers who perform these missions traditionally do so by invitation from the host country, while the mandate of the operation is authorized by the Security Council under Chapter VI of the UN Charter.

First-generation peacekeeping operations usually occur after all parties agree upon a military cease-fire and negotiate the presence of military observers. In such operations the UN observer is usually, although not always, unarmed. She performs such activities as monitoring truces between two hostile parties, observing troop withdrawals, facilitating contacts between combatant commanders and governments, and establishing buffer zones to enhance political and military negotiations. The observer's responsibilities further consist of reporting, observing, providing good offices, and conducting fact finding on the status of the conflict (Doyle and Sambanis 2000, 781).

In contrast to observational or monitoring operations, multidimensional undertakings are also known as peacebuilding and peacemaking missions. They can be conducted with the mutual consent of the combating sides, or possibly at their request (although not always). Unlike observational missions, however, they involve the implementation of multidimensional peace agreements. Like observational operations, the Security Council under Chapter VI of the UN Charter authorizes multidimensional missions, except when they are performed without the consent of all parties, in which case Chapter VII might be invoked. Peace soldiers operating within this framework deploy within military contingents or other troops to perform civilian, police, and military activities for a six-month rotation period. Doyle (1998, 6) refers to these operations as second-generation missions where "the United Nations is typically involved in implementing peace agreements that go to the roots of the conflict, helping to build a long-term foundation for stable, legitimate government."

Second-generation peacekeepers typically go to war-torn states that are largely unable to perform the normal functions of a sovereign nation-state. Second-generation peacekeepers step into the power vacuum and facilitate the creation of a security environment that adheres to minimum standards. Officers deployed to such missions must be prepared to face war-like situations, although their charter remains building peace, rather than making war. As Thakur and Schnabel (20001, 13) describe it, a UN multinational force "is prepared for combat action if necessary, and is given the mandate, troops, equipment, and robust rules of engagement that are required for such a mission. However, the military operation is but the prelude to a *de facto* UN administration that engages in state-making for a transitional period."

Establishing demilitarizing zones, deactivating land mines, assisting with the development and formation of new armed forces, safeguarding strategic objectives, providing security to civilians and UN staff, and policing are among the many military activities that peacekeepers perform during multidimensional operations.[11] They can also help maintain law and order in zones of separation, restore social and political structures capable of preventing the renewal of conflict, monitor elections, protect human rights, build refugee camps, deliver food, set up medical facilities, restore water and power supplies, and perform other humanitarian actions (Boutros-Ghali 1992, 32). Not surprisingly, in contrast to observer missions, peacekeepers in multidimensional missions can be lightly armed.

Finally, this book considers peace enforcement missions, or third-generation operations. These missions attempt to enforce an external solution to a conflict by using or threatening to use military force. Controversy surrounds third-generation operations. Some experts believe that peace enforcement actually resembles war making, which then makes it incompatible with the "peaceful" nature of UN peacekeeping. As Doyle (2001, 533) further explains, "peace enforcing missions—which in effect are war-making— . . . extend from low-level military operations to protect the delivery of humanitarian assistance to the enforcement of cease-fires . . . these operations seek to deter, dissuade, and deny." In these scenarios, the UN Security Council usually identifies an aggressor party and then attempts to force the aggressor to undertake an action or to roll back aggression. Chapter VII of the UN Charter, which discusses the actions taken if and when international peace is threatened, authorizes these measures.

In peace enforcement operations, military personnel predominantly perform military activities, to include applying routines, standards, operations, and strategies that are common in military institutions when they prepare for war. Military activities in peace enforcement operations additionally include carrying out international sanctions, establishing no-fly zones, delivering air or missile strikes, localizing sources of conflict, and eradicating armed formations that refuse to cease fighting.

With a definition of peacekeeping and its three forms now in hand, a final definitional-conceptual clarification needs to be made. I use the concept of military reform to describe four factors: (1) transformations in the military's orientation, specifically missions and roles; (2) changes in doctrine, tactics, and training; (3) changes in military professionalism; and (4) transformations in civil-military relations (i.e., enhanced cooperation and integration between soldiers, civilians, and diplomats). I focus on these four innovations or policies because they highlight the relationship between the armed forces' external roles and missions and civil-military relations in newer democracies. In this sense, I focus on just one of the three basic components that make up democratic civilian control, a broad concept that includes the institutional oversight of security agencies (such as police and intelligence), military effectiveness, and military roles and missions.[12] As argued above, different types of missions may socialize soldiers in divergent ways, while the incentives to perform different tasks can lead to equally diverse forms of self-identification. Consequently, this study does not examine security sector reform per se, which is a much broader concept that captures an additional, equally complex dimension of the civil-military relationship. Instead, and among other things, it analyzes the mechanisms by which military and foreign policy come to intertwine (or not, as the case may be) as a result of a military's peacekeeping experiences.

## Broader Implications

*The Myth of the Democratic Peacekeeper* contributes both to international relations theory and to substantive issues in civil-military relations and comparative politics. It not only provides a novel argument about how peacekeeping works but gives further insight about how international factors affect domestic politics. First, this volume contributes to the second image reversed tradition, developed by Gourevitch (1978), which focuses on how the third level of analysis (international system) affects domestic structures (second image or second level of analysis). As Gourevitch (1978, 900) argues, "students of comparative politics treat domestic structure too much as an independent variable, underplaying the extent to which it and the international system interact." Scholars have long debated the influence of international factors on domestic politics in a number of areas, including human rights, trade, military intervention, regime types, and political coalitions. Yet little is known about how international security institutions affect the armed forces of member states. In fact, the second image reversed tradition has not been widely applied to studies on civil-military relations in democratizing states, or on works related to peacekeepers.[13] Through the examination of peacekeeping participation and its effects on democratizing states, this book begins to fill the gap in international security studies on how international variables affect (positively and negatively) the security institutions of democratizing states.

Second, I draw attention to a variable that has received insufficient attention in civil-military relations: the role of externally oriented missions. Scholarship on civil-military relations claims that civilians are more capable of controlling their armed forces when they serve on missions overseas. For authors such as Desch (1999, 12), an environment dominated by external threats tends to menace the whole state but unifies the government and focuses everyone's attention (including the armed forces) outward. An externally oriented mission thus enables civilians to control and manage domestic politics more effectively without having to face the challenge of military intervention or insubordination. In a critical review of the civil-military relations literature, Pion-Berlin and Arceneaux (2000, 417) summarized the externally oriented mission argument as follows: "As the military prepares professionally to face external challenges, it is increasingly preoccupied with matters strictly of a defensive nature, and thus lured away from domestic politics." It therefore makes sense for civilian leaders to emphasize externally oriented missions. Desch (1999, 122) argues, "civilian leaders in these newly democratizing states ought to encourage their militaries to adopt externally oriented, defensive doctrines. The Argentine government . . . has recently been having the military participate in international peacekeeping missions. This is a realistic and beneficial post–Cold War military mission."

The most comprehensive and well-known study about peacekeeping effects on military institutions, Charles Moskos's *Peace Soldiers: The Sociology of a United Nations Military Force*, supported this conventional wisdom. He asserted that additional professional skills were gained by engaging the armed forces in international political crises that could be solved with intervention but did not require war. For Moskos (1976, 137), peacekeeping provides a positive and enhancing experience that "is clearly a progression of military professionalism along managerial lines."

While this volume does not fully question the assumptions and claims made in previous studies in civil-military relations, it does find problems with the relationship between mission orientation and civilian control. It raises concerns about how current and contemporary peacekeeping operations (which have become more complex than those analyzed by Moskos four decades ago) can generate unintended consequences, especially when civilians lose control of the armed forces as they perform blue helmet tasks overseas.[14] The findings in this book raise the possibility that civilian control can be frequently undermined when the armed forces are abroad.

Finally, this study contributes to our understanding of how international institutions affect democratizing efforts. Debates in international relations theory have focused predominantly on whether international institutions influence membership in democratizing states. On the one hand, realists have been traditionally skeptical about the independent role of international institutions. For structural realism in particular, institutions only matter at the margins and are little more than symbols of state power. As Mearsheimer (1994, 7) argues, "realists maintain that institutions are basically a reflection of the distribution of power in the world. They are based on the self-interested calculations of great power, and they have no independent effect on state behavior." Realism conceives of states as actors who rarely, if ever, allow institutions to dictate domestic policies; instead, powerful states determine institutional paths. It is therefore not surprising that structural realists regarded NATO's enlargement in the late 1990s with disbelief, because in their view institutions had no democratizing potential in Europe or elsewhere. Reiter (2001, 67) argued in an article published more than a decade ago that "NATO did not push democratization during or after the Cold War, and there is no reason to believe that it will do so in this decade."

On the other hand, neoliberals and constructivists describe international institutions as independent actors that can shape state preferences, behavior, and identity. For these two schools of thought, multilateral institutions can indeed enhance the democratic processes and norms of its membership, either through cost/benefit incentives or normative discourse and socialization. For neoliberals such as Keohane, Macedo, and Moravcsik (2009, 3), "involvement with multilateral institutions often helps domestic democratic institutions restrict the power of special interest factions, protect individual rights, and improve the quality of democratic deliberation, while also increasing capacities to achieve important public purposes." According to Pevehouse (2002a, 527), "security-oriented organizations can help persuade the military to acquiesce to democratization by not only providing externally supported guarantees, but by helping to reorient officers away from their interest in domestic politics."

For constructivists, institutions often define liberal norms and affect member states by inducing them into the norms and rules of a given institutional community. From this perspective, an institution like NATO played a key role in the reconstruction of central and eastern European democracies, as the alliance first persuaded and then educated its new members to adopt liberal and democratic norms of governance (Gheciu 2005).

This book shifts the debate from whether institutions matter to how they matter—or, more specifically, how they actually affect democratizing states through their multiple and divergent effects. In so doing, it challenges the extreme position that treats international institutions as epiphenomenal, but it also questions the liberal bias that conceives of multilateral organizations as agents of liberalization and democratization. In fact, as mentioned above, international institutions can generate unintended consequences and run counter to democratic norms, leading to different implications for state behavior, preferences, and identities. To argue that organizations such as the UN can have divergent effects on its members suggests that attention has to be paid to institutional variation—why institutions have varying effects. Overall, this book makes a contribution to the study of variation in institutional effects, which has until recently been neglected by conventional international relations theory.[15] At the same time, it is important that a study on institutional variation extends beyond the European and NATO focus that has dominated the international relations literature. By focusing on the UN and its non-European members, I hope to throw critical light on whether the claims of European security institutions, made by realists and liberals alike, hold up to universal scrutiny.

## Structure of the Book

This book is organized into six chapters. Chapter 1 analyzes why democratizing states participate in UN peacekeeping missions. To address whether and how peacekeeping exercises an effect, I must first discuss why states send soldiers abroad, exploring why democratizing states have deployed and continue to deploy their soldiers to various UN peace operations. I argue that democratization provides a particularly powerful impetus for countries to join UN peace missions. In fact, engaging in peace operations confers authority to international organizations that are beyond the rough and tumble of local politics. In so doing, peacekeeping creates a political opportunity and an excuse to engage in reform by relying on international strategies. Although states' motivations to participate in UN peace operations vary substantially from case to case, democratizing states commit themselves to peacekeeping operations for three main reasons: signaling and desire for foreign policy primacy, domestic reform, and monetary incentives.

In chapter 2, I draw upon a detailed historical analysis of why the three countries under study embraced peacekeeping after their democratization. I explore the degree to which signaling, military reform, and economic incentives prompted their involvement in UN peace missions. Argentina is the first case study because, of the three countries analyzed, its theoretical motivations for participating in peacekeeping missions were the strongest; it needed to send positive signals about its intentions to the international community, to take steps to reform its military, and to exploit the financial benefits made possible by peace missions. The second section analyzes Brazil's reasons for participating in UN peace operations, an activity that was largely defined by the need to signal international commitment, prestige, and status. Finally, the third section of chapter 2 focuses on Uruguay, a country whose peacekeeping commitment is driven primarily by economic and salary considerations.

Even if leaders in democratizing states are fully committed to military reform, domestic politics and different forms of socialization in the field are likely to diffuse the effects of peacekeeping. Hence the incentives for states to participate in peace missions are often likely to be different from the actual effects of participation. Chapters 3–6 analyze whether and how peacekeeping exercises an effect on military reform. I devote a chapter to each of the three questions raised previously: peacekeeping and organizational reforms are addressed in chapter 3, the socializing effects of peacekeeping are analyzed in chapters 4 and 5, and the integration of defense and foreign policies is examined in chapter 6. Each of these chapters compares how peacekeeping either did or did not nudge Argentina, Brazil, and Uruguay toward military reform. Chapter 3 demonstrates that peacekeeping has had an impact on the military establishments of all three states, especially in the areas of training and doctrine. Genuine reform of roles and missions has only taken place in Argentina, however, and less so in Brazil and Uruguay.

Chapter 4 highlights how South American troops were first induced and socialized into peacekeeping operations in the early 1990s. While all soldiers served in UN-mandated missions that shared the same institutional framework, the soldiers from each of these countries experienced different types of peacekeeping operations and divergent forms of interaction with multiple actors, which eventually translated into varying levels of socialization. For instance, Argentine blue helmets, who mostly performed observational and peace enforcement operations in Europe, obtained valuable experiences that enhanced their careers, and acquired and developed skills valuable for the military as an organization. By contrast, Brazilian and Uruguayan peacekeepers were sent to various UN peacebuilding missions in Africa and Asia, where their main duties involved policing and internal security functions. This in part resembled their previous mission, which focused primarily on counterinsurgency. The overall effect for these troops was that peacekeeping diluted and even undermined military professionalism.

Chapter 5 provides an in-depth analysis of the UN Stabilization Mission in Haiti (MINUSTAH), where the three South American countries under study played a key peacekeeping role. I demonstrate how professional and integration effects varied substantially among the three countries. Soldiers from Brazil and Uruguay had heavy policing, drug interdiction, and public security responsibilities as part of their peacekeeping tasks. These policing and law enforcement roles generated negative socialization among troops, often leading to serious acts of misconduct and abuse in the mission. But some Argentine soldiers and a handful of Uruguayan troops, who performed mostly peace observing functions, experienced positive forms of socialization and benefited professionally from such an experience. Such mixed results illustrate that a cohort of states may share many common regional features and peacekeeping experiences; however, specific variations beneath these broad commonalities—different types of socialization, varied types of missions, and different forms of monitoring—can lead to a mixed bag of reforms.

Concerning foreign and military policy integration, the news is not uniformly bad. Chapter 6 examines how Argentina (and Brazil to a more limited extent) experienced positive integration trends. Diplomats interacted more actively and cooperated more intensely with soldiers when the defense and foreign policy establishments jointly coordinated peacekeeping missions. Nevertheless, I also show that a deepened involvement of the Uruguayan military services in UN peacekeeping generated the opposite effect, whereby members of the diplomatic establishment were in fact segregated and isolated from the decision-making process.

Finally, in the concluding chapter, I explore the reasons for diplomatic and military segregation by summarizing the findings and discussing the implications for both theory scholars and policymakers. My major finding is that the largest peacekeeping, troop-contributing countries in this study—Uruguay and to a lesser extent Brazil—are the ones that have benefited the least from the experience, at least in terms of military reform, socialization, and integration.

# 1

## Why Do Democratizing States Participate in Peacekeeping?

Peacekeeping has become the UN's key instrument for maintaining world peace and order. Given the prominence of this tool, a significant portion of international relations research has inevitably focused on the relationship between peacekeeping, the durability of peace agreements, and the end of interstate and civil wars (Fortna 2003, 2004a, 2004b, 2004c; Greig and Diehl 2005; Walter 2002; Werner and Yuen 2005). In the wake of this focus, however, little attention has been paid to analyzing why states choose to participate and contribute troops to UN peacekeeping operations.

The Charter of the UN (1945, 28–29) requires all member states to help maintain international peace. Article 43 states: "All Members of the UN, in order to contribute to the maintenance of international peace and security, undertake to make available to the Security Council, on its call and in accordance with a special agreement or agreements, armed forces, assistance, and facilities, including rights of passage, necessary for the purpose of maintaining international peace and security." Despite these obligations, most UN members do not fully meet them. Some states provide financial support to UN peacekeeping operations, while others provide troops. Though both levels of participation (financial and military) are equally important for the functioning and success of this type of mission, only a limited number of states second troops to the field, and their numbers vary. The rest of the UN membership typically abstains. They prefer to "free ride" and enjoy the benefits of a general peace without bearing its heavier costs. Such behavior naturally raises the question of why some states are willing to become regular troop-lending countries and others are not, especially since peace is notoriously hard to maintain among rival states or belligerent groups. For authors such as Fortna (2004a, 10–13), the answer is relatively straightforward. Peacekeeping is difficult to sustain because of the conflicting interests and mistrust that exist between the parties involved in a cease-fire agreement. Fortna argues (2004a, 13), "the cease-fire marks a decision to stop fighting, but this does not mean that both sides now prefer peace to victory, only that they have calculated peace to be preferable to the ongoing costs of war, perhaps only temporarily. There is nothing to guarantee that belligerents are not biding their time, waiting for a better opportunity to resume battle." Moreover, reaching a peaceful settlement might be particularly difficult if the war ended because of international pressures exerted by the UN Security Council.

The fact that peace is so difficult to achieve presents an interesting puzzle for those interested in analyzing the supply side of peacekeeping. If peace missions are so hard to maintain, why would any state want to contribute troops to this type of UN operation? Since war can break out at any time, peacekeepers must be prepared to face serious difficulties, including the possibility of being attacked by belligerent groups. And yet some countries continue to supply troops in support of peacekeeping efforts. So, given the obstacles to peacekeeping, why do states deploy peacekeepers? To answer this question, I empirically analyze who contributes to UN peacekeeping operation efforts and then assess their motives. My analysis shows that a new generation of willing peacekeepers has emerged in the past two decades, and that their reasons for participating in peacekeeping operations differ from those of "old-generation" wearers of the blue helmet. Because a considerable number of the recent participants come from democratizing and transitional states—states with fresh memories of military authoritarianism—it is not surprising that domestic imperatives, monetary incentives, and a perceived need to perform political signaling generally drive their commitment to peace operations. The old cadre of blue helmets reflected their developed-country roots. Their common motivations included national security interests, international system power dynamics, and normative considerations.[1] Identifying and exploring these updated motives is an important preliminary step in this analysis. It serves as a necessary prequel to determining broader outcomes; that is, determining whether participation in peacekeeping missions genuinely transforms the military institutions that perform them, especially those originating from fluid, potentially disorienting democratizing states. Some of the downstream consequences of participating in peacekeeping operations can be anticipated if the states involved specify their motives, including eventually persuading their own militaries to accept and perhaps even promote democratization by first reorienting their attention away from domestic politics.

## Which States Participate in UN Peacekeeping Operations?

Before determining what motivates nations to participate in UN peacekeeping operations, it is first important to analyze who contributes to them. Canada originally suggested that peacekeeping be a UN function as a political measure to preserve cease-fire agreements between two hostile armies. Although the peacekeeping literature is voluminous and internally disparate, a cursory reading of the literature during the Cold War period provides certain recurring generalizations on the core issue of who should theoretically participate in these types of operations.[2] These generalizations can be summarized as follows: (1) major powers are inappropriate participants of peacekeeping because of their geopolitical interests; (2) blue helmets should remain neutral and impartial in local disputes; (3) soldiers from midlevel and neutral powers are more likely to perform peacekeeping missions precisely because of their militarily neutral and impartial identities; (4) peacekeepers must exhibit international or cosmopolitan values; and (5) blue helmets must come from professional armies that provide military and diplomatic training (Diehl 1994; Moskos 1976).

Given these requirements, UN peacekeeping came to rely on a handful of states that provided the bulk of the personnel required. These were mostly middle- or medium-sized powers that were sufficiently developed or industrialized, with midrange military capacity and sufficient diplomatic leverage to meet the requirements at hand. The states that met these criteria included Canada, the Scandinavian nations, Australia, and the Netherlands. Larger developing countries, such as Brazil and India, also provided personnel for a substantial share of peacekeeping operations, but they did little to finance them (Bobrow and Boyer 1997, 742).

A product of its time, early peacekeeping changed once the Soviet Union collapsed. Since the 1990s, UN peacekeeping has experienced a sea change in the frequency, nature, and purposes of its missions. During the Cold War era, for example, there were never more than five missions operating at any one time, while after the first Gulf War there were twelve. Troop levels also increased, both initially and later. While following a U-shaped force-sizing pattern, the total number of military personnel in the field increased from 78,000 soldiers in 1990 to almost 100,000 blue helmets in 2011 (UNDPKO 2011).

Not only has there been a dramatic increase in the demand for peacekeepers, there has also been a radical change in the number and quality of the blue helmets supplied by troop-lending countries. The so-called middle powers, for example, no longer provide the bulk of the UN's peacekeeping contingents. Instead, more than half of the top eighteen UN troop contributors are newcomers, almost two-thirds come from the third or developing world, and the majority of these countries have poorly professionalized armies. And while these troop-lending nations may be diverse in terms of their ethnicity and nationality, the political character of UN peacekeeping is still not as cosmopolitan as one might hope. Recently, for example, three of the top forty peacekeeping contributors have been major military powers: France, the United Kingdom, and China. They are also permanent members of the Security Council, which in the old peacekeeping model might have raised questions about their neutrality and impartiality. Additionally, in some cases, the top troop contributors have been regional powers with enduring rivalries, such as India-Pakistan, Argentina-Brazil, and Nigeria–South Africa, or they have been at the receiving end of UN peacekeeping operations, including India, Pakistan, Jordan, Ethiopia, Nepal, and Namibia. What these various permutations confirm is that there is a "before" and "after" to the story of UN peacekeeping operations. In the former case, the UN depended on middle-range powers that had sufficient economic and military weight to be taken seriously as agents of stability, but who were also sufficiently limited in their power to avoid the taint of great power meddling when performing peacekeeping operations. In the post–Cold War environment, the top contributor nations come from the developing world, offer up militaries of varying professional quality, and operate in an environment in which the desired neutrality and impartiality of the past, if not compromised, have increasingly overlapped with the nation-state political dynamics of the UN at large. That said, are the latter dynamics the coherent expression of coherent states?

Among the top sixty-eight peacekeeping contributors in the UN, a significant number have transitioned from authoritarian to democratic rule relatively recently and are therefore still in the process of consolidating their gains. Such is the case for Argentina, Brazil, Namibia, Nepal, Nigeria, the Philippines, Poland, Slovakia, South Africa, South Korea, Ukraine, and Uruguay. These countries have been part of the so-called third or fourth wave of democratization, which has often been explained in terms of international contagion or "demonstration effects."[3] The process started with Portugal and Spain in 1974, and within a decade was followed by five South American nations (Argentina, Bolivia, Brazil, Ecuador, Peru, and Uruguay). Next came Chile and Paraguay in 1988. The wave of democratization then expanded to eastern Europe in 1989—with Bulgaria, Czechoslovakia, East Germany, Hungary, Poland, and Romania joining the list—and crested with the democratization of Namibia, Nigeria, and South Africa in the 1990s. All of these countries now participate in UN peacekeeping activities in one form or another, as shown in table 1.1. Their levels of participation vary from case to case, but many democratizing states are among today's top troop-lending countries in the UN.

## Why Do Some Democratizing States Participate in Peacekeeping?

Peacekeeping, as defined in the Introduction, refers to any international effort that promotes the termination of armed conflict or the resolution of long-standing disputes with the deployment of military personnel (Diehl 1994, 4–5; Fortna 2008, 5).[4] But it is a process that usually takes place within an institutional framework. In the UN system, countries involved in peace missions have developed institutionalized practices that include regular meetings between troop providers, the crafting of rules of engagement, the formalization of codes of conduct, and the codification of institutional procedures for deployment and reimbursement. To some extent, countries that participate in peacekeeping become members of a special UN club. But why do some states participate in peacekeeping? Even more specifically, why do democratizing states want to become active members of the UN peacekeeping system? The traditional literature on international organizations has tended to describe international institutions as facilitators of cooperation, in which membership enables states to discuss, bargain, negotiate, and reduce their transaction costs (Keohane 1993; Lake 2001). Yet little attention has been paid to analyzing how domestic imperatives drive membership of particular international institutions—how domestic politics influence and shape the propensity of states to join and then support international bodies.

Mansfield and Pevehouse (2006) have conducted the most direct analysis of political democratization and international organization membership. They found that a drive for ongoing democratization is an especially potent impetus behind states that join international institutions, especially because these types of states have a difficult time sustaining the liberal reforms needed to consolidate their own democracies. Democratization is often an uncertain

| Ranking | Country | Committed troops | Ranking | Country | Committed troops |
|---|---|---|---|---|---|
| **Tier 1: Top 18 contributors, 90,000–10,000 troops** | | | | | |
| 1 | Pakistan | 84,818 | 10 | Kenya | 15,474 |
| 2 | Bangladesh | 85,579 | 11 | Senegal | 15,061 |
| 3 | India | 66,053 | 12 | South Africa | 14,616 |
| 4 | Nigeria | 41,734 | 13 | Egypt | 13,511 |
| 5 | Jordan | 31,444 | 14 | Morocco | 12,618 |
| 6 | Ghana | 30,634 | 15 | Italy | 12,082 |
| 7 | Nepal | 29,555 | 16 | China | 11,992 |
| 8 | Uruguay | 20,934 | 17 | France | 11,865 |
| 9 | Ethiopia | 17,392 | 18 | Rwanda | 11,008 |
| **Tier 2: Top 19–68 contributors, 9,999–1,000 troops** | | | | | |
| 19 | Ukraine | 9,727 | 44 | Republic of Korea | 3,470 |
| 20 | Brazil | 9,614 | 45 | Guinea | 3,276 |
| 21 | Poland | 8,944 | 46 | Togo | 3,169 |
| 22 | Argentina | 8,633 | 47 | Namibia | 3,109 |
| 23 | Zambia | 7,470 | 48 | Thailand | 3,081 |
| 24 | Benin | 7,208 | 49 | Bolivia | 2,950 |
| 25 | Indonesia | 6,519 | 50 | Canada | 2,861 |
| 26 | Sri Lanka | 6,519 | 51 | New Zealand | 2,170 |
| 27 | Philippines | 6,293 | 52 | Finland | 2,106 |
| 28 | Australia | 6,213 | 53 | Romania | 2,097 |
| 29 | Spain | 6,103 | 54 | Sweden | 1,875 |
| 30 | Austria | 6,061 | 55 | Burkina Faso | 1,744 |
| 31 | Portugal | 5,563 | 56 | Japan | 1,717 |
| 32 | Germany | 5,240 | 57 | Gambia | 1,704 |
| 33 | United Kingdom | 5,198 | 58 | Tanzania | 1,666 |
| 34 | Malaysia | 4,783 | 59 | Peru | 1,642 |
| 35 | United States | 4,723 | 60 | Belgium | 1,603 |
| 36 | Turkey | 4,528 | 61 | Guatemala | 1,503 |
| 37 | Ireland | 4,279 | 62 | Mongolia | 1,447 |
| 38 | Tunisia | 4,225 | 63 | Netherlands | 1,446 |
| 39 | Fiji | 4,219 | 64 | Hungary | 1,386 |
| 40 | Slovakia | 3,842 | 65 | Malawi | 1,145 |
| 41 | Niger | 3,735 | 66 | Denmark | 1,143 |
| 42 | Chile | 3,688 | 67 | Zimbabwe | 1,119 |
| 43 | Russia | 3,506 | 68 | Cameroon | 1,046 |
| **Tier 3: Top 69–100 troop contributors, 999–100 troops** | | | | | |
| 69 | Norway | 975 | 72 | Bulgaria | 833 |
| 70 | Mali | 962 | 73 | Yemen | 683 |
| 71 | Greece | 840 | 74 | Uganda | 667 |

Table 1.1.   (continued)

| Ranking | Country | Committed troops | Ranking | Country | Committed troops |
|---|---|---|---|---|---|
| 75 | Singapore | 655 | 88 | Switzerland | 346 |
| 76 | Croatia | 625 | 89 | Kyrgyzstan | 345 |
| 77 | Cambodia | 622 | 90 | Chad | 255 |
| 78 | Ecuador | 550 | 91 | Samoa | 248 |
| 79 | Paraguay | 532 | 92 | Slovenia | 243 |
| 80 | Cote d'Ivoire | 490 | 93 | Qatar | 239 |
| 81 | Bosnia and Herzegovina | 473 | 94 | Algeria | 238 |
|  |  |  | 95 | Djibouti | 232 |
| 82 | El Salvador | 440 | 96 | Serbia and Montenegro | 188 |
| 83 | Guinea Bissau | 437 |  |  |  |
| 84 | Sierra Leone | 411 | 97 | Burundi | 176 |
| 85 | Mozambique | 386 | 98 | Madagascar | 175 |
| 86 | Vanuatu | 360 | 99 | Honduras | 131 |
| 87 | Czech Republic | 351 | 100 | Jamaica | 112 |

Tier 4: Top 101–131 contributors, 99–1 troops

| Ranking | Country | Committed troops | Ranking | Country | Committed troops |
|---|---|---|---|---|---|
| 101 | Albania | 95 | 116 | Iran | 16 |
| 102 | Central African Republic | 95 | 117 | Timor-Leste | 15 |
|  |  |  | 118 | Libya | 15 |
| 103 | Moldova | 80 | 119 | Mauritania | 14 |
| 104 | Lithuania | 76 | 120 | Venezuela | 11 |
| 105 | Colombia | 54 | 121 | Granada | 9 |
| 106 | Democratic Republic of Congo | 46 | 122 | Lebanon | 8 |
|  |  |  | 123 | Cyprus | 7 |
|  |  |  | 124 | Palau | 6 |
| 107 | Gabon | 42 | 125 | Kazakhstan | 6 |
| 108 | Dominican Republic | 29 | 126 | Luxembourg | 5 |
|  |  |  | 127 | The former Yugoslav Republic of Macedonia | 5 |
| 109 | Botswana | 27 |  |  |  |
| 110 | Mauritius | 25 |  |  |  |
| 111 | Estonia | 23 |  |  |  |
| 112 | Iceland | 21 | 128 | Israel | 4 |
| 113 | Lesotho | 20 | 129 | Cape Verde | 3 |
| 114 | Brunei | 18 | 130 | Yugoslavia | 1 |
| 115 | Tajikistan | 18 | 131 | Honduras | 1 |

Note that the UN does not report a yearly ranking of troop contributions to its operations. Instead, it reports monthly data on the size of individual peacekeeping activities. The data in this table represent the sum of a yearly average for all countries' monthly contributions to UN peacekeeping operations, including troops, military observers, and police from 2000 to 2010. Data were obtained from UNDPKO (2010a) reported statistics.

process involving "undetermined social change, large-scale transformations which occur when there are insufficient structural or behavioral parameters to guide and predict the outcome" (O'Donnell and Schmitter 1986, 6). Political actors can change from one election to another, and in such circumstances there is no guarantee that domestic arrangements or *pacta sunt servanda* (treaties and obligations) will be respected.

Uncertainty is the defining characteristic of democratization. And the strategic choices of key actors—the supporters and opponents of the incumbent government—initially shape that uncertainty. Their agendas often collide with each other, and they do not always have the mechanisms needed to help resolve their disputes. Uncertainty is also shaped by the national-level context. The opportunities that political elites have to mobilize support for democratization, for example, will be greatly shaped by the broader structures that are in place, however transitional they may or may not be. Economic context influences transitions to democracy, where the failure to adjust to economic crises increases the incentives to oppose the regime, thereby making democratization potentially more likely but also more uncertain (Haggard and Kaufman 1995, 7).

Ironically, the instability that is endemic in democratization provides a strong incentive for politicians, especially liberals or pro-reformers, to seek out international support. As agents of democratization, they rightfully perceive international institutions a useful tool, if not an outright scapegoat protector. Local leaders know that it is difficult, perhaps too difficult, to achieve democratic reforms on their own. Why not transfer, or delegate, a degree of authority to an appropriate international institution that is relatively insulated from domestic political influences and that has policy preferences of its own (Martin and Simmons 1998, 752–53). That these preferences are often progressive is all to the good, or so politicians often feel.

To illustrate this gambit, one might consider Andrew Moravcsik's argument that international human rights regimes are often most strongly supported by those democratizing states that most fear political instability: "by alienating sovereignty to an international body, governments may be able to establish more reliable judicial constraints on future non-democratic governments or . . . on future democratically-elected governments that seek to subvert democracy from within" (Moravcsik 2000, 217).

By way of analogy, participating in UN peacekeeping operations is no different for democratizing states than conferring authority to international organizations that are beyond the rough and tumble of local politics. I contend that a key impetus to join UN peace missions originates in the selfsame domestic political arena and that, in doing so, the democratizing nation fulfills three ends: signaling its intentions to both foreign and domestic actors, enhancing domestic reforms, and providing economic benefits during periods of uncertainty.

## Peacekeeping as an External and Internal Tool for Political Signaling

The ability to make credible commitments is central to the process of foreign policymaking. It is a core requirement for a reliable state. Democratizing states unfortunately find it particularly difficult to signal their intentions, for an obvious reason: the general uncertainty about the future of the government in place. Those who put faith in the international commitments of a democratizing state must account for the possibility that a new leader or regime will reject the policies and agreements made by their predecessors. Unlike democratic regimes, which possess stable institutions and well-regulated mechanisms for the transfer of power, democratizing states confront serious challenges in ensuring institutional, political, and policy-centered continuity. Likewise, the absence of consolidated democratic institutions means that there is less transparency in the decision-making process, making it even more difficult for insiders and outsiders to put their faith in transitioning states (Gaubatz 1997, 27–65; Morrow 1999, 77–114).

From this perspective, participation in UN peacekeeping operations can help democratizing states overcome some of the structural and self-inflicted obstacles they face in committing themselves to international agreements. Engagement in peace operations, in other words, can be positively instrumental. It can help a democratic work in progress assert its dependability to a wary international audience by clarifying the direction in which the country is heading. A peacekeeping commitment basically sends a signal that a seismic shift has taken place within the political culture of the state, and that the shift is long term (Pevehouse 2002b, 613–14). A commitment to becoming a troop-lending nation is essentially a marker for the future. The feckless self-image created by a previously authoritarian past no longer applies, as illustrated by the reliable measures and policies now being pursued. The commitment further demonstrates that the democratizing state does not need to keep its troops at home— either to maintain domestic order or to avoid charges of external human rights violations by hostile media "waiting in the wings" or NGOs. For these and other reasons, democratizing states with limited peacekeeping experience have been tempted to glom onto the UN peacekeeping system in order to show to the rest of the world that an irreversible domestic change in their political cultures has occurred.

In addition, the type of political signaling just described is not only valuable in an international setting but also helps reshape national identities, which is particularly important for countries with an authoritarian past. They, and the political cultures they represent, never experience a "clean" death. There is no tidy "before and after." Instead, there is messy overlap. New political practices appear, but past authoritarian practices, dispositions, memories, mythologies, and even obsessions linger on. But reorienting one's foreign policy can hasten the demise of these political pathologies and shore up the internal legitimacy of new transitional democracies (Pridham 1995, 166–203). A state-level commitment to UN peacekeeping thus represents a "twofer." It announces a state's seismic political shift not only to an international audience but to an internal one, as well. It represents, in short, an overt distancing from the external and internal authoritarian patterns of the past. It declares from a constructivist point of view that the state is building a new identity that permits future access to additional international organizations or security communities in which democratic practices are the norm. Additionally, a new domestic political identity will help nudge an authoritarian past further into history.[5]

## Peacekeeping as an Accelerator for Domestic Reform

In discussing the domestic political dynamics of being a UN troop provider, the previous section focused on one issue: the identity-transforming benefits of signaling a political intention to change. There are other domestic benefits to be had, including the reform of civil-military relations. This particular reform is not easy. Because the political institutions of a transitional state are often too divided and weak to push through necessary domestic reforms, their military counterparts have been known to wrest a high degree of institutional autonomy as a condition for their returning to their barracks (Stepan 1988a). The victim of this drive to preserve or expand military domains and prerogatives—if it has not been "victimized" already—is the creation and consolidation of a national democratic consensus (Agüero 1992, 153–98). Absent this consensus, the state may find it difficult to achieve reforms through unilateral action. As a solution to this problem, the democratizing state may want to turn to international institutions, such as the UN, and use them as much-needed catalysts to resolve this core problem.

By elevating their domestic policymaking process to the international level, the leaders of democratizing states can at least in part try to avoid political paralysis by borrowing the trade space they need to carry out a portion of their reform agenda.[6] Yes, they are once again making international organizations instrumental to achieve benefits that are unavailable through unilateral domestic action. Doing so, however, offers additional enticements—the act of joining an international organization comes with rights and responsibilities. By committing to international treaties and norms, political leaders in transitional states can deliberately tie their hands in such a way that domestic actors are forced to comply with external demands while also increasing the costs of reverting to previous policies. Reform can take place by transferring some degree of policymaking to an international institution that is insulated from domestic influence (Mansfield and Pevehouse 2006; Martin and Simmons 1998). UN peacekeeping operations, although not sufficient unto themselves, nevertheless provide three useful arrows in the quiver of pro-democracy civilian elites who are keen for military reform to occur.

First, a democratizing state may perceive international peacekeeping as an opportunity to restructure at least some of its military's traditional roles and missions, if not outright chip away at its old authoritarian doctrine of internal national security. Under such a doctrine, the armed forces must perform numerous public order and enforcement functions, including anti-drug and narcotics campaigns, the control of labor protests and strikes, peasant land seizures, counterinsurgency, and other civic action and development functions.[7] For a transitional state, peacekeeping provides an opportunity to reorient its army away from internal roles and toward external ones. Transferring soldiers abroad is thus part of a diversionary strategy. It preoccupies the military with events and security concerns occurring outside their own country. It also provides civilian elites with the added political space they need to pursue internal democratization, while not being unduly menaced by a military overly preoccupied with national security. As an added bonus, exploiting this political space may help further accelerate military reform, primarily by increasing civilian decision making and security-related oversight.

As argued in the Introduction, scholars of civil-military relations have argued that civilians are better able to tether their armed forces when the latter's attention is centered on external missions. Desch (1999, 122) finds that, in order to ensure military subjugation to civilian rule in peacetime, civilian politicians must encourage their armed forces to adopt externally focused missions, such as peacekeeping.[8]

Second, civilian leaders in democratizing states may conclude that performing peacekeeping operations will change their soldiers' professional self-image through international socialization. UN peacekeeping is a service provided by a donor country, as well as a schoolhouse where a democratizing state's armed forces learn to internalize new roles, doctrines, and social norms. One of these core norms is allegedly adherence to democratic principles, including civilian control over the military. The leaders of transitional states hope (if not outright expect) that international socialization will help persuade the best and brightest members of their military to accept civilian democratic oversight as a natural norm, either by observing the example set by their colleagues or by formal training and education. As Pevehouse (2002a, 528) notes, "regional alliances and military organizations, especially those that conduct joint training operations or maintain permanent institutions, such as NATO, can help socialize military leaders in member states as to the [proper] role of the military in domestic society." While the empirically proven effects of international socialization have yet to be established, the current generation of democratizing states that provide peacekeeping may have been inspired to action by the relative success that multinational institutions like NATO had on military reform efforts in Spain, Portugal, and eastern Europe. In these cases, NATO aggressively indoctrinated deep state militaries to embrace democratic norms and rules through Alliance Membership Action Plans and the Partnership for Peace Program. Through these programs, thousands of officers from former Communist countries stationed abroad received training and instruction on NATO's norms and doctrines (Agüero 1995; Gheciu 2005; Pevehouse 2002b). Although the UN system does not have institutionalized programs as extensive as NATO's for its blue helmets, multiple programs and centers offer peacekeeping training, which is then reinforced through socialization in the field.

Third, civilian leaders in transitional societies may commit themselves to peacekeeping functions, not only to redirect their military away from undesired roles and missions, or to change their soldiers' professional self-image, but also to reduce the policy influence of military commanders by increasingly interjecting themselves into doctrinal debates. For some democratizing states, peacekeeping participation provides this opportunity. It promises civilian leaders to integrate defense and foreign policies while simultaneously arguing that their military broadens their skill set. Noted military sociologist Charles Moskos argued as much in his 1976 study of European peacekeepers, which demonstrated that armed forces accrued additional professional skills by resolving crises through interventions rather than war. The benefits of these added, real-life capabilities, Miller (1997, 447) later argued, "outweigh the temporary deterioration of some combat skills, particularly in the broader political sphere." If the military focuses on external challenges, whether on its own or as a result of civilian prodding, the coordination and cooperation inevitably required of politicians and generals will lead to the greater integration of defense and foreign policies. Such integration in turn nudges military and diplomatic agents to work together not only to identify common national goals but also to open up military doctrine development to civilian influence. These ends can be achieved through ministerial meetings, dual committees, and by appointing attachés to military and diplomatic posts, although they are mostly acquired through the delegation of power and the establishment of delicate oversight systems designed to meet the expectations of principal politicians (Mares 1998, 6–9).

As discussed earlier, using peacekeeping operations as a vehicle to integrate civil-military policies, and the way in which they are formulated, parallels how they are used for international signaling. The extent to which political signaling is successful will depend on how well integrated a nation's foreign and defense policies have become. Theoretically speaking, a transitional state should be better able to signal its intentions when its leaders speak with one voice, meaning that military and diplomatic preferences must be well coordinated, aligned, and thus integrated.

A note of caution is in order. There is no intrinsic reason why the armed forces should acquiesce to civilian control because they are engaged in peacekeeping. The following chapters discuss how participation in peacekeeping operations can lead to a number of unintended and even divergent consequences, even while democratizing states participate in UN peace missions in order to induce domestic military reforms through foreign policy commitments and pressures. What I intend to reveal here are the potential incentives that peacekeeping offers to democratizing states; that is, why transitional countries commit troops to UN peace efforts (Sotomayor 2010a).

### Peacekeeping as a Monetary Incentive

If performing peacekeeping functions permits a transitional state to send clear political signals both externally and internally, and if it helps the state to accelerate possible domestic reforms—particularly in its own military—it also can provide monetary incentives. Budgetary politics play a role in shaping the incentives to participate in peacekeeping operations. The UN General Assembly (UNGA) approves a peacekeeping budget every other year to sustain its multiple peace missions around the world. In 2009, the adopted budget reached an unprecedented $7.8 billion for the period between July 1, 2009, and June 30, 2010. This amount, which provided the financial resources needed to sustain fourteen peacekeeping operations, came directly from state contributions, of which the United States was the biggest donor, followed by Canada, China, France, Germany, Italy, Japan, Mexico, the Netherlands, South Korea, Spain, and the United Kingdom (UNGA 2009). These contributions were then used to pay troop-lending countries, which finally remunerated their own deployed troops and police forces according to their national rank and salary scales.

UN reimbursement policies for military personnel, however, distinguish between troops; that is, members of units, such as battalions or infantry groups, and military observers, who are officers usually seconded by their country and deployed to peace missions individually. The UN pays an allowance rate, along with any supplementary payments for troops, which the UNGA standardizes and approves. The current monthly rate of pay for troops is $1,028 per soldier, including $68 for personal clothing, gear, and equipment and $5 for personal weaponry. The rate for observers is allocated by a per-diem system that varies from mission to mission. It also factors in such variables as the threat level faced, costs of living, and travel expenses within the area of operation. Depending on his level of seniority and the mission in question, a military observer can earn from $2,500 to $6,500 per month. According to the UNDPKO, the approved peacekeeping budget represents only 0.5% of global military spending and is thus far cheaper than other options, such as unilateral intervention.[9]

The UN also reimburses member states for the use and depreciation of their own equipment during a peacekeeping operation. The organization defines contingent-owned equipment as "major and minor equipment and consumable[s] owned or leased, and operated by a troop-contributing country's contingent in the performance of peace-keeping operations" (Abraszewski et al. 1995, 20). Major equipment consists of ground vehicles and trailers, aircraft, naval vessels, and specifically identified "stand-alone" specialist equipment. Minor equipment includes that used for catering, accommodations, nonspecialist communications, and engineering. Unfortunately, the reimbursement process in place for the use and depreciation of equipment is slow, and it often takes years to work its way through the UN system.

While the approved UN peacekeeping budget amounts to a mere 0.5% of the world's military spending, and the allowances paid to soldiers are perhaps too low for developed countries, some states do profit from UN peacekeeping budgeting, both from a financial and institutional reform standpoint (Jackson 2007). In fact, the availability of financial resources for military purposes can be irresistible for democratizing states that face budgetary reductions and diminished expenditures. This problem is especially acute for militaries that held political power for a long time but were unable to sustain their budgetary autonomy as a quid pro quo for returning to their barracks. Under such conditions, civilians and politicians alike have typically withheld funds to punish the armed forces for past abuses. Finally, the return of election cycles and congressional politics means that defense budgets will be subjected to increased public scrutiny and competition for resources.[10] As Hunter (1997, 96) points out, "electoral competition gives politicians virtually irresistible incentives to attract voters through patronage. In order to finance these 'goodies,' they need to claim resources, even at the expense of the military." In fact, this effort to guarantee electoral success compels even those politicians who do not have any particular aversion to the armed forces to reduce their share of the budget.

Whatever the reasons for them, reduced military expenditures and budgets may be welcome news to liberals and democrats, but they can also fuel civil-military tensions, thereby leading to increased levels of uncertainty in states undergoing democratic transitions. In response to budgetary cuts, for example, the military may refuse to do their work, fail to conduct their normal missions as ordered, or even conduct missions more intensively than instructed, all of which lead to less civilian control.[11]

Participation in peacekeeping operations may not necessarily eliminate all of the above challenges to democratization, but it does provide an incentive to use such operations as a source of income for the military. First, depending on the level of national income and military spending, democratizing states can use peacekeeping resources to cover individual military salaries. As mentioned above, the UN will reimburse member states for their peacekeeping costs, with the exception of military observers who are paid directly on a per-diem basis. This means that each troop-lending contributor is responsible for designing a reimbursement system for its troops. Some countries pay all the UN funding directly to their blue helmets, distribute it evenly among its troops at home, allocate it to their defense budget, or add funding in order to provide compensation for overall peacekeeping costs. Ultimately, however, participation in peacekeeping operations increases military salaries. Second, the incentive to earn money in a foreign currency can motivate troops and can even help recruit capable young men into the armed forces. Finally, UN reimbursements offer resources, however minimal, to sustain operational costs and perhaps even purchase military equipment.[12]

## Conclusion

The number of states involved in UN peacekeeping operations has increased over the past two decades. Some might argue that the reason for such an increase is the large demand for peacekeepers in the post–Cold War era. Yet many of the states that have increased their participation in peacekeeping seem to share one feature: most underwent recent processes of democratization. While UN peacekeeping operations often assist recipient states in building their own democracies, little is known about how peacekeeping might affect those who are involved in keeping the peace. Does democratization drive participation, for example? I have provided a number of possible reasons why democratizing or transitional states may want to participate in UN peacekeeping operations (figure 1.1). The reasons confirm, at least from a theoretical standpoint, that democratization is an especially potent impetus for joining peacekeeping

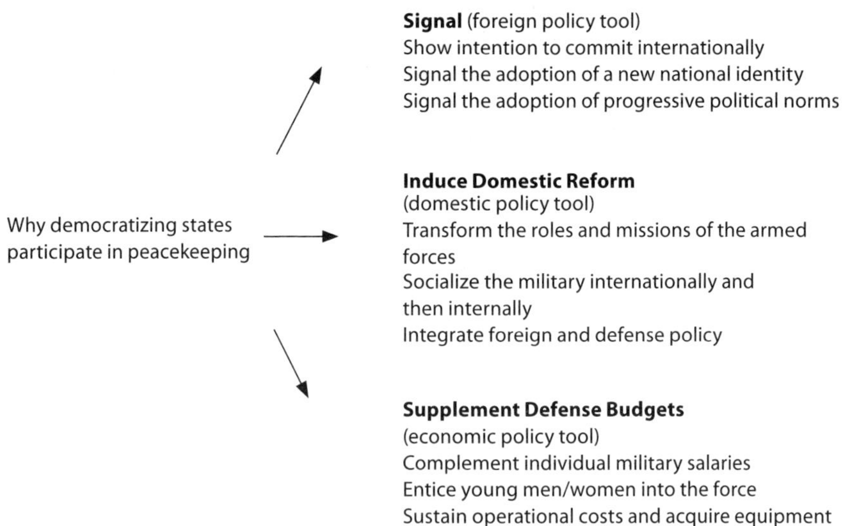


*Figure 1.1.* Reasons that democratizing states participate in peacekeeping

missions. Transitional states are likely to contribute blue helmets because they often "have difficulty credibly committing to sustain liberal reforms and the consolidation of democracy" (Mansfield and Pevehouse 2006, 138). Peacekeeping, in other words, offers these states the possibility of improving the clarity of their internal and external political signal sending, enhancing their capacity for internal military reform, and increasing their defense budgets in times of contraction, all of which are necessary in order to have the military acquiesce to civilian democratic leadership and control.

These motivating factors do not need to be present at all times and in all cases. Some troop-lending countries will be more enticed by the economic incentives of participation, while others might join UN peacekeeping missions in order to introduce domestic reforms. In the next chapter, I present detailed and nuanced evidence of how democratization imperatives prompted Argentina, Brazil, and Uruguay to actively participate in peacekeeping.

But this is not to say that a national-level commitment to UN peacekeeping operations will necessarily exercise the desired effects on military reform, foreign policy, or defense budgets. The incentives for participation in peace missions are often likely to be different from the actual effects of participation. Jervis (1997, 61) informs us that foreign policy actions have consequences, even though the effects are not always seen in the areas anticipated by policymakers. Even if leaders in democratizing states are fully committed to military reform, different forms of socialization in the field, the complexity of peace missions, and various military reactions to peace missions are likely to diffuse the effects of peacekeeping. The remainder of this book strives to determine the type and direction of these effects.

2

# What Is the Evidence from South America?

While chapter 1 covered the rationale for democratizing states' participation in peacekeeping operations, here I provide an empirical evaluation of the same themes, examining how signaling, domestic reform imperatives, and budgetary motivations have affected peacekeeping activities in South America in diverse ways. I trace in depth the participation of Argentina, Brazil, and Uruguay in peacekeeping missions. In addition, I emphasize various sequences of events by specifying the beginning and end of each country's peacekeeping contributions. Finally, I offer an assessment of the causal relationship between countries' commitments to UN peace operations and the democratization trends we see within them.

Argentina is the first case study because, of the three countries analyzed, its theoretical motivations for participating in peacekeeping missions were the strongest: it needed to send positive signals about itself to the international community, to take steps to reform its military, and to exploit the financial benefits made possible by peacekeeping missions. I analyze Brazil's reasons for its participation in UN peace missions, an activity that was largely defined by the need to signal international commitment and prowess. Finally, I focus on Uruguay, which has deployed large numbers of peacekeepers to different regions of the world, primarily for economic reasons.

## Argentina: From Military Coups to Peacekeeping

Of the three countries examined in this chapter, Argentina was the most eager to participate in peacekeeping missions. It wanted to signal its willingness to promote peace on the international stage; to use peace missions in order to promote domestic reforms, particularly within the military; and to cope more

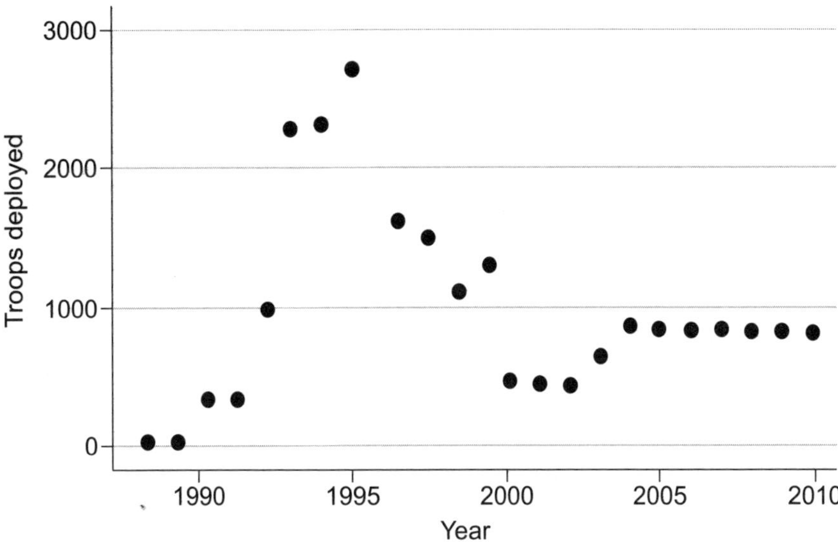


*Figure 2.1.* Argentine troops deployed in UN peace operations, 1988–2010

effectively with budgetary constraints. Still, it is important to point out that these motivations have not always existed nor been constant. In fact, the nature of Argentina's involvement in peace operations has evolved and varied over time. Since its redemocratization in 1982–83, three different trajectories or historical sequences shaped the country's commitment to peacekeeping. First, between 1990 and 1995, Argentina ranked as a major troop-lending country in the UN peacekeeping system. Signaling, domestic reform, and budgetary considerations mattered the most in this first phase. In contrast, between 1995 and 2003, the country's participation in UN peace missions declined substantially as its economy collapsed. Finally, between 2004 and 2010, the desire to use peacekeeping missions as a way of sending positive international signals became more acute (figure 2.1).

## Phase I of Argentina's Peacekeeping Activities, 1990–95

Argentina's proactive approach to peacekeeping first began in August 1991, when two Argentine frigates with 450 navy crewmembers deployed to the Persian Gulf from the Argentine port of Belgrano. Their aim was to contribute to the UN-sanctioned blockade of Iraq.[1] In the aftermath of the Gulf War, Buenos Aires then pledged to send a nine-hundred-man battalion to the UN

Protection Force in Former Yugoslavia (UNPROFOR). Also during this period, the Argentines made three other significant troop commitments in Cyprus, Iraq-Kuwait, and Haiti. According to data from Ejército Argentino and Consejo Argentino para las Relaciones Internacionales (CARI), in less than a decade, Argentina would send over fifteen thousand soldiers to participate in twelve peacekeeping operations worldwide (Ejército Argentino 1997; CARI 1997). In total, about 40% of the country's commissioned officers gained some kind of peacekeeping experience during this period, making Argentina the most active Latin American peacekeeping contributor and one of the top five UN troop suppliers between 1992 and 1996.[2]

This trajectory may initially seem insignificant. After all, the country was merely fulfilling its responsibilities as a founding member of the UN. Recall that the country's naval deployment to the Persian Gulf in 1990 occurred only months after the attempted coup against the democratically elected government of President Carlos Saúl Menem. Paradoxically, the very military institution that had revolted at least three times against the re-emergence of Argentine democracy was now engaged in a mission thousands of miles from Buenos Aires. This was no accident. Argentina's engagement in UN peacekeeping missions clearly coincided with the government's efforts to realign the country internationally and to restructure its restive armed forces. In this first phase, Buenos Aires wanted to broadcast its new role as a democratic player on the international stage, to promote and consolidate internal political and military reform, and to defray the costs of its military institutions.

The above process started when Menem took office as president of Argentina in 1989. His election reflected both a turbulent transition to democracy and the collapse of the national economy, which had brought down the previous elected president, Raúl Alfonsín (1983–89). At the time, Menem's Argentina faced high levels of external debt, economic stagnation, and hyperinflation. It desperately needed Washington's economic support to renegotiate its debt and obtain fresh international credit.

The country's external image was equally damaged by the legacy of its authoritarian past (1976–82) and its aftermath. In the eyes of Argentine foreign policy experts, including Andrés Fontana, the war against Great Britain in 1982, the development of the Condor II medium-range missile project, and the navy-led covert Argentine nuclear program all negatively affected Argentina's international image and damaged its diplomatic attempts to renegotiate its foreign debt.[3]

In this context, peacekeeping participation became a prime way for Argentina's emergent democratic government to send clear and far-reaching signals of its commitment to change. The government in particular tried to participate in peace-observing and peace enforcement missions in order to secure greater American support and international exposure. The move expressed not only tacit support for U.S. policies abroad, but also tacit alignment with Washington. Peacekeeping engagement was therefore an explicit strategy on the part of Argentine decision makers. This policy was designed to "bring Argentina from a very low level of agreement with the U.S. superior only to Cuba in Latin America, to a very high level of correspondence" (Norden 1995, 339). So great was the need to realign Argentine foreign policy with U.S. imperatives that Guido di Tella, Menem's foreign affairs minister, once publicly acknowledged that his country aimed to develop nothing less than "carnal relations" with Washington.[4] It did so by deploying troops to missions in the Persian Gulf, the former Yugoslavia, and Haiti, all of which the U.S. government duly noted and valued. According to two astute observers of Argentina's foreign policy, "the area of reform that proved most fruitful for U.S.–Argentine relations was cooperative security. Argentina's participation in international military missions, especially through the United Nations, not only coincided with the broader post–Cold War trend in this direction, but particularly aided the United States. Argentina's troop contributions both helped lower the manpower costs for the United States and gave U.S.-led missions the added legitimacy of a multilateral appearance" (Norden and Russell, 2002, 45).

On a broader level, Argentine engagement in UN peace operations was also a way to improve and redefine its abysmal human rights record acquired while under military rule. Although Argentina could have used regional organizations to signal its new resolve, its leaders determined that the UN was the most appropriate forum, in part because it had come to embody an unstinting commitment to human rights norms and values. As Diamint argues (2010, 670), "the Argentine government in Buenos Aires was not merely interested in reestablishing cordial relations with its North, South and Central American neighbors, it also had a broader desire to reconnect to the international community." The deployment of Argentine troops to UN missions thus had an important symbolic meaning: the need to signal unequivocal intent to its allies and the desire to transform the country's broader international identity.

Argentina initially deployed troops to UN peace operations whole hog under Menem, with the goal of looking like a reliable partner who could follow U.S.

cues. Civil-military reform was not part of the original intention or motivation; in fact, the impulse to resocialize troops by sending them abroad came as an afterthought, once the first group of soldiers returned from the mission in Kuwait. It was only after key foreign policy decisions about U.S.–Argentine relations that the Menem administration turned to peacekeeping as a means to resolve its stickiest internal concern: military rebellion (Lagorio 1998, 123–27; Norden and Russell 2002, 45). In fact, between 1982 and the early 1990s, Argentina's armed forces experienced a period of professional crisis characterized by defeat, scarcity, exclusion, fragmentation, and punishment.

A series of legislative and judicial measures aimed at reforming their spheres of influence was effective in reducing the military's power, but the measures also generated discontent. The Alfonsín administration's negotiation of a national defense law with the Argentine Congress in 1988, which abrogated the military's responsibility for internal security, particularly provoked consternation. The police force and other internal security agencies were placed under a separate civilian authority, and the new legislation specified that the only mission of the armed forces of a democratic Argentina was to defend the state in the case of an external attack.[5] In theory, the country's military could have merely devoted itself to external defense; almost immediately after Alfonsín took power, however, Argentina signed peace agreements with Chile and co-founded a civilian-led nuclear agency with Brazil, which inspired the establishment of Mercosur.[6] Because these diplomatic initiatives highlighted the lack of imminent external threats to the country at the time, the military ultimately struggled to surmount what then seemed like an ill-defined mission.

Things only got worse in 1987 with the human rights trials directed at military officers accused of both torture and murder during their dictatorship.[7] Fraga (1988) points out that the number of military men prosecuted for human rights violations reached 450 by 1987, not including the seventeen hundred officers still awaiting trial. Although not all officers participated in the La Guerra Sucia (Dirty War) between 1976 and 1982, a large percentage of them feared that either they or one of their colleagues could stand trial. In fact, Norden (1996a, 103) has highlighted that the number of officers prosecuted by Argentine courts in 1987 represented about 20% of the country's active officer corps. Because the judicial system was unable to process all these claims quickly and effectively, and because the armed forces were unwilling to tolerate the trials, the circumstances ultimately triggered three revolts in 1987, 1988, and 1989. They were organized by a group known as the *carapinta-*

*das* (painted faces), largely made up of middle-ranking and junior officers who stood up to their senior commanders, revealing that factionalism and indiscipline were rampant in the armed forces. Eventually, military insubordination, hyperinflation, and social revolt forced Alfonsín in 1989 to transfer power to the newly elected Menem six months earlier than expected.[8]

In an attempt to avoid the fate of his predecessor, Menem pardoned all officers who had led the uprisings against the Alfonsín government. Yet military factionalism and fragmentation prevailed, as did military disobedience. In December 1990, on the eve of an official visit to Argentina by President George H. W. Bush, a group of approximately one hundred *carapintadas* took over the Libertador building, the headquarters of the Ministry of Defense, just next to the Casa Rosada, or presidential house, and attempted to stage a coup. Unlike previous revolts in which officers concentrated on removing their service commanders, the 1990 coup was organized directly against President Menem. Insubordinate officers and soldiers explicitly agitated for both political and military change.[9]

The lesson from all this political maneuvering was that amnesty was not an effective means of halting military unrest. By then, it was clear that the military required a general purpose, and the direction of the military needed redefining, which led to discussions about new military missions. An initial plan proposed by the United States was to establish an antinarcotics and antiterrorist military task force led by military officers and noncommissioned officers who had participated in the first revolts against President Alfonsín (Zagorski 1994, 426). The idea was for the government to appease insubordinate officers by keeping them busy with military activities. But there was a lack of consensus over whether drug interdiction was an appropriate mission for the military, especially since the constitution now required the armed forces to exclusively focus on external defense. As a consequence, the U.S. initiative was discarded on the grounds that it represented an internal rather than external security mission.

Happily for the Argentines, a new opportunity soon presented itself in 1991 when Iraq invaded Kuwait, which prompted the UN to issue a troop request. Argentina responded to this request eagerly; it was still keen to establish a more positive role for its military in the aftermath of yet another coup attempt. The country sent a navy destroyer, a frigate, and several air force cargo planes to support the UN-sanctioned blockade of Iraq and, by deploying troops to Operation Desert Storm, it became the only Latin American state to aid the United States and its NATO allies in this mission (Neves 1995, 50–62). To the surprise of many, the soldiers returned satisfied with this new endeavor. The move significantly changed the national debate on military affairs. Politicians and soldiers now shifted their attention away from rebellion and legal pardons to UN enforcement missions abroad.

In this sense, peacekeeping not only enabled Argentina to signal its dependability as an international actor, but also enabled it to begin rehabilitating its armed forces by exposing large numbers of its troops to out-of-area missions conducted by multinational forces. The government soon began deploying observers, units, and even full battalions to various UN peace missions. Troops deployed to UNPROFOR, UN Confidence Restoration Operation in Croatia (UNCRO), UN Peacekeeping Force in Cyprus (UNFICYP), and UNIKOM (UN Iraq-Kuwait Observation Mission). Figure 2.1 illustrates how Argentina increased its peacekeeping contribution from barely thirty peacekeepers in 1989 to almost three thousand in 1995, representing a hundredfold increase in less than six years. Argentine military officers became ubiquitous peacekeepers in Central America, Africa, and Europe. The country also became the most active Latin American peacekeeping contributor and one of the top five UN troop suppliers for the period under discussion here.

Finally, in Phase I, monetary considerations played a key role in Argentina's pursuit of a UN peacekeeping role. Budget reductions intensified the internal disorder of the armed forces, almost causing institutional paralysis. In a period of less than twenty years, there was a general decrease in Buenos Aires' military spending of approximately 66.25%. Pion-Berlin (2001, 148) found that it represented at the time "the world's largest reduction in military spending for any country whose total defense budget exceeded \$100 million." Not surprisingly, such budget cuts then reduced the number of active-duty military personnel and the resources made available to them. More than 100,000 soldiers (or 58.28% of the force) were discharged in less than twenty years. The army was the hardest hit, losing 45.0% of its manpower between 1983 and 1987, as compared with a 30.1% drop in the navy and an 11.1% loss for the air force. In barely one generation, Argentina went from being a heavily militarized country to fielding one of the smallest armed forces in the Southern Cone of Latin America.[10]

In this context, peacekeeping participation provided both a political and economic opportunity to different tradeoffs. As I explain in chapter 3, the army was the prime beneficiary of the country's participation in UN peacekeeping, but it was also the hardest hit by lower budgets and force reductions. Menem used peacekeeping resources as "carrots" to reduce military unrest and to make it easier for the military to cope with economic scarcity. The Ministry of Economics and the Ministry of Foreign Affairs, which saw the missions as an integral part of the nation's foreign policy, for example, funded the salaries and operational costs of troop deployments to UN missions. At the same time, the Argentine government usually provided its peacekeepers with a $1,000 monthly allowance and an additional 25% pay increase. The standard payment for a peacekeeper at the rank of army sergeant was thus $1,400 per month, including the UN salary and supplement. When one considers that a sergeant in Argentina received $760 per month (before the 2001 devaluation), the peacekeeping pay supplement was critical. Military observers were paid on a different scale and system, receiving a per diem directly from the UN, ranging from $85 to $120, depending on the mission. The same sergeant described above could make the tidy sum of $3,000 a month by serving as a peacekeeping observer in Cyprus or Kuwait, the best-paid UN missions.[11]

## Phase II of Argentina's Peacekeeping Activities, 1996–2003

The dynamism of Phase I did not last. By 1996, troop commitments began to decline and fewer soldiers were sent abroad. The decline reflected a second phase in Argentina's peacekeeping history, in which domestic reform was less of an imperative and not forcefully implemented. Diamint (2010, 670) argued that "the role of peace operations on the Argentine political agenda has varied throughout the democratic period. While during the Carlos Menem administration (1989–99), the strategy was centrally aimed at reintegrating Argentina into the global community, for the next government (Fernando de la Rúa, 1999–2001) peace operations served to assign a mission to the military in the absence of a clear defense policy."

So why did Argentina reduce its peacekeeping contributions in this period? In 1997, while President Menem was still in power, the country began to experience the first symptoms of what would become a severe economic crisis, which subsequently prompted the government to reduce its force levels abroad from almost three thousand in 1995, to fifteen hundred in 1996, to fewer than five hundred in 2000. While peacekeeping initially provided economic blandishments to the armed forces, the operational costs of some of these missions became too expensive to sustain in the face of economic adversity. In some cases, such as the UN mission in Croatia, the government poured in more than $42 million—1.6% of the country's entire military expenditures for 1992—making it Argentina's most expensive peacekeeping mission in the 1990s. A small company of engineers in Kuwait cost almost $9 million to deploy, while the 1994 mission in Haiti, where troops deployed but never disembarked, absorbed more than $5 million.[12]

By 2002, the number of Argentines in blue helmets dropped to 454 worldwide. The devaluation and subsequent collapse of the Argentine peso in December of 2001 drastically affected the country's armed forces. In 2002, for example, 63% of all military personnel were now making less than 716 Argentine pesos a month (approximately $250), and the number of Argentine staff on UN missions was cut in half (Gallo 2002). These economic reverses obviously occurred in the broader society, too. As a result, Argentines became enraged, and confrontations between the police and citizens grew. For the first time that anyone could remember, the military did not intervene to halt the political chaos. At least five civilians occupied the presidential seat within a year: Fernando de la Rúa, Federico Ramón Puerta, Adolfo Rodríguez Saá, Eduardo Oscar Camaño, and Eduardo Duhalde. As Watson (2005, 64) argues, "what could go into peace operations for a military that cannot be completely funded by external sources is money that can go into keeping Argentines off the streets and from looting stores and business establishments . . . It would appear that peace operations will remain a low level of interest for the Republic as long as the severe economic turmoil persists." This phase was thus shadowed by the economic uncertainties that prompted Argentina to reduce its international commitment to peacekeeping. The armed forces were not considered responsible for this crisis and did not intervene, but the absence of political leadership once again forced them to focus their attention on the domestic turmoil that surrounded them.

The fact that Argentina was able to sustain a peacekeeping force of four hundred amidst such political and economic turmoil was in itself surprising. Five different presidents from at least two different political parties (the Radical Civic Union and the Justicialist Party) managed to supply a small yet stable number of UN troops between 2001 and 2003. What this case illustrated at a minimum was the difficulty of sustaining Argentine participation in peacekeeping missions at the time. Multiple Argentine governments were willing to deploy a minimum number of soldiers to demonstrate their enduring commitment to the UN in a time of economic crisis, but at the same time Argentina almost lost its voting rights in the UN General Assembly because of a $215 million debt.[13]

## Phase III of Argentina's Peacekeeping Activities, 2004–10

Argentina embarked upon a third and final phase of its peacekeeping trajectory in 2004, once the political and economic crises had died down. President Néstor Kirchner's request for congressional permission to deploy a full battalion and a unit of observers—totaling 1,103 soldiers—to the UN mission in Haiti fueled a new impetus for the country to participate on the international stage. It was the first large deployment after the crisis and the third-largest national contingent in Haiti from a South American nation (it later became the fourth-largest contingent in Haiti; see chapter 5).

What was Argentina trying to signal? The decision-making process behind this large deployment was complex, because at the time Kirchner had little interest in foreign policy matters and was heavily focused on the domestic agenda. However, Defense Minister José Pampuro and Foreign Affairs Minister Rafael Bielsa convinced an apathetic Kirchner to use peacekeeping as a foreign policy tool to signal two goals.

First, Argentina increased its peacekeeping commitment in order to promote subregional military cooperation with its South American neighbors, of which Brazil and Chile were the most influential. Kirchner requested congressional authorization not only to deploy troops abroad, but also to allow Argentine forces to cooperate actively with Chilean and Brazilian soldiers in the field.[14] Although the country's diplomatic relations with Chile and Brazil had been stable and peaceful, military-to-military cooperation was limited among these South American nations. Peacekeeping also served as a means of signaling commitment to regional defense integration by compelling the armed forces to participate in joint peace efforts. This was a particularly sensitive issue for Argentine-Chilean relations, given their historical mistrust and differences over sovereignty and territory, for which they almost fought a war in 1978 for the Beagle Channel. In that sense, a joint peacekeeping force with regional neighbors provided an important foreign policy mechanism with which to signal the arrival of a new era of regional relations. This signal culminated in the creation of an Argentine-Chilean binational force for peace operations known as Cruz del Sur (Southern Cross), which "opened up the prospect of further defense cooperation and helped to definitively end mutual conflict scenarios" (Diamint 2010, 671).

As for the second goal, Ministers Pampuro and Bielsa persuaded the president to use Argentina's active role in Haiti as an opportunity to establish a new division of labor between the region's middle power (Brazil) and the United States. In the view of these decision makers, peacekeeping would permit a minimum level of cooperation with the administration of President George W. Bush, with which Argentina had a tense and difficult relationship owing to Washington's steadfast refusal to support a bailout for Argentina.[15] Hence peacekeeping was once again used to signal reliability and credibility, especially when U.S.–Argentine relations were at their lowest ebb. To date, Argentina maintains a battalion and an air force unit in Haiti, and it is still South America's third-largest contributor to the UN mission there.

## Brazil: From Isolation to Global Player

Brazil has historically also been one of Latin America's major troop contributors, having deployed UN observers and troops to missions such as the UN Emergency Force in the Suez, the UN Operation in the Democratic Republic of Congo (DRC), the UN Military Observer Group in India-Pakistan (UNMOGIP), and UNFICYP. Between 1957 and 1967, Brazil deployed an infantry battalion (approximately six thousand soldiers) to the Gaza Strip.[16] Between 1947 and 1988, Brazil was among the top thirty-two contributors, supplying regular personnel for a substantial proportion of these operations, although it did little to finance them directly (Bobrow and Boyer 1997, 742).

But between 1968 and 1988, Brazil did not actively participate in the UN system, following a similar path to that of its neighbors Argentina and Uruguay.[17] This assessment was influenced by the Brazilian military coup of 1964, which effectively installed a dictatorship that would last for more than two decades. Like most bureaucratic-authoritarian regimes in Latin America, Brazilian military leaders reasoned that isolationism would silence international criticism for a poor human rights record. Although Brazil joined international military missions through the OAS during the dictatorial regime, it did not commit UN blue helmets until after its redemocratization in 1984.[18]

The return to democracy brought Brazil back to UN politics. As the country democratized, the Ministry of Foreign Affairs (also known as Itamaraty) increased its presence in the international organization. Democratization has played an important role in shaping Brazil's multilateral policy, and foreign and domestic policy imperatives, in which a perceived need to send signals internationally and domestic reform have been the key factors, largely motivated its return to peacekeeping affairs.

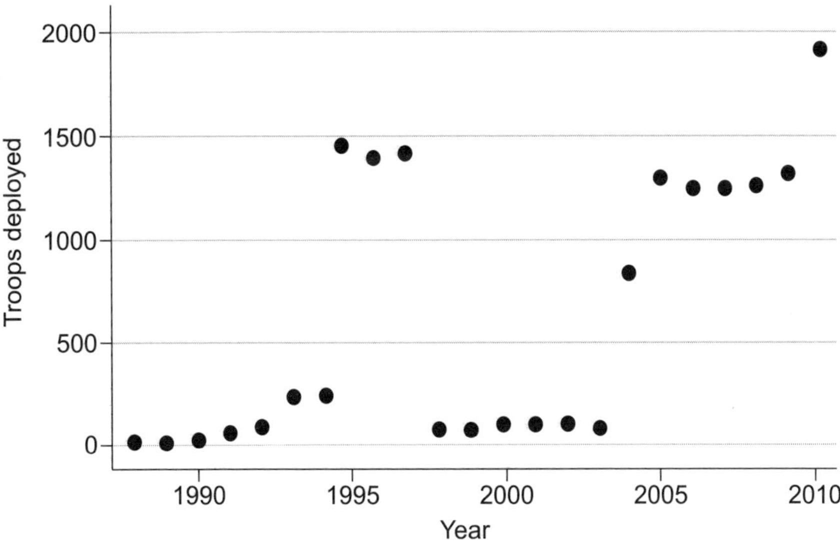

*Figure 2.2.* Brazilian troops deployed in UN peace operations, 1988–2010

In contrast to Argentina, however, peacekeeping in Brazil had been conceived as a mechanism to help integrate defense and foreign policies, which in turn enabled the country to effectively signal its aspiration to be considered a global power. Signaling and domestic reform (integration) thus provided an impetus for Brazil to join UN peace efforts. The country's peacekeeping trajectory, represented in figure 2.2, reflects three distinct historical phases. The first, from 1988 to 1996 or thereabouts, covers the early process of democratization in Brazil. The second goes from 1997 to 2003, when the country reduced its troop contributions during the economy's financial collapse. Finally, Phase III covers the period from 2004 to 2010, when Brazil embraced a commanding position in the UN mission in Haiti. Signaling and domestic reform play key roles in the first and third phases, while economic incentives were of greater significance in the second phase.

### Phase I of Brazil's Peacekeeping Activities, 1988–96

In its first decade as a democratic state, Brazil pursued a strategy in which international signaling was key, given the uncertain nature of the country's domestic politics at the time. While Brazil did not experience a traumatic transition to democracy by collapsing, as its neighbor Argentina did, its democratization was uneven and at times rocky. The country's first democratically elected president, Tancredo Neves, died before assuming the presidency in 1985. As part of a compromise, the vice presidential candidate, José Sarney, served as president for the next five years, despite the fact that three quarters of the electorate wanted his term to end sooner. President Fernando Collor de Mello was the first elected president of Brazil to take office in the postdictatorial era; his term began in 1990, but his administration faced a serious political and economic crisis, leading to his impeachment by Congress in 1992. Another interim president, Itamar Franco, followed until Fernando Henrique Cardoso was elected as president in 1995.

There was also uncertainly about the role of the military. The armed forces continued to exercise autonomy and intervened actively in politics during this period. Linz and Stepan (1996, 169) found that "on numerous occasions the military unilaterally decided whether or not to send military units to quell strikes. Active duty army officers continued in control of the National Intelligence Service. Congress discussed none of Brazil's controversial militarized nuclear projects. The military played a major role in setting the boundaries to agrarian reform." Political crisis and economic instability dominated the first democratic decade in Brazil.[19] As analyzed in chapter 1, political and economic crises offered the ideal context for elected leaders of democratizing states to join international organizations to credibly commit to reform.

So what was Brazil trying to signal? Participation in UN peacekeeping was part of a broader strategy intended to achieve two related foreign policy goals: to increase the country's visibility in the UN system after years of isolation and to encourage the internationalization of its economy after decades of import substitution. First, peacekeeping helped signal credibility and commitment in UN politics. As the country democratized, Itamaraty increased its participation in the UN, publicly announcing the country's intention to regain a prestigious position on the Security Council. Brazilian diplomats and politicians alike engaged in an international public relations campaign to push for a rapid UN reform, which would grant Brazil the desired permanent seat on the Security Council.[20]

To signal interest in UN affairs, Brazil gradually increased its UN peacekeeping troop contribution in the late eighties and early nineties. In December 1988, Brazil sent sixteen military observers of UNAVEM I (UN Angola Verification Mission) to verify the redeployment and total withdrawal of Cuban troops from the Angolan territory. In 1991, President Fernando Collor de Mello increased Brazil's military presence in Angola by sending 120 observers to verify the peace agreement established between Angola's government and the National Union for the Total Independence of Angola (UNITA). A year later, Brazil accepted an invitation to participate in ONUMOZ (UN Operation in Mozambique) to help implement the general peace agreement signed by the local government and the National Resistance Movement. In 1994, when ONUMOZ's mandate formally came to an end, two hundred Brazilian military officers had performed monitoring and observational activities in Mozambique (Campos Tarrisse da Fontoura 1999; Sena Cardoso 1998). These constituted the first deployments of Brazilian combat troops to a foreign country since the 1967 peacekeeping participation in the Suez. Interestingly enough, these commitments were made precisely when Brazil was experiencing its worse postdictatorial political and economic crisis.

The scale of these deployments was minute compared with what would come in the second half of 1990. In 1995, Brazil sent its first army battalion to UNAVEM III to assist the government of Angola and UNITA in restoring peace and achieving national reconciliation (a peacebuilding mission). The battalion was made up of nine hundred officers and noncommissioned officers, the first of several who would serve in the area. The mission ended abruptly in 1997; by then, over four thousand Brazilian Army soldiers and forty-eight Brazilian Navy officers had been involved in UNAVEM III (see more on socialization in UNAVEM in chapter 4).

While the forces in Angola and Mozambique undoubtedly represented Brazil's largest contingents abroad during this first phase, the various democratic governments of Brazil deployed observers and troops to other UN missions, too. From 1994 to 2003, the military sent sixty-three observers to ONUSAL (UN Observer Mission in El Salvador), thirty-nine officers to UN Mission in Guatemala, and more than five hundred blue helmets to East Timor (Aguilar 2002; Borges and Couto Gomes 2004).

By far, Brazil's largest troop contributions during this initial period supported UN missions in Africa and Asia, including the peace operations in Angola, East Timor, Ivory Coast, Liberia, Mozambique, and Uganda-Rwanda. With regard to a commitment for troop presence, Brazil explicitly chose Portuguese-speaking Africa and Asia. In total, 4,942 Brazilian officers and noncommissioned officers participated in UN peace missions during this period.

While Brazil was internationally active, it also behaved cautiously. When the UN requested troops for the missions in Haiti and Yugoslavia, Brazil refused to join. During this initial phase, Brazil was reluctant to support peace enforcement operations and adamantly opposed the establishment of a force that, although designed for peacekeeping, could possibly be drawn into peace enforcement, especially in complex emergencies where prevailing conditions verge on chaos.[21]

Second, Brazil approached international institutions like the UN in part because it was signaling its intention to change its national economy and global strategy. Pro-reform politicians in Brazil, such as Collor de Mello and Fernando Henrique Cardoso, wanted to abandon the nationalist-developmentalist and isolationist model that had been followed by the previous dictatorial regime.[22] In that sense, peacekeeping was an attempt to integrate defense policy into the country's new grand strategy. For Brazil, however, unlike Argentina, military reform was not the main objective of its signaling strategy. Guedes da Costa (1998a, 232) argued that "Brazil's international military presence has not been the subject of internal debate, whether as part of the consideration of foreign policy or in specific discussions of the role of the armed forces. Peacekeeping activities are viewed as part of the international role of the country."

Instead, participation in the UN and in other international forums was part of the country's broader agenda to reform the national economy, not the armed forces. The advent of democracy in Brazil failed to bring about a dramatic transformation of the economy. So liberal Brazilian leaders designed a foreign policy intended to implement once and for all a liberal economic regime by signing international agreements, founding regional institutions, and actively participating in existing global forums such as the UN. Regionally, Brazil was pursuing economic integration with its neighbors Argentina and Uruguay through Mercosur.[23] Globally, it was assuming an active role in multilateral affairs in efforts to embrace and project a new international identity through peacekeeping, joining the Security Council, and hosting the 1992 UN Conference on Environment and Development (also known as the Rio Summit). Solingen (1998, 147–54) and others have branded these moves as the internationalist revolution in South America, in which pro-liberal politicians (including Mello and later Cardoso) seized the opportunity to join international forces to address domestic and social agendas. Peacekeeping was thus part of a much larger Brazilian strategy to embrace international forces and to engage heavily in international transactions with those who shared the same liberal and pro-democratic norms.

## Phase II of Brazil's Peacekeeping Activities, 1997–2003

By 1998, UN troop levels decreased substantially from one thousand to barely fifty soldiers, marking a second phase in Brazil's peacekeeping trajectory. Three factors explain this sudden withdrawal of Brazilian troops. First, the UN decided to leave Angola in January of 1998, after four years of vain attempts to prevent fighting among warring factions. At the time, Brazil was the second-largest troop-lending country to the mission in Angola after India; the withdrawal of UN blue helmets from UNAVEM drastically reduced the number of Brazilian forces in peacekeeping.

Second, similar to Argentina, Brazil experienced a financial collapse in 1999, leading to a traumatic devaluation of the national currency and high inflation rates. The financial crisis made it extremely difficult for President Fernando Henrique Cardoso, a staunch supporter of Brazil's peacekeeping engagement and a former head of Itamaraty, to deploy troops abroad. Like Argentina, Brazil faces high operational costs when it sends soldiers overseas. For instance, the government allocated roughly $217 million for maintaining its battalions in Angola (Campos Tarrisse da Fontoura 1999, 210). Because of the high cost of deployment, Brazil was only able to maintain a handful of military police officers (fewer than sixty-two peace observers per year) in East Timor between 1998 and 2003.

Third, shortly after President Cardoso took office in 1995, service commanders complained about salary and force reductions.[24] The armed forces also expressed reservations about future peacekeeping deployments, especially after the unpleasant experience in Angola, where Brazil had deployed a full battalion. In this context of military discontent, President Cardoso proposed a number of legislative amendments in the area of defense policy. And during this process, the president and the armed forces focused predominantly on domestic politics and not on UN peacekeeping operations. In fact, Cardoso formally institutionalized peacekeeping policies by introducing them into a broader defense policy known as the National Defense Plan, which served to create the first civilian-led Ministry of Defense in Brazil. Among other things, the proposed plan determined that the armed forces should support the country's foreign policy.[25]

Financial troubles and domestic reform kept Brazil temporarily out of major peacekeeping deployments between 1997 and 2003. But an important foundational base was set up in this period that ultimately provided the institutional setting under which Brazil would make its most important commitment to peacekeeping in 2004.

## Phase III of Brazil's Peacekeeping Activities, 2004–11

Brazil once again deployed troops to the UN in 2004 under the administration of President Luiz Inácio Lula da Silva, marking the third and final phase of the country's peacekeeping trajectory. It substantially increased its role that year by sending more than one thousand soldiers to Haiti, a non-Portuguese-speaking nation. The decision to deploy Brazilian troops there came in response to a formal request from the United States and France to assist with the stabilization of the Caribbean island in the aftermath of Jean Bertrand Aristide's controversial resignation as president of Haiti. In an attempt to secure the country and put an end to escalating civil conflict between Aristide's supporters and opponents, the UN Security Council authorized a three-month multinational interim force in February of 2004. U.S. marines as well as French, Canadian, and Chilean troops who were heavily armed initially comprised the force. Yet the growing controversy over Washington's role in persuading Aristide to go into exile fueled international criticism of the Bush administration. Human rights groups and member states of the Caribbean community strongly questioned the legitimacy of the mission, which took place only one year after the equally contentious U.S. invasion of Iraq.[26] In March 2004, amidst the political crisis in Haiti, French President Jacques Chirac reportedly asked President Lula to assume command of the mission (Diniz 2007, 102–4). The United States and France were to some extent trying to persuade local and regional stakeholders to participate in the operation in an attempt to legitimize the overall enterprise. In the absence of Caribbean supporters, they turned to South America. Surprisingly, Lula committed a force of over one thousand soldiers, which lead to the creation of MINUSTAH in April 2004.

The force appeared to be relatively small, but it had symbolic significance. In the space of six years (2004–10), 5,960 Brazilian soldiers participated in MINUSTAH, making it Brazil's largest foreign military commitment since the Suez mission in the 1950s and World War II. Also for the first time, Brazil was given the general command of a UN mission, composed of roughly seven thousand soldiers and sixteen hundred police, half of whom came from Latin American countries. Moreover, it was the first time that soldiers from the Brazilian Army participated in a mission mandated under Chapter VII of the UN Charter, about which Itamaraty had previously expressed reservations. Finally,

President Lula was deploying forces to take over from American and French forces on a Caribbean island with few, if any, cultural, linguistic, or political linkages to Brazil.[27]

Why did Brazil make this ambitious commitment? It wanted to send signals to the international community, even though the signs and the message differed from those sent in the past. Brazil was no longer engaging in UN peace operations to signal reliability and credibility in the face of political adversity. Instead, it used the mission to help publicize Brazil's commitment to international accord and to demonstrate that it had sufficient commanding skills to be considered a so-called global player or emerging power. In other words, participation in UN missions helped a transitioning state to redefine its global identity. Domestic considerations appear to be secondary, but they played a role in explaining Brazilian motivations. In particular, the Lula administration sought to improve intrabureaucratic coordination between soldiers and diplomats by forcing both establishments to work jointly in peacekeeping. Decision makers have thus come to realize that if Brazil is to increase its recognition of its status as a global player, it needs to synchronize the messages and activities of its various bureaucracies, especially its most visible ministries.

MINUSTAH coincided with the UN reform process of late 2005, in which Brazil publicly reiterated its aspirations to have a permanent seat on the Security Council, together with Germany, India, and Japan. Participation in MINUSTAH gave Brazil a political platform to support its long-standing request for a seat on the Security Council. In this sense, the key distinction between Lula's foreign policy and the foreign policies of previous administrations was its willingness to assert itself and to be more proactive on the international stage.[29]

With a total force of almost 300,000 soldiers, roughly seven times that of Argentina, Brazil could have deployed far more troops than it actually committed. The current Brazilian deployment in Haiti (about one thousand) is small compared with those of the largest troop-lending countries. States like Pakistan, Bangladesh, and India deploy eight times more soldiers per year than Brazil, while much smaller countries such as Nepal and Uruguay (analyzed below) supply three times more. Brazil has never been among the top five troop-lending countries to the UN (it is ranked twentieth; see table 1.1).

Brazil not only expressed a willingness to commit and sustain troops in Haiti, it also signaled its intention to lead and command the mission, to go beyond its linguistic and cultural sphere of influence, beyond a mere Chapter VI peacebuilding mission. Whereas Argentina was motivated to join the

MINUSTAH mission to signal a willingness to cooperate with neighbors, Brazil was primarily driven by its own global ambitions (Rohter 2004). In Brazil, peacekeeping is ultimately part of a broader international marketing strategy to signal intention, interest, and commitment to play a larger global role.

Similarly, domestic imperatives appear to play a supporting role in Brazil's peacekeeping strategy. Unlike the country's first phase of participation in peace operations, which involved no discussions about military reforms, its current engagement in Haiti has been the subject of a much broader national debate on the role of the armed forces and the use of national resources.[30] In places like Haiti, the military is not merely a tactical supporter of Brazil's foreign policy. It is also largely responsible for the policy's strategic implementation on the international stage, which is expected to force diplomats and soldiers to coordinate policies and to thereby increase interagency collaboration, or service jointness. Ultimately, this should improve foreign policy cohesion at a time when Brazil is in the international spotlight. It should also help enhance relations between civilians in the Brazilian government and uniformed personnel. (I explore and test this hypothesis in chapter 6.)

For the *Economist* (2004a), peacekeeping is a means of modernizing the armed forces. With democracy firmly established, the Brazilian Army needs a new job, and peacekeeping can facilitate the process. Citing a Brazilian geopolitics expert, the *Economist* (2010a, 52) claims that "peacekeeping encourages the democratization of the military mindset. The old generation is all about war and security. In another generation we'll have a new military, with an international outlook and new ideas about conflict prevention, civilian government and the rule of law."

The unintended consequences and negative effects of peacekeeping participation are the focus of the following chapters. In them I critically assess to what extent peace operations are changing the Brazilian military's mindset. The fact is that many in Brazil see peacekeeping missions as providing incentives to reform an institution that has, until now, been predominantly preoccupied by its own internal order, public security, and a lack of transparency.

## Uruguay: From Guerilla Warfare to Profitable Peacekeeping

In 1992, Uruguay sent its first peacekeeping battalion to Asia as part of UNTAC (UN Transition Authority to Cambodia). In total, 1,330 soldiers (about 5.5% of the country's total armed forces) deployed in four military units across the various provinces of Cambodia. Uruguay had previously participated in peacekeeping missions during the 1950s and 60s, when it sent military observers to missions in Sinai and India-Pakistan (Ejército de la República Uruguay 1999, 20–38; León 1996). But the 1992 decision to participate in UNTAC was significant for two main reasons. First, it was the first large-scale deployment abroad, involving troops and contingents from different services. Second, it symbolized a radical departure in military politics, as it shifted the focus of the armed forces away from domestic politics toward international affairs. The deployment took place only six years after the country's return to democracy and after thirteen years of dictatorial rule. The military dictatorship that ruled Uruguay from 1973 to 1985 was not as brutal as Augusto Pinochet's regime in Chile or the Argentine military junta, but guerrilla and labor repression and the percentage of people detained for questioning by the military was higher than in any other country of the Southern Cone of South America.[31] It was therefore somewhat ironic that the Uruguayan military, once responsible for state repression, was now involved in UN peacekeeping.

Within a decade of the 1992 deployment, Uruguay became one of the world's largest troop-contributing countries. The number of blue helmets sent to UN missions increased from fewer than one hundred observers in 1982, to more than a thousand peacekeepers in 1993, to over two thousand blue helmets in 2010. In 2010, this small South American state was involved in nine different peacekeeping operations. By late 2011, 24,335 of the country's soldiers had been involved in at least one UN peacekeeping mission. In relation to its population (fewer than four million people), there is one Uruguayan peacekeeper for every 280 citizens. This makes Uruguay the world's largest UN troop contributor per capita. As UN Secretary-General Ban Ki-moon said during a visit to Montevideo in June 2011, "Uruguay's commitment to global peacekeeping is without rival . . . When adjusted for population, no country contributes more troops than Uruguay" (MercoPress 2011a). In absolute terms, Uruguay was the eighth-largest UN troop contributor between 2000 and 2010. It was also Latin America's leading supplier of blue helmets.

Why does this small South American state supply such a large number of soldiers to UN peacekeeping operations? The Uruguayan case can be compared with those of Argentina and Brazil on the basis of important control variables. Like its two big neighbors, Uruguay underwent a democratization process that motivated an internal interest in international affairs. The three nations are also all members of the same subregion and have experienced similar authoritarian regimes and parallel democratization processes. The similarities are not as intriguing as the differences, however. In contrast to Argentina and Brazil, Uruguay has not relied on peacekeeping as a signaling strategy. Instead, participation in UN peace operations has primarily helped fund the armed forces and, by extension, justify their existence in a democratic era.

Uruguay's participation in peacekeeping missions can be divided into two distinct phases (figure 2.3). The first was during the early phase of democratization from 1992 to 1998, when, in the face of a serious military identity crisis, it deployed a large number of military staff members to Cambodia and Angola. Mission transformation and budgetary considerations motivated this first peacekeeping trajectory. The second phase spans from 2002 to the present day, during which time Uruguay has engaged in major deployments in the DRC and Haiti. Economic incentives provide the main impetus for participation in this second phase.

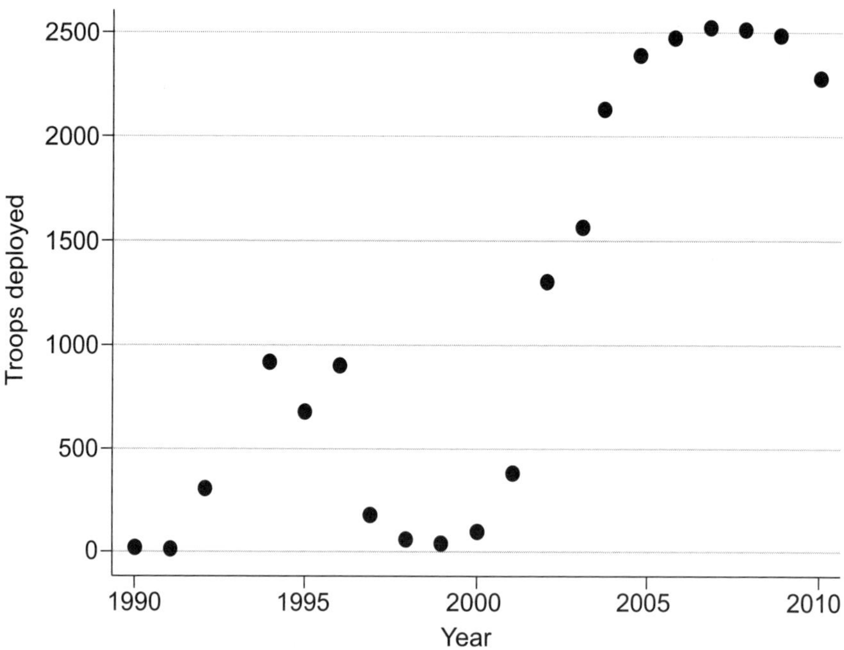


*Figure 2.3.* Uruguayan troops deployed in UN peace operations, 1990–2010

## Phase I of Uruguay's Peacekeeping Activities, 1992–99

Understanding Uruguay's involvement in UN peacekeeping during the 1990s requires an assessment of its domestic process of democratization. Uruguay would probably not have volunteered blue helmets had it not been for two fundamental crises within the armed forces themselves: an identity crisis and a budgetary emergency, both of which were brought on by democratization.

Unlike Argentina's transition to democracy, which took place as a result of the collapse of the military in the 1982 Falklands/Malvinas War, and Brazil's transition to democracy, which was agreed with the military, the redemocratization of Uruguay stemmed from domestic and international pressures that forced the military government to withdraw from direct rule and to hold extrication elections (Caetano and Rilla 1987, 65–75; Linz and Stepan 1996, 65–75). Civilian opposition from the left and the right forged alliances that in turn led to massive street demonstrations against the dictatorial regime in 1983. The military was forced to engage in negotiations with the opposition, producing the Naval Club Accord and culminating with the democratic election of Julio Maria Sanguinetti as president in 1985. Fifteen years after the establishment of an authoritarian-bureaucratic regime, and after five years of intense negotiations with the military, Uruguay re-established liberal democracy and the rule of law.[32]

The circumstances of Uruguay's democratization in 1985 afforded civilians both political leverage and influence. In contrast to Brazil, where the military and their conservative allies in part handled the transition, in Uruguay the democratization process ultimately remained in civilian hands. Linz and Stepan (1996, 158–59) explain, "one of the reasons that the military was not very powerful in Uruguayan politics after free elections was that they had virtually no allies." Hence the democratization process did not provide the military with the degree of autonomy required to proactively assume the role it deemed necessary.

Slowly but surely, civilians began to introduce an unprecedented number of initiatives that diminished the role of the military. The Uruguayan police forces were demilitarized, and the military was unable to award itself constitutional responsibilities for the maintenance of law and order. The National Security Council was abolished, as was the Commission for Political Affairs, both of which were formerly managed by the intelligence services and the military (Stepan 1988a, 116–18).

One consequence of redemocratization was the army's identity crisis, which in large part stemmed from an incapacity to define its political mission. It was exacerbated by the absence of leftist guerrilla movements, which rendered obsolete the Communist threat that the military had devoted years to combating and defeating.[33] Military reform in Uruguay has always been debated, not only in terms of reorientation but also in terms of changing tactics, doctrine, and national security culture. By the time the redemocratization began in 1985, the Communist guerrillas had been defeated, so the military had no explicit domestic threats to combat.

At the same time, the erosion of regional rivalries in the Southern Cone brought the military's main external mission into question: the defense of the nation from external attack.[34] Without a doubt, the Argentine-Brazilian reconciliation brought into question the military's raison d'être, which had been to protect Uruguay in the event of an armed dispute between its two huge neighbors. Mercosur played its part, too, since Uruguay joined the organization and its capital, Montevideo, became the headquarters of the new regional institution. In this new era of regional integration, Uruguayans began to seriously question the need for armed forces, effectively transforming the conventional national security doctrine and altering the national security culture that prevailed within the armed forces.

To make things worse for the military, a budgetary crisis emerged. Politicians and soldiers clashed over the size of military budget shares in Uruguay's new democracy, with defense spending proving to be a low priority for most politicians. Year after year, politicians diverted funds from the military to initiatives that were more highly valued by their constituents. Military expenditures dropped from $482 million in 1994 to $200 million in 2002. The military's share of the central government's expenditure underwent a steady contraction. In 1981, at the peak of the dictatorial regime, the central government was spending 15.4% of its budget on the military, which represented 4.0% of gross national product (GNP). By 1999, military expenditures amounted to just 4.1% of the total government's expenditures, or 1.3% of GNP (U.S. Arms Control and Disarmament Agency 2000).

The Uruguayan military was caught in a severe financial crisis. It faced a shrinking budget and a relatively large force that needed to be fed and paid. The absence of purpose, low salaries, and decreasing budgetary allocations led to a downward spiral of morale. For the civilian politicians alone, economic constraints compelled the military to implement reforms. Civilian leaders reasoned that, in the face of scarcity, the armed forces should be reorganized and restructured (Pion-Berlin 1997, 190–94). Mariano Brito Checchi, minister of defense from 1990 to 1993, stated: "There was a degree of inconformity among some retired military officers regarding economic compensation and retirement pensions. But we had to rationalize our budget and we reduced expenditures within the rule of law, with norms, and compensations."[35] For military officers, however, the economic constraints translated into operational and professional decay. In their view, civilians were not following a rational policy sequence, because reorganization could not come prior to the development of a military mission and doctrine.

In this critical domestic context, participation in UN peacekeeping provided an opportunity to cope with the institutional crisis in the military. The need to reform the national security culture of the armed forces prompted an interest in peacekeeping affairs, and a small window of opportunity emerged in 1991. That year, Venezuela accepted a UN invitation to join the mission in Cambodia by sending a contingent of approximately one thousand peacekeepers. The following year, a failed military coup organized by then-Colonel Hugo Chávez impeded Venezuela from deploying its troops to UNTAC,[36] giving Uruguay the justification to assume Venezuela's role. In 1992, Batallón Uruguay I—a battalion of close to one thousand men that included army officers, noncommissioned officers, and navy personnel—deployed. Uruguayan peacekeepers held positions across four Cambodian provinces, with military units occupying six border patrol positions (Ejército de la República Uruguay 1999). The deployment represented one of Uruguay's largest peacekeeping contributions, both for the number of soldiers and for the logistics required. The operation entailed transporting forces, vehicles, ships, hospitals, and aircraft sorties from Montevideo, via Bangkok, to Boung Long, in the providence of Ratanakiri, on the northeast side of Cambodia.[37]

The decision to allow the armed forces to participate in UNTAC was made by President Luis Alberto Lacalle in consultation with Minister of Defense Mariano Brito. Economic and military considerations prompted the government's decision. Military advisors in Uruguay reasoned that UN peacekeeping was a relatively inexpensive mission that could divert the focus of the armed forces away from domestic politics and budgets to external roles, effectively transforming the dominant national security culture of the armed forces (which had focused mostly on internal missions). Peacekeeping provided an ongoing role that was more likely to be funded by some version of international assistance.

Decision makers in Uruguay thought that UN peacekeeping would also help alleviate budgetary ailments by providing additional salaries and operational resources. Individual military personnel had strong monetary incentives to join UN efforts because their salaries can more than triple during peacekeeping service. For example, a lieutenant colonel receives roughly $700 per month in Uruguay, but while on a UN mission, the same officer can make up to $6,000 monthly owing to all the extra incentives the state provides, such as a 50% pay hike. A navy noncommissioned officer makes $100 per month, but the same soldier can make up to ten times that amount while on a UN mission.[38] But the government did not realize that UN payments were slow and that it could take up to two years to be fully reimbursed. Former Minister of Defense Brito revealed that "we prepared the material, including vehicles, and we even painted the equipment; but the UN paid with some delay."[39]

After UNTAC, Uruguay engaged in two other deployments in Africa. In February 1993, Uruguay sent an infantry battalion to the southern region of Mozambique as part of the ONUMOZ mission. In January 1996, Uruguay followed in Brazil's footsteps, deploying an infantry battalion to UNAVEM II and III. In total, ninety-six military observers and 2,389 army officers and noncommissioned officers were sent to help verify a cease-fire agreement and an electoral process. But in 1997, the UN ordered all peacekeepers to withdraw, leading to a drastic decline in participation by Uruguayan blue helmets. This marked the end of the first phase of Uruguay's peacekeeping history, in which a declining military institution progressively embraced UN peacekeeping as an alternative mission.

## Phase II of Uruguay's Peacekeeping Activities, 2000–2011

Uruguay had not fully recovered from UNAVEM III when, in February 2000, the UN Security Council expanded the mandate and objective of MONUC (UN Mission in the Democratic Republic of Congo). Given Uruguay's peacekeeping experience in Africa, Secretary-General Kofi Annan requested that Uruguayan blue helmets form part of the mission. After domestic deliberations, Jorge Battle, the newly elected president of Uruguay, accepted the invitation and deployed the country's fourth-largest peacekeeping force. Between 2000 and 2004, over five thousand Uruguayan soldiers participated in MONUC. By

2004, the South American state became the leading troop contributor to MO-NUC, providing 21.32% of all UN military personnel. Since this deployment, Uruguay has maintained close to 11% of its military strength in UN peacekeeping operations.[40]

The deployment in the DRC began a gradual transformation of Uruguay's engagement with UN peacekeeping. Whereas in the first phase Uruguay supplied troops, it assumed a much more active, logistical role as a peacekeeper in the second phase, taking over tasks that included not only the deployment of troops but also the provision of services for the UN peacekeeping system. For instance, in MONUC, Uruguay maintains three battalions responsible for air and river transportation. A corps of army engineers has also been responsible for installing water treatment plants that supply drinking water to all UN units in the DRC (Angelero 2008). Today, there are six plants operating in the DRC and four in Haiti (Resdal 2010a). Uruguay gradually established a way of keeping its armed forces busy as well as a niche specialty area in the UN peacekeeping system, which has proven to be profitable.

The number of Uruguayan soldiers abroad has increased since 2004, mainly as a result of the country's contribution to MINUSTAH (González 2010, 293). In fact, Uruguay doubled its military strength by deploying close to thirteen hundred soldiers to Haiti, all while maintaining a similar force of peacekeepers in the DRC and a handful of observers in other UN missions. By 2010, Uruguay had become the second-largest troop-lending country in Haiti, second only to Brazil but larger than Argentina and Chile.[41]

The irony is that Uruguay was not originally included into the core group of South American states involved in MINUSTAH (i.e., Argentina, Brazil, and Chile—or ABC, as they are sometimes known). This group coordinated the political aspects of participating in MINUSTAH and formally became the $2 \times 3$ coordination mechanism, which regularly gathers two deputy ministries (foreign affairs and defense) from its three member states ($2 \times ABC = 2 \times 3$). The ABC excluded Montevideo from the bargaining table, in part because the country believed that it was already overcommitted in DRC. MINUSTAH was by no means a Mercosur initiative, although its members converged in Haiti by chance and then cooperated in an ad hoc manner. Chile (a non-Mercosur member) was the pioneer state to get involved in Haiti early on because of its close relationship with the United States. Brazil and Argentina followed suit. Uruguay, the largest Latin American peacekeeper, was left aside.

Why did Uruguay join MINUSTAH when it was already fully committed in MONUC? Perhaps because it was drawn into peacekeeping by its neighbors, following a regional diffusion pattern that prompted "contagious" behavior, in which proximate states emulate and imitate the strategies, policies, and practices of their fellow neighbors.[42] But Uruguayan peacekeepers deployed at a time when regional relations and integration within Mercosur were at their worst. Uruguay was knocked off course by Argentina's economic collapse in 2001, which led to a run on its banks and a deep recession in 2002–3. By 2004, Uruguay began exporting elsewhere, mainly to North America and the United States.

Furthermore, 2004 was the year that a diplomatic conflict emerged between Argentina and Uruguay, when the latter authorized the construction of two paper mills on the banks of a river that both states share. Buenos Aires eventually took the case to the International Court of Justice and sued Uruguay in 2006, leading to a freezing of diplomatic relations between these two South American neighbors.[43] If anything, bad neighborhood relations distanced Montevideo from the rest of its regional peacekeeping counterparts.

The 2002–3 financial crisis almost drained the country's foreign exchange reserves, forcing the government to close banks and negotiate a loan with the International Monetary Fund. Public spending was drastically cut, again affecting the budget of the armed forces. As in the previous phase, peacekeeping helped cushion the impact of this recession. In 2003, Yamandú Fau, then Uruguay's minister of defense, declared in testimony to Congress that the country had received $129 million over the past eleven years for its troop contributions. And Colonel Álvaro Picabea, the director of peacekeeping operations in the army's general staff, explained that "peacekeeping provides jobs that are needed when the country is facing its worst economic crisis."[44] In 2002 alone, the government received $20 million for supplementary peacekeeping salaries of participants in the UN mission in the DRC (Instituto de Ciencia Política de la Universidad de la República 2003). Peacekeepers were the country's second most profitable export product, after beef exports. By 2004, the Uruguayan economy was still recovering, and the UN mission in Haiti offered yet more resources and foreign currency.

There are no public data available on how much money Uruguay receives for its peacekeeping services, but it does get a generous amount of money in terms of UN allowances. In 2010 alone, Montevideo had on average close to twenty-three hundred soldiers abroad participating in different peace missions. This translates into $2.3 million per month, or $27.6 million a year, in UN allowances; compared with its defense budget, it represents close to 8% of the total budget for 2010 ($375 million; González 2010; Resdal 2010a). This figure does not include the reimbursement for equipment that had depreciated in value, nor does it take into account the compensation soldiers received for services, such as water treatment, provided to the UN. But, given that at any time 11% of the Uruguayan armed forces are abroad while another 11% are training for the next deployment (troops are rotated every six months), it appears that peacekeeping partially helps maintain at least a quarter of the force and may finance even more. In this sense, peacekeeping has become a true military profession, as its practitioners are paid generously for performing their duties.

## Conclusion

In all three case studies, it appears that democratization trends drive the supply of peacekeepers. Argentina and Uruguay were not motivated by geostrategic and security considerations to deploy troops to the UN. Not one of these countries committed uniformed personal in order to promote public goods or to lead by example. In fact, Uruguay is all but a regional or middle power. Although the countries vary in terms of size and capabilities, they all seem to share one intrinsic quality: they are still in the process of democratic consolidation. While Brazil's peacekeeping activities have promoted its status as an emerging power, its democratization process has been slow. In all three cases, troop commitments have increased as the domestic demand for democracy intensified.

A comparison of these cases sheds light on some of the hypotheses outlined in chapter 1, and supports the notion that democratization creates strong incentives to commit blue helmets. Table 2.1 provides a comparison of how different motivations associated with the democratization process shaped peacekeeping commitments across cases and in different historical phases. The need to signal a credible commitment to peace and cooperation amidst domestic instability motivated Argentina and Brazil to play a larger role in UN peace missions. In both cases, but in different historical periods, participation of the armed forces in UN-sanctioned operations signaled the arrival of a new era of foreign policymaking, thus shaping national identities. The desire to reform the military and to shape their roles in a postauthoritarian age has encouraged Argentina, Uruguay, and to a lesser extent Brazil to join peacekeeping efforts.

*Table 2.1.* Motivations in Argentina, Brazil, and Uruguay

| | Signaling | Domestic reform | Economic incentives |
|---|---|---|---|
| **Argentina** | | | |
| Phase I, 1990–95 | Government deployed troops to show its commitment as a reliable U.S. partner. | Politicians supported peacekeeping as a means to transform the mission and orientation of the military. | Peacekeeping increased salary incentives for soldiers. |
| Phase II, 1996–2003 | | | Government reduced its UN troop commitment due to a financial collapse. |
| Phase III, 2004–10 | Politicians committed troops to the UN to support regional partners (Brazil and Chile) in joint peacekeeping efforts. | | |
| **Brazil** | | | |
| Phase I, 1988–96 | Government committed troops to signal reliability as a new democracy. | Multilateral institutions were purposely sought to liberalize and internationalize the country after decades of inward-looking policies. | |
| Phase II, 1997–2003 | | | Brazil reduced its UN commitments due to the 1998 financial crisis. |
| Phase III, 2004–10 | President Lula used peacekeeping to signal Brazil's new "emerging power" status. | Domestically, the government utilized peacekeeping to incentivize service jointness and interagency cooperation between soldiers and diplomats. | |
| **Uruguay** | | | |
| Phase I, 1992–99 | | Civilian politicians used peacekeeping to transform the orientation of the military in a postdemocratic era. | For the military, peacekeeping alleviated budgetary ailments by providing additional salaries and operational resources. |
| Phase II, 2000–2011 | | | Peacekeeping deployments increased military revenues and organizational resources. |

In all three cases, engagement in peacekeeping provides juicy economic enticements for uniformed personnel and for the armed forces (mostly individual salaries), especially when military budgets are subject to drastic cuts imposed by newly established legislatures.

It is also clear that commitments to peacekeeping have not been constant or stable. UN troop contributions vary over time and between states, mainly because of associated or overlapping domestic trends. Economic instability and financial crises forced Argentina, Brazil, and even Uruguay to pull a substantial number of their forces out of various UN missions in the 1990s. The cases suggest, however, that domestic politics can drive democratizing countries to contemplate participation in peacekeeping.

Chapters 3–6 examine whether these countries' participation in peacekeeping had the intended effect. A sequential analysis of the three cases has generated numerous observations and assessments of the impact of peacekeeping, and having identified their incentives to participate, we can inquire about the consequences. Did peacekeeping reform the armed forces in Argentina in 1995, Uruguay in 1999, or Brazil in 2010? Was the outcome similar in Argentina and in the other cases? How different were the effects of peacekeeping engagement in Brazil during its first phase in the 1990s, and its second phase in 2004? How have increased peacekeeping commitments modified the armed forces in Uruguay? What have they learned from those various deployments? Has peacekeeping increased foreign and defense policy integration in all cases and over time? I now turn to whether (and if so, how) participation in UN peace missions affects military organizations and foreign policy integration.

# 3

## Does Peacekeeping Reform Military Organizations?

Having analyzed why democratizing states participate in peacekeeping operations, I now turn to how peacekeeping affects the military as an organization. As I discussed in chapter 1, the desire to induce military reform can motivate states to join international peacekeeping efforts. Conventional wisdom argues that participation in internationally mandated peace operations presents the armed forces of participating countries with numerous opportunities for reform. First, peacekeeping can help democratizing states upgrade and enhance military professional skills. In addition to providing budgetary benefits, peacekeeping is said to offer the added advantage of placing participants in an operational environment in which they can gain valuable hands-on experience (Palá 1998, 137). Second, such operations provide military officers with opportunities to modernize their doctrines, tactics, and capabilities through UN exercises and training. On a broader level, these missions also contribute to the transformation and gradual democratization of military participants and their national institutions. Loveman (1999, 267) contends that "it might even make young officers more cosmopolitan, less nationalistic, and more resistant to calls for military 'salvation' via coup in times of crisis." UN missions may theoretically intensify participants' exposure to democratic principles and practices, making them more receptive to notions such as the democratic control of the military.

This chapter examines such assertions and assesses the impact of participation in international peacekeeping missions on military organizations. I investigate how peacekeeping may affect training military exercises and mission orientation in troop-contributing nations. I ask whether these training exercises equip soldiers with new, transferable skills and enhance their general professionalism, and whether they gradually modify the orientation of a nation's armed forces as a growing proportion of its members engage in peace operations. I also discuss whether, if conventional wisdom holds, it is possible to detect the first signs of organizational change in a nation's military institutions immediately after its military personnel have participated in a UN mission. After all, such training sessions could well expose soldiers to novel doctrines and tactics while enhancing their logistical capabilities. Ultimately, a fundamental axiom must be respected—if peacekeeping is to be effective, participation in peace missions should divert the orientation of the armed forces away from internal security (counterinsurgency, quelling social protest, and maintaining public order) and toward international security.

In analyzing the impact of orientation and training exercises in military institutions, I emphasize the role of national decision makers in peacekeeping and the nature of their interactions with military institutions. Since elected leaders often make the decisions to participate in peace operations, they are also likely to determine how military institutions will integrate such experiences into their operations. This research reveals that outcomes typically hinge on whether the decision makers in troop-contributing countries act as active or passive managers of peacekeeping policies.[1]

I first review the literature on international peacekeeping and its potential effects on military organizations, which will be referred to as "the conventional wisdom." In addition, I elaborate on why UN peacekeeping operations are inherently distinct from other types of missions performed by international organizations such as NATO. The second section analyzes the three case studies, focusing primarily on how peacekeeping has affected (or not affected) training and orientation in troop-contributing nations over time.

## Why Training and Orientation? (And Why Peacekeeping Is Different)

In this chapter I focus on how peacekeeping operations affect military organizations in terms of training and mission orientation. I chose these indicators of military reform for two main reasons. First, a large body of literature on civil-military relations has paid overwhelming attention to issues related to military training. Prospective professional military leaders theoretically must undergo rigorous education and training programs in order to acquire a status that would deem them worthy of promotion, which makes training an intrinsic component of the military profession. As a result, advocates of military professionalism school contend that a highly trained soldier will not only be more professional than one who has not been professionally trained, she will also understand the imperatives of civilian control to a far greater extent (Huntington 1957; Janowitz 1960).

While this literature has been subject to academic criticism for the past decade, in the policy arena, professional military training continues to shape strategy and operations.[2] As previously stated, the conventional wisdom claims that engagement in international operations increases professionalism in part because it provides an environment in which soldiers can be trained to conduct a variety of tasks abroad. The acquisition of such expertise is thought to generate positive changes in military leadership and management systems at home. To examine this in greater depth, Moskos (1976) explored the attitudes of European national contingents with regard to their participation in UNFICYP in the 1970s. His study revealed that officers deployed there valued the training and tasks assigned to them. He asserted that members of the armed forces acquired additional professional skills if they engaged in international political crises that authorities were seeking to resolve by peaceful means and not through war: "Peacekeeping is clearly a progression of military professionalism along managerial lines . . . The peace soldier is one who is able to subscribe to the precepts of absolute minimal force, a reliance on compromise and negotiation, and the recognition of the elusiveness of permanent political solutions" (Moskos 1976, 137). In line with Moskos's insight, recent studies of the post–Cold War NATO have highlighted the virtues of the training and teaching mechanisms used by the alliance to help central and eastern European militaries gradually accept liberal democratic norms of governance (Gheciu 2005; Zagorcheva 2001/2002).

If such accolades about the power of military training are true, they should also apply to peacekeeping training, which provides participants with specialist training in peace observation, peacebuilding, and peace enforcement. Theoretically speaking, soldiers should receive diplomatic and mediation skills, concepts of humanitarian law and human rights, and basic UN rules. Such is the model Moskos envisioned, which ultimately helped to transform "the war manager" (the classic professional soldier) into "the soldier diplomat" (the postmodern soldier) more focused on preventing wars than on fighting them (Corn 2009; Moskos 1976; Moskos, Williams, and Segal 2000).

This brings us to the second reason why training and orientation are often considered important: they can help define a scope of military action. Some scholars believe that they help ensure that the armed forces do not stray beyond their officially set professional limits. In this respect, democratizing states would be wise to steer clear of so-called national security doctrines, which can involve the nation's armed forces in public order and enforcement functions—such as antidrug and narcotics campaigns, control of labor protests, strikes, peasant land seizures, and counterinsurgency—in addition to other civic action and development functions. Such a broad remit of responsibility may heighten their sense of self-importance and potentially reduce the speed of democratization (Stepan 1973, 46–65; Welch 1976).

Much of the scholarship on civil-military relations claims that civilians are better able to tether the military when they are assigned to missions overseas (Desch 1999, 120–33). In a critical review of this literature, Pion-Berlin and Arceneaux (2000, 417) summarized the argument posed by the conventional wisdom as follows: "As the military prepares professionally to face external challenges, it is increasingly preoccupied with matters strictly of a defensive nature, and thus lured away from domestic politics." For organizational purposes, mission orientation is as relevant as training, since it can define the military's fundamental national role (Hunter 1999).

Consequently, if peacekeeping is to be meaningful at an organizational level, it should also be able to contribute to keeping the military away from national security doctrines and policing roles, and more involved in externally oriented missions. In other words, peacekeeping operations should ideally have a doctrinal effect, serving as a mechanism for democratizing states to induce change, not only in their foreign policy but also in the military's overall orientation. Military routines, operations, and roles should thus be affected by the increased international interactions they experience during peace operations.

But UN peacekeeping is different from other missions performed by international organizations like NATO. Surprisingly, an official UN peacekeeping doctrine has never been established. The UN Charter does not even mention peacekeeping. The UN requires that soldiers meet two basic conditions: (1) that they have minimal foreign language credentials, such as fluency in English; and (2) that they be volunteers. UN experts agree that, while peacekeeping lessons have been learned and applied in practice, there is no comprehensive doctrine (Ahmed, Keating, and Salinas 2007). In the absence of a unified and centralized peacekeeping doctrine for all blue helmets, the UN has recently published *UN Peacekeeping Operations: Principles and Guidelines*, which provides basic directives and standard procedures for peacekeepers. As stated in UNDPKO (2008, 9):

> The document is intended to serve as a guide for all UN personnel serving in the field and at the UN Headquarters, as well as an introduction to those who are new to UN peacekeeping. Although it is intended to help guide the planning and conduct of UN peacekeeping operations, its specific application will require judgment and will vary according to the situation on the ground. Peacekeeping practitioners are often faced with a confusing and contradictory set of imperatives and pressures. This document is unable to resolve many of these issues; indeed, some have no clear, prescribed answers. Instead, it provides a handrail to assist planners and practitioners maneuver through the complexities of contemporary UN peacekeeping operations.

UN guidelines emphasize basic principles for peacekeeping, including consent of the parties, impartiality, nonuse of force, legitimacy, credibility, and promotion of national and local ownership (UNDPKO 2008, 31–38). Yet the UN does not prescribe member states how they are supposed to train their soldiers to follow these guidelines when they are assigned peacekeeping posts. Similarly, the UN does not offer specific procedures for how to prepare for more complex peace operations, such as those involving enforcement or Chapter VII mandates.

As a result, the UN does not formally train or instruct national contingents on how to conduct peacekeeping missions. Joint exercises are not mandatory, and no common training is formally required. The UN does not certify national training centers, nor does it send its own staff members to prepare future contingents. Ultimately, training and doctrine are dependent on national and domestic policies, which leaves each member state responsible for preparing, training, and indoctrinating their personnel, causing divergence—not convergence—of both UN training practices and doctrine. As each country is responsible for training its own peacekeepers, case-by-case analysis is appropriate. In the remaining sections of this chapter, I analyze the impact of soldiers' participation in peacekeeping missions upon organizational structures in Argentina, Brazil, and Uruguay.

## The Organizational Effects of Peacekeeping: Argentina

Of the three cases studied, Argentina is the only one in which peacekeeping had an impact on training and orientation, especially in the period between

1991 and 1996 during the Carlos Menem administration. Participation in peace operations appears to have had a lesser effect on Argentina's defense operations between 2004 and 2010. Here I focus on its impact in the 1990s and during MINUSTAH.

## Phase I of Argentina's Peacekeeping Activities, 1991–96

Chapter 2 referred to Argentina's first large-scale engagement in peacekeeping operations, which took place in 1991 during the first Gulf War after a number of domestic military revolts. Less widely known, however, is the fact that in 1991 Argentina did not have a specialized peacekeeping unit that met the UN's minimum requirements (fluency in English and being a strictly volunteer service). Huser (1998, 57) argues that "no existing unit was close to being prepared, since formations of this size (regiments, in the Argentine infantry nomenclature) were geographically based and consisted of relatively small professional cadres and large complements of conscripts; even those personnel were in short supply and not suitably trained for blue helmet units."

Therefore military training and education were reformed to comply with UN requirements. In 1994, President Menem eliminated the conscription system and ordered the establishment of a specialized training facility for Argentina's professional peacekeepers. As a result, CAECOPAZ (Argentina's Joint Peace Operations Training Center) was founded in 1995 in Campo de Mayo, an army garrison located in the outskirts of Buenos Aires, where some of the military revolts of the late eighties and early nineties first originated. The center was established to familiarize officers and soldiers with standardized concepts and to facilitate interoperability with foreign forces once a peacekeeping troop deployment was authorized. As Major Carlos Solcín, head of the education and doctrine department at CAECOPAZ, explained in an interview in 2002, "there was a need to internalize UN common procedures, which are sometimes different from national procedures."[3] The founding of CAECOPAZ also enabled officers who had previously served in peace missions to continue serving an institution with a similar ideological base.[4]

Officers who attended the school learned about theories and concepts that were not part of the standard training program in each of the country's service schools. The center ran a range of peacekeeping courses for UN military observers, UN company commanders, and UN staff officers and commanders, to name a few. Prospective peacekeepers usually underwent training for four to twelve weeks depending on their military rank and assignment. The curricula included such courses as UN logistics and administrative issues, operational communication, driving skills, cultural and religious awareness, diplomacy, international law, and medical care, including HIV and other illness prevention. Some of these courses were intended to help peacekeepers maximize their effectiveness in the societies they sought to serve. Another set of courses included UN background and principles, which familiarized peace soldiers with the structure and functioning of the UN system and other organizations connected with peacekeeping operations, such as NGOs. Interestingly, English language courses were not part of the core curricula. Officers simply needed to have passed an English proficiency exam before attending CAECOPAZ. The center's most unorthodox training courses focused on conveying negotiation techniques to participants, aimed at helping them prevent conflicts from escalating and teaching them about human rights and public affairs.[5] Officers attending CAECOPAZ were now learning about aspects of human rights that may well have been beneficial twenty years earlier during the Dirty War.

CAECOPAZ was institutionally underdeveloped from the outset and continues to be so today, especially when compared with the Canadian or Scandinavian peacekeeping training centers, which have developed doctrines and schools of thought and are fully integrated, effectively incorporating civilian components into peacekeeping training.[6] There is no Argentine peacekeeping doctrine, in part because CAECOPAZ operates more as a training center than as an academic institution. Nevertheless, inspired by the Canadian Pearson Peacekeeping Center, which some Argentine instructors attended, CAECOPAZ introduced programs for civilians, including a yearly workshop for journalists in conflict resolution and peace missions. The instructors include military staff as well as practitioners, diplomats, journalists, civilian scholars, and even psychologists, who help reintegrate soldiers with their families and units after service in peace missions.[7] Visiting scholars from universities in nearby Buenos Aires teach international and humanitarian law. As a consequence, several civilian components permeate the center. Internationalism also prevailed at the Campo de Mayo training facility, as U.S. military assistance helped support the facility until 2001, when the Argentine peso's financial collapse distanced Washington and Buenos Aires. CAECOPAZ was the first joint peacekeeping training center in Latin America and the first in the region to organize joint peace exercises with the U.S. Southern Command.

In the years following its foundation, the center provided training to Bolivian, Chilean, Paraguayan, and Peruvian visiting officers.[8]

CAECOPAZ had its limitations, however. Though numerous officers participated in peacekeeping missions between 1990 and 1996, the training offered at the center was not extended to other military programs. CAECOPAZ is unconventional in its teaching methods, emphasizing the importance of peaceful negotiation, but the schools run by each service offer a traditional and orthodox military education, of which antiguerrilla tactics and counterinsurgency were still a part in the 1990s.[9] "Officers were encouraged to learn English and increasing numbers began to pursue this option; however, overall, the armed forces had not reoriented their preparation towards the new internationalism" (Norden 1995, 344). When asked why these training sessions were not combined, senior officers revealed that the two systems could not be fully integrated because peacekeeping seemed to emphasize the softer aspects of military science while maintaining low levels of technical warfare skills.[10] In other words, two different perspectives dominated the Argentine military establishment, namely those held by staff who had participated in peacekeeping missions and whose outlook was typically more cosmopolitan and "civilian," and those who lacked such experience and tended to represent the perspectives of military nationalists and traditionalists.

The impact of CAECOPAZ was most evident in the relationship between soldiers and authorities, primarily because the center encouraged decision makers to act as managers. Until CAECOPAZ was founded, it fell to the relevant branch of the armed services to take responsibility for training. In the Argentine military system, recruits usually received their basic training in their assigned units. They then received further specialized training in military colleges and schools, but each service was in charge of maintaining its own training facilities. By contrast, the Estado Mayor Conjunto, or Military Joint Staff in the Argentine Ministry of Defense, managed CAECOPAZ, effectively empowering the ministry to prepare joint military strategies, operations, and training programs for UN peacekeeping.

Peacekeeping participation modified the relationship between the service commanders and the Ministry of Defense, particularly the Military Joint Staff, which is an advisory unit within the Ministry of Defense. Its function is to counsel the defense minister on joint military strategy and operations. It is staffed by active-duty officers but is independent from the services and their commanders. The Military Joint Staff was a weak agency in part because it clearly reflected the symptoms of "a more widespread and deeply rooted maladies of the state itself" (Pion-Berlin 1997, 142). To a limited extent, however, peacekeeping did affect the working procedures of the Military Joint Staff. The Ministry of Defense delegated peacekeeping logistics and operations authority to the Military Joint Staff, effectively empowering its staff vis-à-vis service commanders and enabling civilians at the Ministry of Defense to exercise more direct control over policy by undermining military autonomy.

The country's military had no previous experience of deploying major combat units abroad. In fact, the last time that a major movement of troops had occurred there was ten years earlier, during the Falklands/Malvinas War, which had not been categorized as a foreign deployment. So the coordination of logistics and forces for peacekeeping missions fell to the Military Joint Staff, which empowered its bureaucracy to make relevant deployment decisions.[11] As the army's commander in chief explained, "in Croatia, in less than 45 days, we had to send 106 vehicles, 900 men in a location 12,000 kilometers away" (Balza 1994, 6–7). Since military personnel had to be rotated, this task was performed every six months for almost seven years. One battalion was sent abroad while a new one was formed and trained at home. By the time the mission had been accomplished in 1995, more than seven thousand Argentine officers and non-commissioned officers had been exposed to peacekeeping and the CAECOPAZ training experience. The Croatian deployment was one of the few instances in which the three branches of the armed services were placed under the de facto control of the Military Joint Staff. Other joint operations they directly monitored included UNFICYP and UNIKOM.

In interviews conducted in Buenos Aires in 2002, Colonel Alfredo Berner, then director of peacekeeping operations in the Military Joint Staff, admitted that the army's dominance of peace missions provoked criticism among the other two forces. Nevertheless, he also recognized that the Military Joint Staff had been relatively successful in achieving its goals. As he explained, "because of our experience in previous peace missions, today we can perform joint operations better than a decade ago. The level of integration that we have achieved today is higher than when we engaged in war in 1982."[12]

What about mission orientation? Did peacekeeping help modify the overall inward-looking tendencies of the armed forces? Peacekeeping forced the military to introduce changes in its training processes and recruitment policies, which ultimately affected the institution's orientation. Argentina had to enlist military volunteers from several different national units. These recruits included officers and soldiers, mostly colonels, majors, captains, and noncommissioned officers. One of the Argentine battalions deployed to Croatia comprised fourteen senior officers, 113 junior officers, and 757 noncommissioned officers (Huser 1998, 58). Although the Argentine blue helmets came from each of the three military services, the substantial majority of the peacekeeping force was recruited from the army, which contributed 81% of all Argentine peacekeepers, while the navy (14%) and the air force (5%) participated to a far lesser extent. By 2002, approximately 40% of all army officers and 60% of all noncommissioned officers had acquired some kind of peacekeeping experience. Of all army officers, only 5% were generals or senior officers. The rest were junior officers.[13]

The recruitment process, which favored the youngest generation of army officers and soldiers, affected the structure and unity of the force. As Rosendo Fraga explained, "our peacekeeping units were not very cohesive because of the UN requirements, which forced us to recruit men from very different geographic companies."[14] This lack of cohesion had an effect on all national units and companies. Because of the UN language requirements, peacekeepers were the best the armed forces had to offer. The *crème de la crème* were spending most of their time abroad, at some distance from the unit to which they were originally assigned. Military cohesiveness was hence weakened at home, too.

So why did the armed forces sacrifice unit cohesion for peacekeeping missions? Peacekeeping served as a tool with which civilians could divide and conquer. The recruitment process benefited the very same cadre of officers and soldiers that had revolted against the government and the military leadership in the past: young, junior army officers and noncommissioned officers (from which most of the *carapintadas* or rebels originated). Peacekeeping was part of Menem's strategy to purge his forces of insubordinate staff by sending large numbers of soldiers abroad and keeping them busy in an activity that was radically different from their previous mission. In the Argentine case, peacekeeping was a diversion that effectively defused the domestic power of the military by changing the role and focus of a particular group of uniformed personnel away from domestic issues and toward external functions. Menem's defense policy consisted of reducing the size of the armed forces and dividing up the various groups so as to eradicate the source of future military revolts. Menem had a strong incentive to claim ownership of peacekeeping policies, and he used it to strengthen his own authority vis-à-vis the army.

But the recruitment process favored English proficiency over and above other skills, so military leaders excluded officers and soldiers who lacked foreign language skills but were competent in other areas, which generated division and antagonism between the "haves" (those with peacekeeping opportunities) and the "have-nots." By 2001, 10% of all Argentine peacekeepers had participated in two or more peace missions. The benefits and effects of peacekeeping were hence exclusive and far from universally shared.[15]

Even so, peacekeeping participation modified perceptions of military missions. In a survey conducted in 1985, Fitch (1998, 119) found that 70% of those interviewed listed internal security as a responsibility of the armed forces, in most cases second only to external conflicts. Seven years later, Fitch conducted the same survey and found that only one-third of the respondents on active duty listed internal security as a military mission. By 2001, the controversy regarding internal missions had largely disappeared. In a survey of 6,607 army officers, a Buenos Aires–based consulting firm found that 45% of those interviewed indicated that forming part of a peacekeeping mission was a priority for the armed forces, 39% perceived such missions as important but not primary, 15% considered peacekeeping as an unimportant mission for the force, and 1% expressed no opinion (Römer and Associates 2001). Argentina's *Book of National Defense*, first published in 1999 by the Republic of Argentina and its Ministry of Defense, formally documented these changes in perception, stating that "the Armed forces are expected to be used in defense of the nation's vital interest, in the framework of the UN and other international organizations, in support of security, and in support to the national community or friendly countries" (Republic of Argentina, 1999, 81).

## Phase II of Argentina's Peacekeeping Activities, 2004–10

As described in chapter 2, a serious financial crisis eroded Argentina's peacekeeping contribution between 1999 and 2003. During this period, only a handful of Argentine blue helmets deployed on peacekeeping missions. A lack of resources and the depreciation of the Argentine peso made it extremely difficult to keep CAECOPAZ afloat. The training center survived the economic debacle, but many of its programs were curbed as a result of multiple budget cuts. An official visit to CAECOPAZ in 2010 assessed its effectiveness after the financial crisis. The impact of the economic crisis upon the quality and form of the center's facilities was obvious. It had fewer permanent faculty members or resources to train prospective peacekeepers. Only soldiers with no previous peacekeeping experiences were required to attend the school, whereas those who had completed a second or third peacekeeping tour (who usually constituted the bulk of Argentina's peacekeeping contingents) were exempted. The training programs for troops had also been shortened from three months to only six weeks, and the outreach program to civilians (such as the training program for journalists) had been reduced, too. Training on human rights, humanitarian law, health issues, HIV, and other related programs continued.[16]

Despite the cutbacks, CAECOPAZ introduced two innovative features as a result of Argentina's re-engagement with peacekeeping in 2004. First, beginning with the authorization of MINUSTAH, Argentina introduced a series of policies to improve gender relations within the armed forces. They include a number of legislative initiatives and executive resolutions that focus on providing women with access to opportunities and equal standing within the institution, such as the ability to serve in higher-ranking positions or as military attachés to Argentine embassies (Ministerio de Defensa 2009a). These policies also strive to eradicate violence against women in the military.

CAECOPAZ has played a key role in ensuring the implementation of this new gender policy. The UNDPKO selected Argentina to develop a nationwide pilot plan to prepare and train the first cadre of female UN force commanders (Ministerio de Defensa 2009b). Argentina is the only Latin American country to have formally established a training program for women in peacekeeping operations. Women can now serve aboard warships, facilitating gender-integrated policies within the armed forces themselves. Decision makers expect that Argentina will be in a position to appoint the first Latin American female UN force commander, potentially affecting the organizational structure of its military and that of the UN itself.[17]

CAECOPAZ's second innovative policy created an Argentine-Chilean binational force for peace operations known as Cruz del Sur (Southern Cross). In this framework, two former regional military foes now conduct joint training exercises for peacekeeping operations in CAECOPAZ and CECOPAC, Chile's peacekeeping training center. Chile established CECOPAC in 2002 by emulating the policies of its Argentine neighbor. Diamint (2010, 670–71) determined that "Cruz del Sur . . . opened the prospect of further defense cooperation and helped to definitely end mutual conflict scenarios. Apart from difficulties that hampered both Argentina and Chile in uniting their respective armed forces—ranging from historical mistrust and suspicion to differences in eating habits—both countries had to overcome the skepticism and suspicion of DPKO officials."

In the post-2004 context, peacekeeping contributed to reforming Argentina's military policy to be more inclusive of women and to reshaping the country's doctrine and orientation toward Chile. While peacekeeping is no longer the military's most visible external mission, as it was in the early 1990s, the overall focus of the armed forces remains externally oriented.

## *Plus ça change, plus c'est la même chose*: Brazil

The case of Brazil contrasts with that of Argentina and highlights the divergent effects peacekeeping participation can have on military organizations. As I explained in chapter 2, international primacy and signaling motivated Brazil to participate in peacekeeping missions. Still, since the country's 2004 engagement in Haiti, peacekeeping has played a prominent role in Brazil's military policy. Some experts believe that its commanding role in MINUSTAH will eventually affect its military domestically. For instance, Clóvis Brigagão (qtd. in *Economist* 2010a, 42) has argued that "the old generation of soldiers is all about war and security. In another generation we'll have a new military, with an international outlook and new ideas about conflict prevention, civilian government and the rule of law."

Evidence gathered from the field contradicts this account, however. In spite of peacekeeping (or because of it), the Brazilian armed forces are predominantly inward looking, and their training and professional ethos still focus on public security. Furthermore, decision makers have assumed a laissez-faire approach to issues regarding doctrine, training, and organization for peacekeeping. Here I analyze how Brazil's peacekeeping policy has evolved from one of no training in the 1990s to one of conducting training sessions to promote public order in the post-2004 context.

### Phase I of Brazil's Peacekeeping Activities, 1988–2004

There is little evidence that military training and orientation changed during Brazil's first and second phases of engagement in UN peace operations (1988–2004). Brazilian military academies have historically played a key role in shaping the country's security policies; changes in the country's military education system would therefore represent a promising sign of transformation in Brazilian civil-military relations. But there is no indication that such reforms are taking place.

The Escola Superior de Guerra (or Advanced War School, an equivalent of the U.S. Army War College) has typically served as the academic and intellectual source of military policy in Brazil. The school transformed the country's old-style professionalism, which focused on ensuring territorial defense and creating a politically neutral military, into new-style professionalism, which placed a premium on internal security and highly politicized the officer corps.[18] Between 1988 and 2004, the Advanced War School continued to offer academic courses for officers and civilians at its headquarters in Rio de Janeiro, but peacekeeping was never formally incorporated into its curriculum. Most related discussions were integral components of courses in high political studies and strategy. However, a core course or seminar on peacebuilding was rarely organized by its faculty, which was made up primarily of retired and active-duty officers. I searched for primary sources and found a relatively small number of theses and research papers on UN peacekeeping in the army's School of Command and Chief of Staff.[19]

During this period, peacekeeping training took place through ad hoc and informal procedures. There was no public official policy for the selection of candidates, and each service decided autonomously who would join a peacekeeping force. In the army, the unit commander led the recruitment and selection processes. In theory, soldiers should have known English before their deployment. In practice, however, few Brazilian peacekeepers spoke English, as foreign language proficiency was not a mandatory component of the armed forces' education. Brazil has not always enforced language proficiency requirements as stipulated by the UN. Military observers and commanders were more likely to satisfy UN language requirements than noncommissioned officers. This policy has not changed in the post-2004 environment, so the criteria for selection remain the same.

Once selected from various national units, both officers and noncommissioned officers were sent to Brasilia for ad hoc training. Military personnel from the army's Joint Chief of Staff, for example, received two weeks of training on UN terms, standard procedures, and logistics before their deployment. But some Brazilian peacekeepers said they had never received formal training in preparation for their missions abroad. Some received information on UN peacekeeping procedures by mail, while others conducted their own research on the UN and the mission. The soldiers who did receive formal training, particularly those who joined UNAVEM III, attended Centro de Preparação e Avaliação, the army's training center in Brasilia.[20] The peacekeepers' general military and physical skills were assessed here, but the content of the exam was not made public, and few outsiders knew that it took place at all. Meanwhile, the rest of the training, which prepared participants both physically and psychologically, took place at either a specialist school of the armed forces or of the specific service to which soldiers were originally assigned.[21]

Unlike Argentina, where the Military Joint Staff was in charge of peacekeeping training, in Brazil the decision makers simply made the services' authority responsible for designing the soldiers' academic and professional curricula. As a result, with the exception of the Advanced War School and the army's School of Command and Chief of Staff, civilian scholars rarely taught courses to young Brazilian soldiers. Peacekeepers did not receive any sort of formal training on conflict resolution, mediation, or international law.

The Brazilian Army and Navy did not develop or establish peacekeeping training centers for their soldiers and officers until 2007. Colonel Sergio Wençeslão, then head of the army's Department for Peace Operations, indicated that additional training would not be necessary because his officers regularly underwent joint exercises like Operation South Cruzeiro, which was conducted biannually in partnership with Paraguay.[22] Similarly, General Benedito Leonel, the former head of the Armed Forces General Staff, argued that Brazil's peacekeepers were "well trained for specific types of missions. For instance, our troops in the Amazon are highly prepared to perform missions in jungles and can effectively serve in African countries."[23]

The Amazon would (and continues to) shape the army's organizational structure, serving as its focal point. There was no peacekeeping training center in Brazil at this time, but a specialized training school did exist in Manaus in the state of Amazonas. Known as the Center for War Instruction in the Jungle, the school prepared soldiers in the rainforest to safeguard Brazil's natural assets. There is little public information available on the school's doctrine and curriculum, but its official mandate was to prepare soldiers for rescue activities and for the deneutralization of guerrilla movements in the Amazon (Sucena do Carmo 1998). The units that served both in the UN missions in Mozambique and later in Angola were first recruited from this training facility in Manaus and from other units in the Amazon.

Consequently, participation in peacekeeping did not initially empower civilians or allow political leaders to designate roles for their armed forces. Decision makers assumed a passive role in peacekeeping affairs, enabling the military to focus on their preferred internal missions. The final outcome is not surprising; peacekeeping had no positive effects on training. On the contrary, the military's role in the Amazon influenced and shaped training for peace operations.

Did peacekeeping modify the military's typically inward-looking tendencies? The redemocratization of Brazil in 1985 failed to change the perspective of the armed forces, at least initially. Internal security functions guided Brazil's military operations over the next two decades.[24] Federal troops routinely helped placate social protests and rallies. In some cases, the military repressed social demonstrations in Rio de Janeiro without even consulting police forces (Mesquita Neto 1999).

The Brazilian military had been successful in identifying new domestic roles and functions for its ranks, which may suggest that they were relatively autonomous in defining their institutional mission. Luis Bitencourt argued "there is really no external mission, no notion of external deployment. The main mission seems to be the protection of homeland, particularly the Amazons."[25]

In principle, securing and defending the country's northern borders (the Amazon is the natural frontier between northern Brazil and six other South American countries) appear tantamount to guaranteeing national sovereignty. According to the military, the Amazon had to be protected against international intervention, drug trafficking, and guerrilla warfare. The problem was that the challenges in the Amazon required the armed forces to do far more than mere defense. In fact, the area was militarized and the army became the largest landowner in the Amazon, deploying almost 40% of its entire personnel to the zone. Soldiers built schools, hospitals, and housing, and also provided services and performed activities otherwise reserved for other state agencies. In so doing, they may have made up for the limited presence of the state in the Amazon, but they also reinforced their own inward-looking orientation.[26]

In this initial phase, many of Brazil's politicians and scholars believed that observation and peacekeeping missions were similar to Brazilian military missions in the Amazon. After all, Brazilian soldiers went to far-off jungle destinations to help build bridges and schools while helping the state consolidate its presence and authority there. Hunter (1999, 4) found that decision makers saw "an added benefit in relocating army units and their internal security functions away from Brazil's large urban centers to the remote Amazon region." In other words, performing peacekeeping was merely seen as an extension of the military's internal mission. Nevertheless, less than 2% of Brazil's military was involved in UN missions between 1988 and 2004. By contrast, 40% fully deployed in the Amazon in the same time frame. This contrasts considerably with the situation in Argentina, where almost 40% of the army officer corps deployed overseas in the 1990s.

This does not mean that civil-military relations have not changed since the democratization of Brazil in 1984. Civilian control was in fact stronger during the administration of President Fernando Henrique Cardoso (1995–2003), when a civilian-led defense ministry was finally established in 1999. But this change would appear to stem from domestic impulses, in which peacekeeping policies played no part in decision-making processes.[27]

## Phase II of Brazil's Peacekeeping Activities, 2004–10

As mentioned in chapter 2, Brazil decreased its UN peacekeeping commitment in 1998 following a severe financial crisis. Interest in UN missions did not re-emerge until 2004, when the country took command of MINUSTAH. Unlike the phase between 1998 and 2004, Brazil's more recent peacekeeping engagements have been the subject of a much broader national debate over the role of the armed forces. No doubt, the government participated in peacekeeping missions primarily because it sought to signal its international primacy to the world. President Luiz Inácio Lula da Silva also sought, however, to improve interagency coordination, especially between the Ministry of Defense and Itamaraty. To date, such attempts to reform military policy have failed.

In his efforts to reform the military, President Lula introduced a number of initiatives. Perhaps most notably, in 2008 he signed the National Defense Law, which went into effect in 2010. In this period, he sought to improve the interoperability of the joint forces by creating the Joint Command of the Armed Forces within the Ministry of Defense (Ministério de Defesa 2008). He hereby attempted not only to improve coordination and "jointness" between the various branches of the armed services but also to strengthen the Ministry of Defense, which has suffered from institutional weakness since its creation in 1999. Each force has traditionally managed policy issues, such as deployment, procurement, training, education, and recruitment processes independently.

The ministry has not been able to effectively override the power of the individual services or to formulate defense policies without continuous intervention from the various force commanders.[28]

The new law did not address issues concerning military training or orientation, however. Unlike in Argentina, where CAECOPAZ was founded outside the command of the services and within the Ministry of Defense, Brazil's civilian leaders granted the armed services autonomy on matters related to peacekeeping training, education, and professionalization. Indeed, civilian authorities delegated the implementation of their policies to the armed forces without any oversight. Brazil is a latecomer in terms of peacekeeping training centers. Its first school for peacekeeping operations opened in 2007, long after the creation of MINUSTAH. But instead of forcing a change within the military, Brazil's decision makers gave the services what they wanted: they authorized the creation of two peacekeeping centers, one for the navy marines known as Corpo de Fuzileiros Navais (School for Peacekeeping Operations), and one for the army, also known as the Peacekeeping Training Center. Ironically, both centers were located in Rio de Janeiro, but each had separate commands, instructors, and audiences. This outcome reflected Brazil's traditional service rivalry, in which the army and navy have historically followed different organizational cultures, leading to intense bureaucratic battles over resources and missions.

In practice, the armed forces had two distinct approaches toward peacekeepers. One form of training focused on the Fuzileiros Navais, the all-professional, elite force whose officers have been exposed to several years of military training and education. Its training school had a much more specialized approach toward peacekeeping, precisely because it focused on training professional soldiers, mostly sergeants and captains. As one of the instructors mentioned in an interview, "ours is an all-volunteer force and close to 90% of our officers have already participated in at least one peacekeeping tour. They no longer require basic training, since they have already spent time in our academies and are familiar with peacekeeping. They are already knowledgeable on human rights."[29]

The army offered a second form of training, which puts an emphasis on troops and noncommissioned officers who for the most part constitute the "hard-core" component of Brazil's contingent in Haiti. In fact, less than 20% of Brazilian Army officers have served on a peace mission since 2004. But the army's training program has not been without controversy. Even critics within the army have raised concerns about the methods used to train recruits for peacekeeping. In 2007, Tailon Ruppenthal, a retired soldier who served as a blue helmet in one of the first units sent to Haiti, wrote a scathing critique about the routine violence in Haiti and the harsh training process imposed by the Brazilian Army. The point of the training program was not to instill appropriate skills for the peace mission, but to ensure discipline within the ranks by exposing the soldier to harsh conditions (Ruppenthal 2007).[30] Language, humanitarian law, and negotiation skills were not part of the training packet offered to the army's noncommissioned officers. Soldiers recruited for peacekeeping were trained following the same standard procedure used in other homeland security missions.

In 2010, both training centers were eventually integrated into Brazil's Joint Peacekeeping Center, named after the late UN Ambassador Sergio Viera de Mello. It appears the army won the bureaucratic battle over command against the navy. But this move did not necessarily improve the Ministry of Defense because the command of the peacekeeping center was, as usual, delegated to the army, much to the chagrin of the marines. The center resides in the same army headquarters as the army's Peacekeeping Training Center and comes under the same army commander. In practical terms, the school changed its name, but not how it functioned. Staff members and instructors come entirely from the military, with no full-time civilian faculty. Civilian guest speakers occasionally lecture on specific issues, but the army mostly instructs courses, including those on humanitarian law and human rights. The entirety of the student body is made up of uniformed personnel, so there is no sign of civil-military integration in the training process itself.

The country's engagement in MINUSTAH serves as a training ground for developing the military's urban operations skills, with a view to using the forces for the so-called pacification of *favelas* (slums). In this case, the emphasis is not on developing new professional skills to help reorient the armed forces toward external missions; rather, the focus is on developing skills to reinforce the military's traditional inward-looking approach.

Peacekeeping training thus emphasizes policing skills, including protest control, urban anticrime efforts, contraband interdiction, and antinarcotics. Army General José Nardi, the new head of the recently created Joint Command of the Armed Forces, explained the training procedures in an interview to the Mexican journal *Reforma* (qtd. in Armendáriz 2011):

The military has more than two months of special training to act amid a civilian population, which is not the same as facing a conventional military enemy. Our troops specialize in the use of non-lethal weapons (pepper spray, tear gas and rubber bullets); they are educated into criminal law to know the limits of action and are trained to patrol the *favelas*, mount checkpoints and dealing with children in schools and mass media.[31]

During an international seminar on peace missions organized by the Fuzileiros Navais in 2009, the marines conducted a peacekeeping exercise that consisted of a scenario in which a large and unruly group of protesters confronted blue helmets. The potential Brazilian peacekeepers then displayed their skills at dispersing the demonstration, first by using tear gas and then by relying on rubber bullets.[32]

The acquired training for peacekeeping is then used as a model for the military's domestic mission, as it is applied not only in Haitian slums but also in Brazilian *favelas* in the so-called pacification strategy (Barnes 2010). Pacification involves the deployment of a large number of security forces, including army and marine troops as well as military police, to clear the slums by hunting members of violent gangs and drug traffickers. This deployment is then followed by months of heavy patrols in which several state agencies and civil society organizations provide basic services to slum inhabitants. Ideally, the pacification works in such a way that it allows for the withdrawal of security forces, leaving behind functioning civilian and peaceful neighborhoods. Training efforts for pacification are moreover intended to retrain soldiers from using excessive force. In practice, however, the pacification strategy has led to an almost-permanent presence of military troops, as well as to serious allegations of police corruption and human rights abuses in which the use of force is the common practice.[33] The implementation of urban pacification strategies, which are allegedly inspired by peacekeeping practices, has utterly failed.

Perhaps the most widely known case of pacification took place in December 2010, when eight hundred military troops and eighteen hundred riot police joined forces to pacify the Complexo do Alemão, a group of thirteen large and mostly violent *favelas* in Rio de Janeiro. During the operation, the troops captured 692 pounds of cocaine and four hundred weapons but comparatively little cash ($68,000). Thirty-seven people died, most of them bystanders, while more than four hundred drug traffickers escaped, most likely assisted by police forces who allegedly drove them away in squad cars in exchange for cash. Since police forces are scarce and not fully trusted by Brazil's local inhabitants, the military forces have now been permanently stationed in the *favelas* "despite complaints from civic activists that the soldiers were not fit for a policing role and might only anger residents" (Barrionuevo 2010).[34]

Most of the military staff members that participated in the "pacifying" operation ironically had been trained for and participated in UN peacekeeping. Sergio Cabral, governor of Rio de Janeiro, made the request for soldiers when he argued (qtd. in *Economist* 2010c) that "many of the troops have performed peacekeeping duties in Haiti." Likewise, General Fernando José Lavaquial, appointed by the Ministry of Defense to be in charge of the Complexo do Alemão, was a former brigade commander in MINUSTAH.

The use of the military as peacekeepers or "*favela* pacifiers" is not exceptional or sporadic. The pacification strategy has expanded to more than twenty federal states. Rio de Janeiro is at the center of this strategy, in part because it is under intense international scrutiny to reduce its high crime rate after being chosen as the venue for the 2014 World Cup and the 2016 Summer Olympics. Military policing roles in Brazil are literally up and coming, and all highly reinforced by peacekeeping.

The internal focus of the armed forces can be easily traced by comparing the number of forces overseas with those deployed at home. Brazil has a total force of almost 300,000 soldiers—roughly seven times that of Argentina. Of these, fewer than two thousand deploy each year for peacekeeping; the remainder stay at home, mostly performing internal and homeland security missions. Brazil's military could deploy far more troops for peacekeeping missions than it actually does, but its internal focus keeps them busy at home.

The Brazilian case is critical because peacekeeping provides strong incentives to reinforce inward-looking military missions and contributes to what Zavarucha (2000, 8–31) once referred to as "the militarization of public safety." Such militarization is a process by which military models, methods, concepts, doctrines, procedures, and personnel are applied to public nonmilitary spaces such as policing, public security, law enforcement, judiciary, politics, and now peacekeeping. In this context, peacekeeping adds an additional layer of legitimacy to the military by fostering the general perception that if troops are being trained, used, and even authorized by international bodies to "pacify" slums abroad, they can be used at home for a similar purpose. In the Brazilian case, peacekeeping is not reforming military organizations. Rather than importing new doctrines and training programs from overseas, Brazilian troops export their conventional policing roles and apply them to peacekeeping strategies with unintended consequences for democratic civilian control.

## An Externally Oriented Mission with No Military Reform: Uruguay

Chapter 2 elaborated on Uruguay's economic motivations to participate in peacekeeping mission. In it, I argued that the country was able to profit from its international commitment to UN efforts. But Uruguay is not only a profiteer; it is the eighth-largest troop supplier to the UN system and Latin America's most active participant in peace operations. Of the various case studies, it should be the most likely case for military reform precisely because the armed forces have been so heavily exposed to UN missions for almost two decades, and because they actually embraced such operations with the specific intent of reforming their operational mission. Yet, as I show, the impact of peacekeeping in this small South American country differs from that in Argentina and Brazil. On the one hand, between 1992 and 1999, the armed forces fully embraced peace missions, a move that contributed to modifying their orientation. On the other hand, while peacekeeping became the military's main mission (circa 2000), it did not radically modify their organization or training approach. Here I explain how peacekeeping changed military orientation but then failed to induce reform.

### Phase I of Uruguay's Peacekeeping Activities, 1992–2000

UN peacekeeping helped ensure the survival of the Uruguayan military at a time when it was desperately seeking resources and a relevant role (see chapter 2). Slowly but surely, the armed forces transitioned from being an inward-oriented institution (focused mostly on antiguerrilla tactics) to an outward-oriented military, massively committing troops abroad while assuming an entrepreneurial role in the provision of peacekeeping services.

In interviews conducted in 2003, several Uruguayan officers rejected the idea that peacekeeping had de facto become the military's main mission. Colonel Roberto Urrutice explained, "we continue to value our traditional mission. We still defend the national sovereignty, as described in our Constitution."[35] With the attention focused exclusively on formal institutions and written documents, there was little evidence that peacekeeping had become a strategic mission. In Uruguay, there is no white paper on national defense, there are no peacekeeping manuals, there is no official peacekeeping doctrine. The army's official website specifies that its mission is to "guarantee, in all circumstances and against all forms of aggression, the security and integrity of the nation, its institutions and its inhabitants." The website does have a link for peacekeeping, but it appears as part of what the army calls "solidarity missions," which involve providing assistance to local communities and international peace missions.[36]

Nevertheless, it is difficult to dispute the claim that, since 1992, peacekeeping has become the military's raison d'être, especially when more than 11% of the military's personnel are serving in nine different UN missions. In addition, an equal number of soldiers are presently training for the next peacekeeping tour; troops are rotated every six months, with troops sent abroad for half a year and then returned home to be replaced by another unit. Uruguay is actually one of the few Latin American countries with an all-volunteer, professional force. Yet Uruguay does not have a specialized peacekeeping unit. Instead, blue helmets are enlisted from different services and military divisions nationwide, posing challenges for military cohesion. Ultimately, this means that close to 25% of Uruguay's military—some twenty-five thousand men and women—is fully committed to peacekeeping missions every year.[37] There is no doubt that UN peacekeeping is now part of the army's role. The organizational purpose of the military as an institution is focused on addressing issues related to logistics, deployment, training, and budgeting for peace missions that take place miles away from Uruguay's borders. In other words, UN peacekeeping became "institutionalized" within the armed forces.

## Phase II of Uruguay's Peacekeeping Activities, 2000–2010

Much like in Argentina and Brazil, peacekeeping in Uruguay has contributed to improving the coordination and jointness within the branches, but military reform remains elusive. Like its neighbors, Uruguay suffers from service rivalry in which the army, navy, and air force jealously guard their centers and resources while preventing attempts to merge or reassign assets. Peacekeeping is an exception to this rule because, as General Hebert J. Figoli explained, it "helps our three forces to operate jointly."[38] Their ability to operate jointly in peace missions appears to be the common organizational contribution of peacekeeping participation. But two problems persist in Uruguay: the military enjoys the institutional autonomy with which to design peacekeeping policies, and its peacekeeping training program includes remnants of the old national security doctrine.

Peacekeeping has become part of the military's exclusive area of influence (a reserve domain) in which civilian authorities have virtually conceded full autonomy. In other words, civilian leaders assume the role of passive managers and take a laissez-faire approach. Much like when Brazil and Argentina transitioned to democracy, the Uruguayan Ministry of Defense was born with inherent political and institutional weaknesses that contributed to enhancing military autonomy. Besio (2008, 289) argues that "once democracy had returned, and the national security doctrine had been wiped out from the legal framework, basic structural definitions had not been made from political institutions, so as to establish clearly the institutional character of the defense and the Armed Forces . . . Clearly, the political space always has to be occupied and, due to the lack of political leadership as to national defense matters, military bureaucracies have been gradually filling up the emptiness."

The Ministry of Defense had little institutional capacity to design defense policies. Instead, there is the National Defense Council, which consists of the minister of defense and the commanders in chief of the army, navy, and air force. It acts in an advisory capacity to the president in the formulation of defense policy, but it relies heavily on the service commanders. In practice, the council informs the minister of defense but relies on the services. As a result, each service has de facto operational and political leeway to shape defense and, by extension, peacekeeping policies.

The Uruguayan presidency decreed the creation of the National System for the Support of Peacekeeping Operations (SINOMAPA) in 1994. SINOMAPA resides within the National Defense Council and coordinates peacekeeping policies between military organizations and governmental agencies. Its goals are to ensure that the units are prepared to start the mission; to make sure that deployment takes place as quickly as possible; and to guarantee economic, political, and technical support for the mission's success once participation has been decided upon by the president and the Ministry of Defense.[39]

Nevertheless, the system has been criticized because civilians are underrepresented. The president chairs SINOMAPA, but its regular attendees are the service commanders. The statutory director of the system is the joint chief of staff, which reports directly to the army's commander in chief. The heads of other executive departments and agencies (such as the Ministry of Foreign Affairs and the Ministry of Economics), as well as other senior officials, are invited to attend meetings of the SINOMAPA when appropriate (Comando General del Ejército 2003, 153–54). The armed forces (especially the army) therefore handle questions regarding peacekeeping logistics, organization, strategy, and doctrine. The system effectively reproduces the structure of military prerogatives in the defense sector and then expands them to the area of peacekeeping, with little effect over civilian control or military reform.

Peacekeeping has ironically impeded Uruguay from undertaking an important reform, namely the modernization of its force. Although Uruguay has a professional military and does not recruit soldiers through conscription, it has one of the highest ratios of armed forces personnel per citizen in the Southern Cone: seven soldiers per one thousand people, as opposed to two per one thousand in Argentina and Brazil.[40] The total number of armed forces personnel did not substantially change after the transition to democracy. In 2010, Uruguay had 24,506 armed forces personnel, only seven thousand fewer than in 1981, when the military was still in power (González 2010, 289–90; International Institute for Strategic Studies 1998–2001). Congress has previously discussed a reduction in the size of the force, but the debate has abated, in part because of fears that such measures would undermine Uruguay's large and profitable peacekeeping contribution (a smaller force would mean fewer blue helmets). Colonel Álvaro Picabea, director of peacekeeping operations in the army's General Staff Office, explains that "peacekeeping provides jobs that are needed when the country is facing its worst economic crisis."[41]

There are also concerns regarding peacekeeping training. First established in 1998 and located in the army's School of Arms and Services, the Uruguayan Peacekeeping Operations School prepares qualifying officers, soldiers, troops, and personnel from military and police services. Depending on their military rank, personnel drafted for peace operations spend from three to six weeks in the school, attending seminars and courses for UN military observers, junior officers, contingents, military police forces, and commanding officers. The training is organized into modules consisting mostly of peacekeeping doctrine as stated in UN documents, operative techniques, history, specialized technical skills (such as the deactivation of landmines), and personal security measures. The school also enables enlisted volunteers to get to know each other and to develop an *esprit de corps* for the mission.[42]

The peacekeeping school is institutionally underdeveloped because the curriculum is not stated in manuals, there are no debriefings, and there is virtually no civilian input. The school does not seem to have developed a national peacekeeping doctrine, either. Colonel Pablo Pintos, director of the school, explained, "structured knowledge is not very useful at tactical and field levels. It is useful at a theoretical level, but useless at a tactical level. Training is better if it relies on real field experience."[43] So training takes place in an informal environment, where the instructor teaches young beginners by sharing her personal experiences of UN peace missions.

Notwithstanding the organizational and innovative advantages of the training center, the army has sufficient institutional autonomy to design peacekeeping curricula with no civilian intervention. All instructors are active officers, and the only civilian students allowed to join the training program are doctors and nurses working for military hospitals and who are also drafted for peacekeeping. One member of the Uruguayan Foreign Service with peacekeeping experience explained to me, "the courses peacekeepers take on international law and human rights are never taught by lawyers or jurists. Even their marketing strategy fails to show the human and civilian dimensions of peacekeeping. What kind of pictures do they bring back from the mission? Tanks and weapons!"[44]

Training procedures have raised questions at home and abroad, particularly since the large Uruguayan force deployment to the DRC. It is worth noting that Uruguay experienced bloody urban guerrilla and counterinsurgency warfare in the 1970s. The radical Uruguayan guerrilla movement Tupamaros ceased to be a threat to the country in large part because the army relied on mass arrests, torture, and large cordon-and-search operations. Military reform in Uruguay has always been debated not just in terms of reorientation, but also in terms of a change in tactics and national security doctrine, with less emphasis on counterinsurgency. Nevertheless, there have been reported incidents in which Uruguayan peacekeepers have been accused of performing actions that resemble antiguerrilla tactics.

Blue helmets from Uruguay have had violent encounters with various active, belligerent groups while performing peacekeeping operations, leading to acts of serious misbehavior. Two officers were kidnapped and killed by the Khmer Rouge in Cambodia.[45] More worrying, in the DRC, Uruguayan peacekeepers were accused of corrupting and torturing civilians (*El Clarín* 2003; UN Integrated Regional Information Network 2003). In Haiti, five Uruguayan peacekeepers were accused of sexual abuse and assault on a teenage boy (BBC News 2011b). (I detail these events in chapters 4 and 5.)

These incidents have led critics to argue that peacekeeping missions have merely transferred military antiguerrilla tactics from domestic to international environments.[46] The incidents in the DRC and Haiti suggest that perhaps the army was training its peacekeeping personnel with some of the old doctrines used during the authoritarian era, such as counterinsurgency and antiguerrilla tactics. One former UN civil servant and Uruguayan native said, "for peacekeeping to be effective, human rights training is required. Most of our peacekeepers, however, have no understanding whatsoever of international or humanitarian law."[47]

Uruguayan military officials insist that this type of misconduct is not a general feature of or systemic among its forces. Statistics compiled by the UN Department of Safety and Security (2011), however, indicate that there were allegations of sexual misconduct against fifty-nine UN peacekeepers in MONUC in 2007, thirty-six in 2010, and at least eleven in 2011. The report did not indicate the nationality of the staff members, but Uruguay was the second-largest troop contributor to the mission.

The army suspended the soldiers and the top officers heading the battalion in MONUC who had been accused of torture in 2004. But Congress did not conduct a formal investigation, and the army did not release an official report. Furthermore, the events in the DRC included criminal misbehavior, and the blue helmets should have been subject to criminal proceedings and not merely punished by their superiors. As an international body controlled by sovereign states, the UN is limited to denunciating acts of misbehavior but has virtually no authority to enforce domestic law when criminal misconduct occurs. It is the responsibility, then, of each country participating in the mission to impose a sanction when their national contingents infringe the law of another state while performing peacekeeping.[48] Ironically, in the DRC incident, the Uruguayan military proceeded in the same way as when accused of human rights abuses at home—with secrecy, denial, and no public trials of any type.

In the Haitian case, the Uruguayan Ministry of Defense has promised to open an investigation into the alleged sexual assault involving Uruguayan peacekeepers. It also relieved of his duties the chief navy commander of the Uruguayan contingent and repatriated all members of the unit (Romo 2011). But the Ministry of Defense responded to the alarm raised by the media and not because of proper civilian oversight. There remains considerable skepticism about the nature of the investigation itself, in part because the armed forces simultaneously played the role of judge, prosecutor, and accuser as military justice—not civilian courts—addressed the case.

Consequently, the Uruguayan government has not reformed its defense and military systems despite its active participation in peacekeeping missions. Civilian decision makers share some of the blame for failing to intervene and then delegating too much autonomy. For almost two decades, conservative moderate political coalitions that tended to support the military ruled the country. In 2005, a leftist and mostly antimilitary political coalition (the so-called Frente Amplio) took power in Uruguay for the first time since the democratization. But even with such political realignment, the government did not alter the strong level of military involvement in UN peacekeeping missions. Congress approved the National Defense Act, which would radically transform and strengthen the Ministry of Defense by eradicating the National Defense Council in 2010, at the end of the first term of the Frente Amplio government. It is now up to the new administration, led by José Mujica, a former Tupamaro leader, to implement the necessary changes.[49] However, even if this change does take place (the law had yet to be enacted in 2011), the evidence indicates that such reform would have taken place in spite of, and not because of, Uruguay's peacekeeping contribution.

## Conclusion

Having traced the process and individually analyzed each case, we can identify some common trends. The central question of this chapter is whether peacekeeping affects military organizations. It does, but only in some cases, and the overall effect is not always the same. In fact, peacekeeping has divergent effects that are particularly noticeable in neighboring South American states sharing similar underlying conditions, but it produces different results. Comparatively speaking, Argentina is the only country where peacekeeping participation transformed military training and orientation, leading to improvements in civilian control. This case seems to partially support the mainstream thinking about peacekeeping and its potentially positive effects. But if the conventional wisdom was right, all democratizing states engaged in peace missions should have followed the Argentine path. Instead, the evidence paints a rather different picture. Uruguay modified the military's orientation, but then failed to induce reforms in training and civilian control. In Brazil, the armed forces managed to keep their traditional internal orientation and training doctrines without affecting the existing levels of civilian control (table 3.1).

*Table 3.1.*    Comparison of organizational
change

Training

|  | New | Old |
|---|---|---|
| **Orientation** | | |
| External | Quadrant 1<br>Argentina | Quadrant 2<br>Uruguay |
| Internal | Quadrant 3 | Quadrant 4<br>Brazil |

Why does peacekeeping engagement generate so much variation? The level of exposure to peacekeeping (how much peacekeeping is done) appears to be inconsequential for the outcome; Uruguay, with the most peacekeeping experience, has reformed its military the least. Argentina and Uruguay, where peacekeeping managed to change the orientation of the armed forces, have different values in terms of civilian control, which tells us something about the relationship between mission orientation and civilian control. Democratizing states will not simply establish civilian control because the military is conducting a mission abroad. The evidence from Brazil and Uruguay indicates that civilians can lose control over the armed forces just as frequently when deployed overseas as when at home.[50]

Previous levels of civilian control cannot explain this divergence, either; all cases (including Argentina) deployed their soldiers abroad at challenging political junctures, when their respective ministries of defense were institutionally fragile. Similarly, motivation cannot explain this policy variation. If a democratizing state (such as Brazil) is not motivated to induce military reform, then peacekeeping will probably fail to modify the armed forces. But even countries that intended to change their military institutions by exposing them to peacekeeping (like Uruguay or Brazil in the second phase) failed to fulfill their expectations: "one cannot infer results from desires and expectations and vice versa" (Jervis 1997, 61). Precisely for this reason, one must distinguish between motivation and effects, or between what decision makers want from peacekeeping and what they actually get.

The difference between Argentina and the others is the role of decision makers. In the Argentine case (especially in the initial phase), civilians seized on the peacekeeping opportunity and resisted temptations to simply delegate peacekeeping missions to the military. President Menem effectively used peacekeeping as a carrot and stick with which to induce change. He used missions abroad and their better compensation packages to reward those who complied with his vision. His administration used UN missions as a policy tool with which to help strengthen a traditionally weak Ministry of Defense and Joint Chief of Staff. Training for peacekeeping provided an opportunity for civilians to intervene in doctrinal matters. President Menem and his civilian leadership managed, claimed ownership, and assumed an active role when implementing peacekeeping policies. In the other cases, civilian leaders assumed a laissez-faire approach, deferring peacekeeping-related decisions to their military commanders while leaving key decisions on organization, training, and doctrine in the hands of the armed forces. In many ways, they assumed a passive role and then conceded institutional autonomy. The military then responded by relying on its own organizational biases, following customary practices, and applying the same criteria of doing things to their "new" peacekeeping duties. In other words, peacekeeping became part of the conventional "militarized" strategy.

Argentina is an exception in that it used peacekeeping as a stick with which to divide and then conquer the strongest component of its armed forces. Participation in UN missions was part of a strategy to clean and purge the army, which had traditionally posed a considerable threat to domestic stability. The consequence of this policy was not only to strengthen the position of the joint chief of staff but to encourage some degree of interservice rivalry, which permitted the various forces to monitor each other and to make sure that one service's power not surpass that of the others. Peacekeeping reinforced civilian control in Argentina because it enabled civilians to manipulate tradeoffs in resources, to divide and conquer the services, or to force decisions to the surface.[51]

In Brazil and Uruguay, peacekeeping policies strengthened, benefited, and then unified the military, especially the army. Peacekeeping appeared to have one common organizational effect in both countries: increased force jointness. Increased integration and rationalization of UN peace operations have diminished internal fights and struggles that would have created additional monitoring mechanisms under other circumstances, as services check each other and civilians trade resources. In these two countries, peacekeeping actually increased the army's leverage vis-à-vis the other services and even civilians.

I revealed how peacekeeping training affects military organizations to some extent. All these governments involved responded to UN demands by establishing national peacekeeping training centers, but they varied substantially in terms of integration and doctrine. The UN certainly plays a role in this outcome, since the absence of clear doctrinal and unified guidelines allows troop-lending states to train their blue helmets on the basis of national (not international or multilateral) doctrines. The absence of conditionality clauses—of the sort NATO has—impedes the UN from making the participation of countries conditional upon their training of peacekeepers in accordance with international standards. As a result, with the exception of Argentina, peacekeeping training had very few positive effects on the military and on civilian control. In most cases, the armed forces responded to training incentives by simply replicating or reinforcing their conventional security doctrines. Peacekeeping was just another way of doing policing and conducting counterinsurgency, jungle, or pacification missions. In that sense, peace operations are not generating a new professional ethos based on the "soldier as diplomat" model.

There is an underlying condition that cannot be overlooked in the Argentine case. Argentina is the only country under study where the military had been previously defeated in war, which might have enhanced an institutional willingness to modify training programs and even doctrine. Argentina's experience in the Falklands/Malvinas War left the armed forces in a doctrinal limbo. This context facilitated civilian intervention into training and doctrinal affairs in ways not seen in places like Brazil or Uruguay. This finding seems to confirm the conventional organizational theory developed by Posen (1984, 57), which argues that undefeated militaries prefer continuity to change, and tend to preserve tried and tested strategies and structures rather than adopting new ones. Unless someone forces a new doctrine and has good reason to do so, peacekeeping alone will rarely change conventional military training. In sum, in order for peacekeeping to be consequential for military reform, two conditions must be met: decision makers must take action, and the military must be willing to comply. As the Argentines would say, civil-military relations are like a dance—it takes two to tango.

# 4

## How Does Peacekeeping Socialize the Military in South America?

I now turn my attention to an examination of how peace missions can impact individual military officers, as people. As Marten Zisk (1993, 21) argues, "It is important to keep in mind the fact that military officers are individuals, not merely bureaucratic and organizational actors." Even if military institutions have strong organizational biases against reform, peacekeeping may have an impact on soldiers' attitudes and identities. Uniformed personnel can sometimes reconsider their organizational identities by bringing new social constructs into line with their personal experiences over the course of their time in service. For authors such as Charles Moskos (1976), peacekeeping can be meaningful at an individual level if soldiers dilute their military organizational interests through their experience as peacekeepers. As a result of cumulative socialized experiences in the field, peacekeepers can potentially cause domestic military leaders to recognize the benefits of civilian control, thereby inspiring a commitment to reform. Through repeated engagements over long periods, blue helmets can grow to accept new organizational roles, adopting the interests—or even possibly the identity—of the international community of which they are now part as peacekeepers. Conventional wisdom suggests that peacekeeping can socialize blue helmets, rendering them more professional as a result of the skills they acquire in the field, and more integrated into civilian components (or civilianized), through the civilian tasks they perform when interacting with diplomats and NGOs in UN missions.

Below I assess these conventional claims about the socializing effects of peacekeeping, and find surprising results. While international socialization may play a role in reforming military institutions, the evidence from the case studies is at best mixed. Peacekeeping has enhanced military professional skills in some South American countries but not in others. Moreover, some blue helmets became more "civilianized" than others through their peacekeeping experience. However, many peacekeepers reinforced their previously acquired skills and confirmed their organizational biases toward civilians.

To enhance our understanding of these divergent effects, I put forward an alternative approach to the subject, building a typology of peacekeeping operations. Peacekeepers engage in a plethora of activities ranging from observational and peacebuilding missions to peace enforcement operations. Each of these operations represents a unique institutional design and environment, with different agents involved, leading to variations in the likelihood and extent of socialization or civilianization of the military. The extent to which peacekeeping affects professionalism or civilianizing trends depends on the type of mission being performed and the agents with whom the soldiers interact. Different types of peace operations and agents thus exercise divergent effects. Consequently, in opposition to the conventional wisdom, I claim that in international institutions like the UN, socialization will not automatically lead to increased professionalism or civilian integration among troops (the so-called policy convergence effect). Participation in peacekeeping will in fact trigger diverse effects and unintended outcomes that often promote policy and interest divergence among its members.

To develop my argument, I trace the history of peacekeeping deployments since the early 1990s and identify general trends. In the absence of opinion surveys, I conducted individual and confidential interviews with thirty-nine young military officers from different services to learn more about their personal experiences during their deployment. The underlying assumption is that rising young officers are on a different journey. They tend to be more outspoken and perhaps more critical of their surroundings.[1] They are also most likely to return home from the mission and diffuse their peacekeeping experiences to fellow service members through various means such as education (in military schools), Internet use, blogging, and after-action reports (socializing the institution to which they belong). I also used articles and reports written by peacekeepers and published in military journals. Additional basic sources of data included conferences, lectures, and documents presented by military officers, especially those with peacekeeping experience. Finally, I used official UN records to evaluate the type of military and civilian tasks that the UN Security Council assigned to the blue helmets.

I first briefly review three arguments about how socialization in peacekeeping theoretically contributes to professionalization and civilianization efforts. I then draw on the case studies to empirically evaluate these stated arguments. Finally, I examine the socializing effects in pre-2004 deployments for Argentinean, Brazilian, and Uruguayan peacekeepers.

## The Logic of Socialization in Peacekeeping

As I argued in the Introduction, little attention has been paid to analyzing how involvement in peacekeeping operations affects soldiers from troop-lending countries. But there is a body of literature on institutional sociology that frames the basic issues at the heart of this argument by referring to the potential effects of international socialization. Here the field of military sociology and a smaller group of constructivists in international relations have taken the lead. Although different in approach, both schools build on a long tradition of research in institutional sociology, emphasizing the socializing effects of certain structures and environments on the individuals who participate in them. These studies often share the meaning of socialization, defining it as the process by which social interaction leads novices to endorse expected ways of thinking, feeling, and acting (Checkel 2005, 804; Johnston 2001, 487–515; Stryker and Statham 1985, 325). Socialization is a process by which actors acquire different identities, causing them to develop new interests through regular and sustained interactions with broader social contexts and structures (Bearce and Bondanella 2007, 706). This process is relevant because, from the viewpoint of both military sociology and constructivism, the individual effects of socialization can also be demonstrated on a more aggregate level, encompassing military organizations and even state interests and identities.

Three main arguments can be drawn from this literature with direct implications for peacekeeping studies. First, peacekeeping socializes its agents by exposing them to increasingly complex environments that require multiple managerial and leadership skills, leading to an improvement of military professionalism. Second, peace operations often require smaller, flexible forces that are highly dependent on civilian support, which ultimately civilianizes the military. Finally, an institutional environment is the most conducive setting for this kind of positive socialization, which reinforces both professionalism and civilianization.

The first of these arguments, on the relationship between socialization and professionalism, is the direct result of studies on military sociology. For this field, the military can be an unusually powerful agent of socialization because "it is often assumed as a total institution, which can isolate its members from society, controls the information to which their members are exposed to, monitors their behavior, and offers material inducements to guide them toward desired behavior" (Krebs 2004, 90). Socializing the rank-and-file officers to specific norms of conduct can shape military preferences.

Janowitz (1960) and Moskos (1976) believed that military officers were more than capable of performing peace missions without eroding their war-making skills. Moskos went even further when he asserted that soldiers could acquire additional professional skills by being engaged in intervention, not war, to resolve international political crises. He believed that peace missions afforded additional professional skills acquired through educational practice and repeated interaction with various international actors during the deployment abroad. Among the many socializing effects that Moskos (1976, 83–115) identified were internationalism, the development of a cosmopolitan view of the world, and a new understanding of the military profession that was more sympathetic toward civilians: "the peace soldier is one who is able to subscribe to the precepts of absolute minimal force, a reliance on compromise and negotiation, and the recognition of the elusiveness of permanent political solutions" (Moskos 1976, 137).

The second argument, regarding the civilianizing effects, also comes from military sociology and from the insights of Moskos, Williams, and Segal (2000) in the immediate post–Cold War period. In essence, they argue that advances in technology and changes in the international environment have drastically modified the basic format of military organizations. In this new setting, dominated by globalization and diffused threats, the armed forces increasingly face multiple missions that go beyond fighting conventional wars. In fact, multilateral organizations more heavily use the military for peace and humanitarian purposes. These new tasks generated a new military ethos and provided the basis for organizational change, in which peacekeeping occupies a central position. The challenges imposed by peace missions make the armed forces dependent on civilians, such as NGOs, contractors, diplomats, and locals. To succeed, the military must not only coordinate more actively with civilians, but also incorporate members of the society it attempts to serve, such as women and minorities. While this trend has perhaps eroded traditional military values, the permeability between civil and military structures has made it possible to democratize, liberalize, and civilianize the armed forces (Moskos 2000, 14–27; Moskos, Williams, and Segal 2000, 1–11).

From this perspective, peacekeeping socializes the soldier, enabling her to become more "civilianized"; that is, for her function to include or be merged with functions that are not inherently military in nature. As a result, the workforce becomes more flexible and enhances civil-military interpenetrability, thereby increasing military capacity and resilience. This takes place when soldiers perform tasks like building refugee camps, providing other humanitarian services, and delivering food and medical supplies (Moskos, Williams, and Segal 2000, 6). Ultimately, socialization in peacekeeping can have a cultural and social impact on the military. Loveman (1999, 267) contended that it "might even make young officers more cosmopolitan, less nationalistic, and more resistant to calls for military 'salvation' via coups in times of crisis."

Finally, the third argument on the institutional setting of socialization is drawn from constructivism. Constructivists suggest that international institutions are often prime agents of socialization because communicative interaction should be more frequent inside institutions than outside of them (Risse-Kappen 2001, 1–39), making them particularly favorable to liberal norm creation "whose own ideology emphasizes cooperation, transparency, confidence-building, and demilitarization" (Johnston 2001, 509).

In their accounts of socialization, constructivists focus predominantly on the logics of appropriateness—the process by which a normative behavior is so deeply internalized as to be unquestioned or taken for granted. Appropriateness occurs through persuasion and dialogue, social influence and emulation, and reputation and prestige factors in international forums (Checkel 2005, 801–2; 2007; Gheciu 2005, 973–1012; Johnston 2001). International security institutions can then assist with the socialization of the military and the move toward democratization by providing externally supported guarantees and by helping to reorient military officers away from their previously constructed identities. "While this may or may not be the goal of membership, this socialization process may occur through interactions in the institution. Socialization amounts to persuading military leaders that the role of the military is not to act as an internal police force, but rather to protect the state from outside forces" (Pevehouse 2002a, 527). Eventually, through repeated engagements and after long periods serving in international security institutions, the individuals involved in the socialization process will accept their organizational roles as "the right thing to do," adopting the interests—or even possibly the identity—of the community of which they are a part (Checkel 2005, 804). It would appear that international socialization can encourage the convergence of interests and policies over time.

These arguments helped assess Western and European cases, where institutions such as NATO and the European Union promoted a liberal form of socialization. By contrast, few studies have analyzed the socializing effects of peacekeeping missions on transitional states beyond the realm of NATO. Socializing effects should hypothetically be stronger among democratizing states that are exposed to international dynamics, precisely because agents from these countries are "newcomers" only just being introduced to a new international environment. Was this the case in South America? Were troops effectively socialized when they were first exposed to peacekeeping?

## Socializing Effects in South America, 1990–2003

Tables 4.1 and 4.2 show the number and percentage of South American soldiers sent to different UN peacekeeping missions between 1990 and 2003. The data are arranged in accordance with the type of mission performed and the country to which blue helmets deployed. It indicates that blue helmets from Argentina, Brazil, and Uruguay engaged in different types of UN missions and that they also socialized with different actors.

Argentine blue helmets were less exposed to peacebuilding missions than the peacekeepers from Brazil or Uruguay. Table 4.1 shows that Argentina mostly deployed soldiers to observational missions (36%) and peace enforcement operations (62%), whereas Brazil and Uruguay tended to deploy its peacekeepers to peacebuilding missions (Brazil deployed about 98% of all its

*Table 4.1.*   South America's UN troop contributions by type of mission, 1990–2003

|  | Peace observation missions | % | Peace-building missions | % | Peace enforcement missions | % | Total |
|---|---|---|---|---|---|---|---|
| Argentina | 4,952 | 35.6 | 390 | 2.81 | 8,521 | 61.59 | 13,863 |
| Brazil | 20 | 0.37 | 5,204 | 97.49 | 114 | 2.14 | 5,388 |
| Uruguay | 173 | 1.68 | 8,350 | 81.43 | 1733 | 16.89 | 10,256 |

*Source:* Data obtained from various sources, including Campos Tarrisse da Fontoura (1999, 210), CARI (1999, 19–63), Ejército de la República Oriental del Uruguay (1999), and UNDPKO (2010a).

*Table 4.2.*   UN troop contributions by mission and country, 1990–2003

|  | Peace observation missions | Peacebuilding missions | Peace enforcement missions |
| --- | --- | --- | --- |
| Argentina | UNIMOG (Iran-Iraq) UNFICYP (Cyprus) | ONUSAL (El Salvador) ONUMOZ (Mozambique) ONUCA (Nicaragua) MINURSO (West Sahara) | UNPROFOR (Yugoslavia) UNCRO (Croatia) UNTAES (Slovenia) UNIKOM (Slovenia) UNIKOM (Iraq) UNMIH (Haiti) |
| Brazil | UNFICYP (Cyprus) | UNAVEM (Angola) UNTAET and UNMISET (East Timor) ONUMOZ (Mozambique) UNAMIR (Rwanda) UNMIL (Liberia) | UNPROFOR (Yugoslavia) UNMOP (Prevlaka) |
| Uruguay | UNFICYP (Cyprus) UNMOGIP (India-Pakistan) | MONUC (Congo) UNAVEM (Angola) UNTAC (Cambodia) ONUMOZ (Mozambique) UNOMIL (Liberia) UNOMSIL (Sierra Leona) | MONUC (Congo) |

*Source:* Data obtained from various sources, including Campos Tarrisse da Fontoura (1999, 210), CARI (1999, 19–63), Ejército de la República Oriental del Uruguay (1999), and UNDPKO (2010a).

blue helmets to such operations). These are not merely semantic distinctions, as the various missions have distinct mandates and entail different activities, goals, logistics, and operations. As a result, differences in the type of mission being performed tended to affect the socialization process for both soldiers and peacekeepers.

## Socializing Effects in Argentina

To determine how the process of socialization took place among Argentine military officers, I relied on interviews with peacekeepers and on their personal accounts published in military journals such as *Revista del Suboficial*, *Revista Militar*, and *Soldados*. As tables 4.1 and 4.2 indicate, between 1990 and 2003, Argentina participated in only two observational operations in the Middle East and in Europe: UN Iran-Iraq Military Observer Group (UNIMOG) and UNFICYP. As indicated in the Introduction, in observational operations, peacekeepers perform activities such as monitoring truces, observing troop withdrawals, facilitating contacts between combatant commanders and governments, and establishing buffer zones to enhance political and military negotiations (Doyle 2001, 532). No substantial evidence surfaced to indicate that military observers in UNIMOG socialized with large civilian groups. The mandate of the operation entailed supervising the cease-fire and withdrawing all Iraq-Iran forces to the internationally recognized boundaries, as established by the UN Security Council.[2] Two articles in *Revista del Suboficial* by military officers deployed to UNIMOG described their activities in Iran during this period (Esteban 1994; Etchehun 1994). Neither mentioned contacts with civilians or engagement in humanitarian activities. Argentine military observers were unarmed during the mission, and their tasks included investigating alleged violations of the peace agreements. For the most part, peacekeepers socialized with military personnel from the two parties in conflict and from other countries. In total, fewer than forty military observers—less than 1% of all Argentine peacekeeping forces—participated in this mission.

By comparison, 4,885 soldiers (over 35% of all Argentine peacekeepers) deployed to Cyprus. The UN established this mission in 1964 to monitor the border between the Greek and the Turkish portions of Cyprus, and the mission has often been perceived as one of the most stable UN operations to date. In Cyprus, there have been no reported armed conflicts, and no military confrontation has taken place since the 1980s. The UN's presence essentially froze the conflict, although the conditions required for troop withdrawal never materialized (Sambanis 1999, 79–108).

Between 1990 and 2002, an Argentine battalion and an air unit deployed to Cyprus through various rotation systems. Official military reports suggest that officers mostly executed military tasks and had limited civilian duties. One report (Ejército Argentino 1997, 218) indicated the following about Argentine patrols:

> [They] generally detected the incidents between the parties in conflict. On an average day there were three or four incidents. The most common were movements of troops, the improvement of the defenses, and the reinforcement of weapons on the cease-fire line . . . The Argentine Task Force Commanding Officer held weekly meetings with the Turkish generals.

Evidence gathered from the field indicated that few military observers in Cyprus were in constant contact with NGOs or civilian staff. Because Argentine observers mostly deployed in a battalion, they predominantly lived their lives in the barracks, socializing for the most part with fellow colleagues in the unit and other international officers. Most interactions with local civilians occurred when observers were not performing peacekeeping duties, although negotiations took place with local government officials. There is no strong evidence to suggest that Argentine peacekeepers were heavily civilianized by their experience in observational missions.

The civilianizing effects of peacebuilding operations upon the Argentinean military were more noticeable than those of the observational missions. Officer reports and interviews indicated high levels of interaction with civilians in ONUMOZ, the UN Mission in Western Sahara (MINURSO) and ONUSAL. In these cases, UN Security Council resolutions stipulated both military and civilian tasks, involving activities such as cease-fires, demilitarization, demobilization, implementation of agreements, and electoral monitoring.[3] For example, military observers deployed to El Salvador had to work with some 140 civilian international staff, 180 local officials, 315 civilian police, and more than nine hundred electoral observers. There Argentine observers were given the task of training brand-new police forces composed of civilians.

Given the multidimensional nature of these missions, the likelihood that soldiers will work with civilians is higher even if they are performing military tasks. As an illustrative example, Major Jorge Carlucci went to Savana, Mozambique, to help with the disarmament process. Although his responsibilities were military in essence, he often engaged in other civilian-related activities. Ejército Argentino (1997, 128) gives a summary of his experience:

> I suddenly found myself in the middle of the jungle, without any kind of support facilities, surrounded by locals and guerrilla forces who were not pleased with the UN presence in the region . . . I had to put up tents, construct the boundary fence, dig holes, build lavatories, carry bags of rice, check and evacuate the sick, play soccer with them and organize them.

Military participants in these missions admitted that their initial contacts with NGOs had a profound impact. As one peacekeeper explained, "it was a cultural shock; we were not used to dealing with NGOs in Argentina, even though there are numerous organizations of that kind in our country. The socialization [process] was different because we were communicating in a foreign language and in a different cultural setting."[4]

Nevertheless, few Argentines participated in peacebuilding operations overall. According to the above data, less than 3% of all Argentine peacekeeping forces assisted with peacebuilding missions. The socializing effects may be too limited to permeate the Argentine defense establishment at an organizational level. Argentina had participated in other well-known UN peacebuilding operations that required police forces, such as the UN Mission in East Timor and UN Civilian Police Mission in Haiti. Yet the Argentine government's official policy is to send police forces (Gendarmeria Nacional) to peace operations requiring policing or electoral assistance and military personnel to operations requiring staff for observational and enforcement tasks. The Argentine military was hence not highly exposed to policing functions in peacebuilding operations. Argentine soldiers were not heavily involved in peacebuilding operations in which one or more of the parties had violated cease-fire agreements. Only one Argentine soldier participated in UNAMIR (UN Assistance Mission for Rwanda) and fewer than forty peacekeepers were sent to UNAVEM II, representing less than 0.2% of all Argentine peace forces.

By contrast, the largest Argentine contingents deployed to peace enforcement missions. Such missions are usually mandated by Chapter VII of the UN Charter and can involve the use of force to compel an aggressor to take an action. In total, 8,521 soldiers (over 65% of all Argentine peacekeepers) participated in a peace enforcement mission between 1990 and 2003. In these operations, the blue helmets mostly assisted with demilitarizing designated areas, monitoring "no-fly zones," deterring border violations, and reporting hostile action. Peacekeepers also participated in the delivery of humanitarian relief and the protection of NGOs. Their main functions in these operations were strictly military in nature, however.

A large number of Argentine soldiers were in constant contact with NATO forces in missions such as UNPROFOR, UNIKOM, and the UN Support Mission in Haiti. About seven thousand Argentine peacekeepers served in the former Yugoslavia: UNPROFOR, over five thousand; UNCRO, 1,960; UNTAES (UN Transitional Authority in Eastern Slovenia), over four hundred; and the UN Mission in Kosovo, 135. The inability of UNPROFOR to enforce order as established in its mandate led NATO to take responsibility for enforcing the peace.[5] So most Argentine peacekeepers who participated in UNPROFOR interacted and then socialized with heavily armed NATO forces.

Similarly, under Chapter VII of the UN Charter, two Security Council resolutions established UNIKOM to monitor a demilitarized zone along the boundary between Iraq and Kuwait.[6] Although the mission was not in copartnership with NATO and included contingents from thirty-seven nations, some of which were not members of the alliance, the largest number of officers did come from the U.S.-led North Atlantic organization.[7] Here, as in the former Yugoslavia, one thousand Argentine peacekeepers (some 7% of all Argentine UN forces) followed NATO's example.

In UNMIH (UN Mission in Haiti), Argentina joined a twenty-thousand-strong, twenty-eight-nation multinational force led by the United States. UNMIH was authorized to use "all necessary means" to facilitate the departure of the military leaders and the return to democratic rule. Argentina originally deployed a small navy force, and Argentine officers embarked on a mission that was never fully completed as originally stipulated by the UN because General Cédras left Haiti after mediation by former U.S. president Jimmy Carter.[8] Those Argentine officers worked closely with their American allies, however, interacting once again with NATO forces.

The Argentine blue helmets' experience of socializing in peace enforcement operations led them to active interactions with NATO forces. Personal accounts and debriefings of peacekeepers in UNPROFOR, UNCRO, and UNIKOM—to which the largest Argentine contingents were sent—suggest that these missions increased the participants' professional military skills.

One young infantry officer commented, "reports, logistics, and accountability were just like the real thing."[9] An air force report on peacekeeping indicates that pilots in UNIKOM flew more than 270 hours under high temperatures and low visibility, transported more than 600,000 kilograms of supplies, and even encountered hostility from Iraqi forces (Fuerza Aérea 1996). A pilot who participated in a mission of this kind simply stated, "we have never flown so many hours in our lives. Any peace mission is a million times better than any mission at home."[10] Another report on UNIKOM from the Argentine Army strongly suggests that peacekeepers mostly engaged in military activities that resembled real war scenarios. Ejército Argentino (1997, 86) describes the conditions of the operation as follows:

> The situation became tense in January 10, 1993, when some Iraqi personnel entered the DMZ [demilitarized zone] going back to their previous ammunition . . .
> From the 13th to the 16th, the coalition forces carried out raids on targets located

within the restricted flight zone imposed by Iraq on August 26, 1992. On the 17th, some targets located near Baghdad were attacked with Cruise missiles launched from U.S. ships.

Interviews with peacekeepers included proud accounts of their roles in enforcement missions and of how they proved their abilities in terms of rapid deployment, interoperability, deactivating landmines, and setting up facilities with absolutely no native infrastructure. One army officer who participated in UNIKOM and UNPROFOR said that his experience introduced him to NATO's logistics and codes of interoperability. As he explained, "the missions I participated in were not peaceful at all; there was a tense calm in the operation. We had to be ready for combat, maintaining high morale."[11]

Lieutenant Colonel Carlos Pérez Aquino joined UNIKOM in the Persian Gulf, and he explained that he believed his most valuable professional experience was to see the operational movement of troops and armies. "It was like seeing the war on CNN, but live. Suddenly we were discussing military plans with American, British and Soviet soldiers."[12] Upon returning from the mission, he authored a book that questions the idea that soldiers become soft during peacekeeping service (Pérez Aquino 2001). As he explains, "these operations are inherently stressful and cover a broad spectrum from minefield clearing to physical security measures to protect the force. Soldiers need to be physically and mentally prepared to deal with the threat level involved."[13]

Army articles and debriefings also emphasized the professional techniques developed by officers in peace enforcement missions. One army major who participated in UNPROFOR wrote: "here we have the possibility of analyzing different types of weapons and integrating our units with other armies" (Castro 1994, 33).[14]

Equally important were the leadership experiences gained in these operations. Argentine officers occupied chief commanding positions in several UN operations, including UNIKOM and UN Mission of Observers in Prevlaka (UNMOP). Articles written by army officials point out that commanding UN troops improved their leadership skills (Moreno 2002, 2–3). Similarly, an article by an Argentine Navy officer reported that interoperability increased as a result of Argentina's exposure to UN enforcement missions (Neves 1995, 50–62).

Interestingly, interviews and written documents on Argentine blue helmets also showed that military officers gained valuable professional skills in UNFICYP. Argentine officers commissioned to Cyprus asserted that their experience increased interoperability between NATO and Argentine forces and enhanced leadership skills. An air force colonel explained, "my participation in Cyprus enabled me to better understand UN defensive doctrine and to establish a working relationship with fellow officers from Australia, Austria, Hungary, Ireland and Sweden."[15] The former director for peacekeeping operations at the Joint Chief of Staff also recognized that interoperability and commanding skills have increased as a result of Argentina's involvement in UNFICYP.[16]

NATO's influence is particularly evident in Cyprus. For almost a decade, the leading troop contributor to UNFICYP was Argentina, followed by the United Kingdom. British elite peacekeeping units, the ones originally studied by Moskos in *Peace Soldiers* (1976), exercised tight control over the operation by commanding and deploying the second-largest number of officers to this mission. As a result, when Argentina first decided to send an infantry battalion to Cyprus in 1993, the troops served under British command. Ironically, ten years after the Falklands/Malvinas War, the two former foes would once again meet on an island, this time in the context of a peace observational mission. Slowly but surely, Argentine troops and civilians replaced British leadership. Oscar Camilión was UN chief commissioner and special representative to Cyprus from 1988 to 1993 (he became Argentina's minister of defense in 1993), and General E. A. de Vergara served as UN force commander from 1997 to 1999. Even the highly specialized British peacekeepers were eventually put under Argentina's control.

In Cyprus, therefore, Argentine peacekeepers interacted mostly with British soldiers. The mingling of Argentine and British troops had interesting cultural and professional consequences. An air force colonel and Malvinas veteran was among the officers first deployed to Cyprus. As he explained, he was sent with the British Royal Navy and boarded a ship that had once disembarked in the Malvinas/Falklands during the 1982 war. The officer described his personal experience as follows: "I will never concede the Malvinas to the British, but I recognize their professionalism. Now I understand why we lost the war."[17]

This comment implies that peacekeepers were learning more than just warmaking techniques. They also developed a sense of corporate identity as soldiers identified with other foreigners of the same profession. Argentine peacekeepers were re-educating themselves using role models as they interacted with armies that were already under firm civilian control. They observed the institutional behavior and personal conduct of professional officers who were experts in their field, shared a sense of organic unity, and performed their missions with responsibility.[18] They saw how American, British, Canadian, and Scandinavian troops carried out their missions professionally and responsibly, even when they disagreed with their civilian commanders. Argentines ultimately emulated attitudes and practices, and internalized the procedures of NATO officers, with the expectation that they would also be acclaimed. As a result, when the colonel asserted that he knew why Argentina had lost the war in 1982, he implied that the involvement of the military in Argentina's domestic politics had been a major mistake and an abandonment of the distinguished character of the military profession.

In recognition of Argentina's commitment to UN peacekeeping, the Clinton administration granted the country the status of major non-NATO ally in 1997 (Sims 1997, A9). But the positive socializing effects on professionalism were not merely the result of the interaction within a specific UN environment. Interaction between Argentina's blue helmets and specific agents from NATO troop-lending countries, who also engaged in UN peacekeeping, contributed to diffusing professional norms among the Argentine peacekeepers. Yet few civilianizing effects were found in Argentina's engagement in peace operations.

### Socializing Effects in Brazil

International socialization in peacekeeping worked differently in Brazil. To assess the socializing effects of peacekeeping, I relied on interviews and articles by Brazilian blue helmets published in military journals such as *Revista do Exército Brasileiro*, *Revista de Defesa Nacional*, *Revista Marítima Brasileira*, and *Revista Verde Oliva*. Most of these documents pertained to the UN missions in Mozambique and Angola.

Tables 4.1 and 4.2 show that only a small percentage of soldiers were involved in observational operations. About twenty officers (less than 0.5% of the entire Brazilian peacekeeping force) joined the UN mission in Cyprus. These observers were sent as part of the Argentine contingent to UNFICYP in accordance with a 1998 bilateral military exchange program between Argentina and Brazil, whereby the two countries exchanged military observers in Cyprus and East Timor, respectively.

An army major, who was also an instructor at the Brazilian Military Institute of Engineering, was one of those twenty officers who joined the Argentine force in UNFICYP in 2001. He described his participation in the UN mission as highly educational and professional. He recognized that his experience did not improve his abilities in combat, but he acknowledged that he gained professional skills during his one-year service in Cyprus. During his work as a military observer, he became familiar with UN logistics and operational procedures such as patrolling, checkpoints, observation post, radio communication, and driving skills. In addition, he improved his foreign language skills through daily interactions with Argentine officers in Spanish and with other peacekeepers and locals in English. He did not fully engage in civilian integrated tasks or functions, but his exposure to UN peacekeeping contributed to his understanding of international politics. Upon his return, he joined a master's degree program in international relations at the Federal Fulminense University in Rio de Janeiro, where he was in constant contact with civilian students.[19]

This case was unfortunately specific to Brazil, as the officer's experience was not broadly replicated among the other blue helmets I interviewed or met. In fact, from 1990 to 2003, most Brazilian peacekeepers participated in peacebuilding operations, which are more complex and involve higher degrees of interaction with civilians. In theory, this meant that civilizing trends more heavily influenced soldiers. But a closer look at Brazil's peacekeeping contributions reveals that, in these operations, a substantial number of soldiers were in charge of the demobilization and demilitarization of active combatants and guerrilla movements in intrastate conflicts, as well as policing roles, leading to a different form of socialization.

Ninety-seven blue helmets (some 3% of all Brazilian peacekeepers) participated in UN operations in Central America. Mission reports from ONUSAL and ONUCA (UN Observer Group in Central America) emphasized that soldiers practiced military tactics such as convoy ambush, the capture or isolation of cities or neighborhoods, reaction to helicopter attacks, use and interception of communications, and others (Danziato Rego 1995; Gomes de Sousa 1994). During these operations, blue helmets also developed negotiation skills as they engaged in peace talks to demobilize governmental forces and the Farabundo Marti Liberation Font in El Salvador. In other words, these experiences appeared to have contributed to the development of the officers' professional skills, particularly in terms of political negotiation.

These peacebuilding operations (the first of their kind, implemented by the UN in the early 1990s) had large civilian components; however, coordination of civil and military efforts was extremely challenging in the field. An ONUCA veteran summarized his experience with NGOs this way: "Civilians did not respect the security zones, as it was planned. They did not follow basic precautions, such as the improvisation of latrines . . . They did not exercise effective control over material, and put obstacles to the required support of vehicle maintenance" (Danziato Rego 1995, 28).[20] Logistics and coordination appear to have improved in El Salvador, where the mission was better funded and enjoyed higher levels of political support from the Security Council. Still, the effects of participation in Central American peacebuilding operations are too limited, or too anecdotal, to suggest that they affected the civilianization of military personnel, since only sixty-three officers served in missions like ONUSAL.

Likewise, it is not evident that soldiers were developing significant military skills in these operations. Peacekeepers in Central America were performing tasks that were common to their traditional military training. Although soldiers used their negotiating skills, they performed functions that resembled those used in missions conducted at home, including the demobilization, internal security, police, and national guard functions.

Brazilian soldiers were more heavily exposed to peacebuilding missions in Mozambique and East Timor. For example, 536 (16% of the peacekeeping force) deployed to the UN Transitional Administration in East Timor (UNTAET) in 1999 and the UN Mission in Support of East Timor (UNMISET) in 2002. These missions exposed them to fluid, constructive, and cordial relations between their civilian and military components. In ONUMOZ, soldiers once again engaged in the demilitarization and demobilization of guerilla forces, such as the Mozambican National Resistance Movement (RENAMO), supported by South Africa's apartheid regime. But in this case, insurgents and the local government showed willingness to accept UN mediation. Similarly, civilian and military components were well organized and coordinated, revealing that the UN was improving its performance and building on previous experiences. Peacekeepers were in charge of verifying the implementation of the military aspects of the peace agreement between the government and RENAMO, as well as providing security for the electoral process (Howard 2008, 179–224). Reports and summaries of the mission indicate that Brazilian blue helmets helped to establish a new national army and also to embark upon a demilitarization process by recovering some 155,000 weapons (Cavalieri 1998, 27–36). Blue helmets involved in these operations put their professional skills into practice in areas not traditionally linked to previous domestic roles. Peacekeepers from Brazil learned to deactivate landmines, to reconstruct national armies, to secure civilian personnel for elections, and to demilitarize a heavily armed society. Performing these military tasks was heavily dependent upon civilians as well as civilian infrastructure.

There were signs of positive civil-military integration in the Mozambique mission. Former Brazilian blue helmets interviewed for this study asserted that a common cultural background and language facilitated their interaction with locals (Mozambique, like Brazil, is a Portuguese-speaking nation). In general, combatants and locals accepted UN and Brazilian good offices, showing willingness to overcome the crisis. As an army major explained, "we were welcomed by the government, the population, and RENAMO, even though there were extremely precarious conditions. The parties were determined to end their political and ideological battles."[21]

Yet Brazilian blue helmets faced challenges with international NGOs, which they had never been properly trained to deal with at home. Interviews with officers revealed that peacekeepers developed negotiating skills in the field, empirically and on a daily basis.[22] But unlike in the case of interactions with locals (who spoke Portuguese), communication with other peacekeepers and with personnel from the UN and international NGOs required a command of English. Most Brazilian blue helmets did not have the foreign language skills required to draft reports or to communicate with force commanders and NGOs. So their work was restricted to helping locals or interacting with colleagues in their troop, and as a result soldiers were not fully integrated into the various missions. The expected effect of mingling civilian and military personnel was limited because only a small number of officers could actively interact with civilian international actors.

Despite the soldiers' predominantly constructive peacekeeping experiences in Mozambique and East Timor, the harsh conditions they faced in Angola cannot be underestimated. Approximately 80% of Brazil's peacekeeping force (4,270 soldiers) served during UNAVEM in the midnineties. UNAVEM I successfully accomplished its mandate and demobilized Cuban troops from the former Portuguese colony. But the second and third phases of the operation, known as UNAVEM II and III, turned out to be failures. Reports by Brazilian officers specify that a conflict situation prevailed between government officials and UNITA, another guerrilla movement. Peacekeepers were in charge of monitoring major violations of cease-fire and peace agreements after a controversial electoral process. The political victory of the governmental party motivated UNITA commanders to launch a nationwide operation to occupy municipalities by force and to remove the government's local administrative structures. This time Portuguese was less useful, as peacekeepers were uncomfortably caught between two hostile parties. During the mission, UNITA forces ambushed peacekeeping troops and kidnapped several military observers, including three Brazilian blue helmets (Carneiro 1996). As a result, the Brazilian soldiers engaged heavily with belligerent groups, which constantly targeted UN peacekeepers. The analogy between this type of interaction and counterinsurgency was obvious; for many Brazilians exposed to the UN mission in Angola, peacebuilding resembled counterinsurgency and policing. For many, the belligerent forces in Angola bore much resemblance to the guerilla forces they might have encountered in Brazil during critical political times.

In several interviews conducted with army and navy personnel, deployed officers confessed that they also had to deal with malaria, dengue, bad weather, poor sanitation, limited supplies, and poor UN logistics.[23] As one army officer explained, "some of us can deal with these conditions during field exercises in the Amazon, but those only last for weeks at a time; then we return to our units with proper accommodations. In Angola, these conditions prevailed for months."[24] In terms of professional skills, soldiers might have learned how to adapt to different environments, but clearly they were not developing highly specialized military skills; they were just trying to survive in a mission that was slowly failing.

Relations between NGOs and Brazilian military personnel in Angola were less cordial than in Mozambique. The UN charges against UNITA's peace agreement violations compromised the international NGOs' neutrality and impartiality. As violence re-emerged, NGOs dissociated themselves from the military institutions that were providing security for the mission, thus affecting the integration between civilians and soldiers. One officer said, "the International Red Cross was adverse to the military and had their own logistics. Other NGOs had religious roots and followed their own political agenda, separate from the UN. In general, the organizations that were financially independent from the UN were adverse to us."[25]

Brazil consequently took a major risk in Angola by deploying a battalion to a UN operation in which the mandate and resources available were inadequate in relation to the complexities of the task, especially in circumstances in which the parties did not demonstrate the necessary political will for peace. The lack of coordination between civil and military efforts strained civil-military relations. The UN publicly acknowledged failure in Angola (UNDPKO 2000), and the mission ended abruptly after UNITA violated the cease-fire agreements in 1997, leading to the withdrawal of UN troops. By then, more than four thousand Brazilian Army soldiers and nearly fifty Brazilian Navy officers had been involved in UNAVEM III, making it Brazil's second-largest peacekeeping deployment in the postdictatorial era (the UN mission in Haiti in 2004 ranks as the largest mission undertaken by Brazil so far). Brazil's experience of peacebuilding in the field could be categorized as mixed, with good lessons learned from the experience in Mozambique, but bad lessons drawn from Angola's failure.

Was Brazil's experience of peace enforcement operations also mixed? Prior to 2003, Brazil had not been supportive of resolutions that involved the UN in coercive interventions. Few officers were exposed to missions invoking Chapter VII of the UN Charter. A handful of Brazilian soldiers were sent to the former Yugoslavia during the early stages of UNPROFOR, but this took place before NATO intervened. In fact, only around 2% of all Brazilian peacekeeping forces served in the UN mission in Yugoslavia. In 1992, just over one hundred Brazilian peacekeepers were sent to help the UN monitor the implementation of a cease-fire agreement signed by the Croatian government and local Serb authorities. By the end of the year, however, the conflict intensified. When the UN Security Council authorized the use of force and imposed no-fly zones, Brazil withdrew its troops. The troops were exposed to violence in the mission, but they did not stay long enough to see the civil war escalate.

Because Brazilian troops withdrew from UNPROFOR early, they did not interact with NATO forces either, the latter having been deployed in January of 1993. Unlike the Argentine peacekeepers, the Brazilian peace soldiers were not (and are not) interoperable with NATO forces. As a result, most Brazilian officers also remained unfamiliar with European military doctrines.

It appears that Brazil's first engagement with peacekeeping operations did not exercise large civilianizing effects, since a significant number of Brazilian blue helmets participated in missions in which cease-fire agreements were violated and in which cooperation with civilian components was extremely limited or compromised by violence. There is also no substantial evidence of large professional effects in peacekeeping operations. Precisely because Brazil was heavily involved in peacebuilding operations, its peacekeepers performed policing and internal security functions rather than strict military tasks. These roles, performed in places like Angola, rest squarely within the tradition of the Brazilian armed forces—to ensure internal law and order. In peacekeeping, Brazilian soldiers carried out the functions toward which they had been oriented at home and for which they had been trained. As a result, international peacekeeping did not seem to civilianize or professionalize the Brazilian armed forces.

## Socializing Effects in Uruguay

Analogous to the Brazilian case, the evidence gathered regarding the Uruguayan peacekeepers indicates that the country had no substantial experience in observational operations between 1990 and 2003. Of the total number of peacekeepers deployed in this period (10,256), only 173 conducted monitoring tasks.[26] The vast majority of peacekeepers, about eight thousand (over 80% of the total Uruguayan peacekeeping force), engaged in peacebuilding operations in missions such as ONUMOZ in Mozambique (24%), UNTAC (13%), and UNAVEM in Angola (23%). Similarly, in 2003, approximately 1,730 soldiers (a full battalion) were sent to MONUC, which began as a peacebuilding operation and eventually became one of peace enforcement.

Uruguay's limited engagement in observational operations does not seem to indicate high levels of civilian integration, because their duties were largely military in nature. Articles by blue helmets in UNMOGIP rarely described contacts between the peacekeepers and civilians or indicated their involvement in civilian tasks. As one report indicates, "sometimes, there were cases where common citizens, individually or collectively, would approach the unit to request UN intervention to solve a problem. For instance, they would request the cease of persecutions against Muslims in India. Our task as observers was to take note and inform the General Headquarters" (Orlando and Viggiano 1989, 49).[27] Blue helmets in Kashmir monitor troop movements on the Pakistani side of the border and supervise a cease-fire agreement, which mostly requires them to fulfill military tasks.

Members of the UN Good Offices Mission in Afghanistan (UNGOMAP), who regularly met with the Afghan and Soviet military representatives, described similar experiences. At these meetings, the observers received information on the ongoing withdrawal of Soviet troops; a Uruguayan veteran of UNGOMAP explained, "I met Russians and Muslims in Afghanistan. I learned about mental flexibility, patience and tolerance, negotiating skills, and even sense of humor."[28] Although military observers were unarmed and developed nonmilitary and negotiating skills, they did not become more civilianized because their responsibilities and daily contacts were military in nature. NGOs and civilian staff played a minor role in these observational operations.

Larger civilianization effects were found among the peacekeepers who participated in UN multidimensional or peacebuilding operations. Civilian interpenetrability was particularly intense in missions in which all parties fully respected the cease-fire agreement. In these cases, officers described their personal contacts with civilians as extremely positive and constructive. Peacekeepers in Mozambique were highly integrated with civilian components. In addition to demobilizing irregular forces, they provided security for electoral monitors and engaged in humanitarian activities with international NGOs. One retired officer described his personal experience as follows: "The population treated us like locals. The interaction was more intense with women than with men, because the former provided food supplies to our contingent."[29] Other officers expressed equally good opinions about the role of NGOs, including one commanding officer who said, "I participated with Doctors without Frontiers in the demobilization and disarmament process. We gave humanitarian assistance to help almost three million people displaced by the war to resettle in their communities. We used humanitarian organizations to achieve our job and we were effectively coordinated."[30] ONUMOZ was, at the time, the biggest and most successful peacekeeping operation undertaken by the UN in Africa, and a substantial number of Uruguayan soldiers (almost 2,520) claimed that they had experienced positive social interactions with civilian components.[31] Other Uruguayan peacekeepers also conveyed their accounts of the missions in East Timor, Guatemala, and Western Sahara, where most UN observers spent a year on the ground, away from the barracks, providing civil services and demobilizing populations as opposed to troops.

Here, too, the missions' civilianizing effects were debatable. While many Uruguayan blue helmets expressed good opinions of UN civilian personnel and NGOs, some were still hesitant to discuss the role of NGOs in Uruguay, particularly those involved with the sensitive issue of human rights. Uruguayan officers seemed to make a distinction between civilians at home and overseas. Many of the interviewees had positive things to say about NGOs in places like Mozambique, but few were willing to share their views about human rights NGOs in Uruguay. Therefore, if civilianizing effects occurred, they were not transferable to the domestic domain.

Civilizing effects were more difficult to observe in peacebuilding operations in which cease-fire agreements collapsed or failed; that is, missions in which a peace agreement or settlement was first negotiated and then violated by one of the parties. Uruguayan peacekeepers were exposed to many such operations, most of which took place in Africa and Asia. Uruguay deployed 5,645 peacekeepers to missions in Angola, Cambodia, Congo, the Ivory Coast, Rwanda, Sierra Leone, and Tajikistan, which have often been classified as UN failures. In these cases, social interaction between UN personnel and locals seemed to have a negative effect on civilian integration or penetration efforts. Uruguay deployed a battalion of 1,330 men to Cambodia, including 850 army officers and noncommissioned officers, as well as 480 navy personnel. Uruguayan troops were positioned across four Cambodian provinces, with military units occupying six border patrol positions, most of them located next to zones dominated by the Khmer Rouge (Comando General del Ejército 2003, 68; Ejército de la República Oriental del Uruguay 1994). Well known for its bloody and repressive strategies, the Khmer Rouge were originally part of the peace agreement, but then defected and refused to canton and demobilize their forces. They instigated violence, mostly in rural areas, and hardened their position toward the UN mission. Blue helmets from Uruguay had violent encounters with the Khmer Rouge—two officers were kidnapped and killed by belligerents during the mission, and one navy officer died of malaria (Cabrera 1994a; 1994b, 56–57).[32]

Likewise, active combatants and militias attacked peacekeepers in Georgia and Angola. These confrontations reduced civil-military cooperation and coordination in the mission, reflected by the words of one officer who said, "we had problems with the Red Cross in Angola because it denied medical services to our peacekeepers. Their position is that in order for them to maintain their neutrality, service is provided to belligerents, but not to peace soldiers, especially in missions under Chapter VI. So we were providing security for them, but there was no reciprocation."[33]

Equally controversial was MONUC, where violence, warlords, and battles over resources once again resurfaced in the summer of 2003, and the UN Security Council modified its mandate from Chapter VI to VII. Reports from international sources portrayed the situation at the time as chaotic. These reports reveal that the levels of internal violence had complicated interactions between Uruguayan peacekeepers and local civilians.[34]

When conflict re-emerged in the DRC in 2003, the Uruguayan military faced increasing problems of corruption and improper behavior among its own peacekeepers. Seven Uruguayan soldiers were investigated for allegedly stealing sacred objects from a church in Bunia, in the east side of the DRC. The Uruguayan soldiers "alleged that the material was removed purely for safekeeping." The report also said, "evidence supports extensive looting by the local population, and the Uruguayan soldiers had indeed stolen some items of value" (UN Integrated Regional Information Network 2003). After the report's release, the army suspended the soldiers and the top officers heading the battalion. A month later, other factions and NGOs accused Uruguayan troops, who tried to contain the fighting in Bunia itself, of human rights violations. According to Amnesty International, "Uruguayan soldiers from MONUC arrested Willy Benguela, an official from the National Intelligence Service and consultant to the UN . . . The soldiers took him to the camp, undressed him, beat him, and then tied his hands and legs" (*El Clarín* 2003).[35]

These incidents ultimately eroded the relationship between UN forces and the local population, effectively damaging civil-military relations and coordination in the field. According to an expert on the Congo, "to the Congolese, the peacekeepers . . . failed to fulfill some of their duties, in particular the protection of the population . . . In 2005, a major sexual exploitation scandal involving a number of MONUC civilian and military staff members dealt a final blow to the UN mission's popularity. Overall, the Congolese often saw MONUC staff as useless parasites, whom they nicknamed 'tourists in a war zone'" (Autesserre 2010, 90).

The evidence suggests that the impact of these missions was ambiguous in terms of their capacity to civilianize, since a large number of Uruguayan soldiers experienced violence in the field and in dealing with active combatants and militias. In cases such as Cambodia, Angola, and the Congo, the military relied on well-known conventional or standard procedures to deter or dissuade violence, often relying on tactics that resembled counterinsurgency. In these circumstances, it is unlikely that peacekeeping would have civilianized the armed forces. For many Uruguayan blue helmets, peacekeeping was essentially about dealing with active combatants, which in their organizational view or framework resembled the old task of deactivating guerrilla movements.

Did peacekeeping enhance professional skills among Uruguayan blue helmets? The evidence from field research suggests that observational missions might have contributed to improving nonmilitary skills such as conflict resolution, mediation, and negotiation. Nevertheless, the number and percentage of soldiers exposed to observational operations were too small to be consequential for the military as an organization. In total, only around 173 Uruguayan peacekeepers occupied UN observational positions, which is less than 2% of the peacekeeping force.

During interviews conducted in Montevideo, both commanders and junior officers expressed a belief that soldiers' skills improved as a result of their engagement in peacebuilding operations. One army commander noted that "soldiers return with vast professional experiences on patrolling, reconnaissance, and UN logistics. Individuals are exposed to different environments in real scenarios."[36] Other officers noted that their skills were not rusty because they had participated in peacekeeping missions; "peacekeeping becomes important in the absence of wartime opportunities."[37] Army officers recognized that their experience increased their leadership skills, especially those who occupied supervision or senior posts.[38] Articles by soldiers in Cambodia, Nicaragua, and Mozambique also indicated that blue helmets developed expertise on landmines, as they were involved in the deactivation of such weapons (Poladura 1998, 31–36).

Nonetheless, there are questions about the quality of professional skills developed by participants in the various missions. In Angola, Cambodia, and the DRC, peacekeepers conducted internal security functions and developed policing techniques as opposed to classical military skills. The fact that they were providing law and order where chaos once prevailed suggests a possible diversion of the military profession. In the DRC, peacekeepers assumed policing and praetorian roles, functions to which the Uruguayan military had been traditionally oriented. For MONUC, success depended largely on the ability of peacekeepers to suppress civilian unrest. For the Uruguayan armed forces, a former praetorian institution, peacekeeping was the equivalent of political arbitration—a function they were used to performing at home during the authoritarian era—which makes it difficult to classify this socializing experience as positive professional enhancement. As one critic argues, "given the general pattern of (peacekeeping) deployment, the fundamental mission of the armed forces, external defense, becomes irrelevant and uncertain" (López Chirico 1999, 277).[39]

What about agency? With whom did the Uruguayan soldiers interact most frequently? They tended to socialize more with various military actors than their

Argentine neighbors. In the DRC, for example, Uruguayan troops interacted and socialized mostly with soldiers from Bangladesh, Ghana, Nigeria, Senegal, and South Africa—the largest suppliers of troops to MONUC. In Bunia, Uruguay's units served next to Bangladeshi and Pakistani contingents. Hence, unlike the Argentine blue helmets, Uruguayan soldiers were not constantly exposed to armies with healthy traditions of democratic civilian control. In fact, most of their social interaction was with officers who may also have come from transitional states. Officers on missions such as that in the DRC did not have the opportunity to emulate the good practices and behaviors of other officers.

## Conclusion

This chapter highlights how South American troops were first induced and socialized into peacekeeping operations in the early 1990s. The cases share some common features. Argentina, Brazil, and Uruguay were all in the process of democratization and all followed the same international trend: to deploy a large number of troops abroad (full battalions and units, not just observers). Yet the similarities are not as interesting as the differences. While all soldiers were involved in UN-mandated missions that shared the same institutional framework, the soldiers from each of these countries were exposed to different types of peacekeeping operations and divergent forms of interaction with multiple actors. These disparate experiences eventually translated into varying levels of socialization that were not conducive to policy and interest convergence.

Socialization in peacekeeping had some positive effects on military professionalism that were particularly evident among Argentine troops, who were mostly engaged in observational and peace enforcement operations. In these missions, officers learned something new and different about their profession, obtained valuable experiences that enhanced their careers, and acquired and developed skills valuable for the military as an organization. Most importantly, through peacekeeping, Argentine soldiers participated in missions that were unrelated to their previous domestic roles yet required training, preparation, and even motivation.

This experience was replicated among some Uruguayan and Brazilian peacekeepers, but was certainly not as generalized as in the Argentine case. Largely through peacebuilding operations, Brazilian and Uruguayan peacekeepers were socialized and exposed to different forms of operational environments. The inherent problem, however, was the type of socialization to which the peace-keepers were exposed. In UN missions in Angola, Cambodia, the DRC, Liberia (UNOMIL), Rwanda, and Sierra Leone, peacekeepers from South America essentially performed internal security missions. Their duties involved policing and internal security functions, sometimes suppressing civilian unrest rather than assisting with civilian reconstruction. In Angola, Cambodia, and the DRC, blue helmets were responsible for deterring or halting active combatants. Their responsibilities in part resembled their previous dictatorial missions, which focused precisely on counterinsurgency, deterrence of guerrillas, and policing.

International socialization, as experienced by Brazilian and Uruguayan peacekeepers, was problematic for professionalism for two reasons. First, in addition to public order, law enforcement, and crowd control, military personnel were tasked with numerous civic action and development functions in UN peacebuilding missions. These tasks ranged from road building and irrigation to the delivery of commodities. Such activities might have helped civilianize troops, but they also diluted military professionalism with nonmilitary tasks, making military institutions responsible for the political and economic outcomes of UN missions.

Second, on missions in places like Angola, Cambodia, and Rwanda, which were first mandated as peacebuilding operations, Brazilian and Uruguayan peacekeepers with little combat experience learned some hard lessons about internal warfare and civil conflict. Such experiences can lead to a perversion of the military profession. These were precisely the types of environments that once led military institutions to intervene in domestic affairs by placing a premium on public order and the surveillance of (and operations against) civilian opponents. For transitioning countries, it is probably best not to expose military institutions to civil conflict overseas in order to wean them away from counterinsurgency and antiguerrilla strategies. In civil wars, the distinction between civilians and combatants becomes blurred. In some of these UN operations, the combatants were not even national armies (like in Yugoslavia or Iraq). Instead, they consisted of rebels and militias who mobilized against a national government, occupied portions of the national territory, were not necessarily uniformed, and had some level of civilian support. In such conditions, armies trained to deal with enemies will most likely treat rebels and militias as enemies or guerrillas that need to be eliminated rather than coerced or persuaded (which is what peacekeeping should be about). This may well explain why peacekeepers from Uruguay have faced serious criticism for their misbehavior while performing peacebuilding functions in places like the DRC.

It is unclear whether peacebuilding missions increased the professional skills of soldiers or simply reinforced previously acquired skills. It seems that, for some soldiers, participating in peace operations is like conducting the functions for which they have been trained and socialized, and from which civilian reformers want to wean them. In other words, socialization in peacebuilding missions did not provide strong incentives to change roles, interests, or identities; instead, it probably reinforced traditional behavioral norms. In the end, there are remnants of the old doctrine.

The evidence gathered for this chapter also suggests that socialization in peacekeeping can have mixed civilizing effects. Yes, complex operations like peacebuilding are increasingly dependent on civilian components, including NGOs, UN civilian personnel, and local staff. A handful of soldiers did interact with numerous civilian components in some peace operations, mostly peacebuilding missions. But such interaction does not automatically translate into fully integrated civil-military missions. Coordination with NGOs can turn sour, and cooperation with locals can become compromised when active combatants fail to adhere fully to peace.[40] Peacebuilding operations were most successful, in terms of their capacity to have a civilizing effect, when all parties to the conflict demonstrated a desire to respect the terms of the peace agreement, as was the case in Mozambique and El Salvador. In those cases, peacekeepers from Brazil and Uruguay experienced positive civilizing interactions. By contrast, in Angola, the DRC, and to some extent Cambodia, failure to commit to peace affected not only peacebuilding efforts but also civil-military relations, as locals lost faith in blue helmets and NGOs distanced themselves from the military.[41] In these missions, the final outcome for Brazilian and Uruguayan troops was civil-military segregation, not integration.

Finally, there is the question of whether the UN was the prime agent of socialization for South American troops. The evidence gathered from the field indicated that the type of peacekeeping mission is as important as the type of agency interaction. Argentina was perhaps the most successful case in terms of socialization, in part because its troops socialized with equally professional troops in multiple observation and peace enforcement operations. The interactions that Argentine officers had with fellow NATO forces in UN operations contributed to reinforcing emulation trends. Argentine blue helmets learned from both the mission and their colleagues which countries had healthy professional and democratic traditions. The lesson of the Argentine case is that positive socialization in peacekeeping is reinforced when there is a higher density of professional soldiers from democratic states interacting with soldiers from democratizing states. This form of experience was absent in the Brazilian and Uruguayan cases. Officers from these countries did not have the opportunity to interact as closely as the Argentines did with NATO troops. Instead, their interactions took place predominantly with contingents from other democratizing and transitional states, leading to a different form of socialization. Krebs (2004, 96) reminds us, "different agents are likely to have different effects on people's basic political orientations and practices in different ways and to different degrees in other countries."

Ultimately, the variations observed within these cases seem to suggest that UN peacekeeping will not always be a potential socializer or an effective tool for projecting proper, liberal, and democratic norms. The logic of appropriateness does not automatically take place within the UN framework. Peacekeeping may involve maintaining peace and building democracy in weak states, but peace missions can also become complex, messy, turbulent, and chaotic. The experiences in Angola or the DRC, where conditions went from bad to worse, indicate that peacekeeping socialization can exercise positive and negative outcomes. We should therefore not automatically expect values to diffuse and converge when actors collaborate on UN peacekeeping missions. Instead, the degree and the nature of socialization that occurs within the UN peacekeeping system can vary tremendously.

# 5

## How Does Peacekeeping Socialize the Military in Haiti?

An in-depth analysis of MINUSTAH helps us consider how peacekeeping missions socialize troops. The mission has a complex set of mandates that combine peace observation, peace enforcement, peacebuilding, and even refugee assistance.[1] Its complexity helps illustrate that peacekeeping is not a one-dimensional activity and that it can have multiple effects on the socialization of ground troops. Also, MINUSTAH brings together contingents from Argentina, Brazil, Uruguay, and other democratizing states. Not only are these the largest troop-lending countries to Haiti, MINUSTAH is the mission to which they deploy their largest national contingents in the UN system (table 5.1). MINUSTAH represents a critical juncture for South American geopolitics and diplomacy. According to Raúl Benítez, the mission "grants Brazil, Chile, Argentina, and Uruguay a position in the region as guarantors of security" (qtd. in Kenkel 2010a, 592). Given this reality, one might assume that the mission would promote policy convergence between these four states as a result of their common interaction in the UN framework and in Haiti. In fact, there is limited quantitative and qualitative evidence of this trend. The mission's influence upon the various peacekeepers in terms of civilian integration and professionalism varies hugely, leading to policy divergence.

From a methodological perspective, and in order to establish a more three-dimensional picture of the socializing effect of peacekeeping missions, this chapter seeks to answer three main questions: Where did the peacekeepers go? What type of peacekeeping functions did they perform? How did their experience influence domestic moves toward civilian integration and military professionalism, if at all? To answer these questions, I rely on a number of primary and secondary sources. I refer to the findings of field research trips conducted in Argentina and Brazil in 2009, and at UN Headquarters in New York and Port-au-Prince, Haiti, in 2010. These field trips allowed me to monitor recent peacekeeping trends and to observe the blue helmets in the field. In addition to visiting the mission headquarters, I also paid a visit to three international displaced persons (IDP) camps and Cité Soleil (a slum in the heart of the capital). Here the blue helmets provided a number of services ranging from control checks to public security and refugee assistance. I also conducted confidential interviews with a variety of nonmilitary actors, including civilian staff and NGO representatives. This chapter begins with some background information about MINUSTAH. It then compares the impacts of the mission on troop contingents from the three countries under study.

## MINUSTAH: Background

The UN has been active in Haiti since 1990, when it launched the UN Observer Group for Verification of Elections in Haiti, followed by a multinational force led by the United States to depose a military junta in 1993, and a peacebuilding mission to facilitate the return of a legitimately elected, civilian government in 1994 (UNMIH). Throughout this period, the UN was relatively successful in its efforts to oust the military and to return Jean Bertrand Aristide to power. Aristide, a former Catholic priest who led the pro-democracy movement, became Haiti's first elected president in 1991. He served two terms as chief executive between 1994 and 1996, and again between 2001 and 2004.[2] In February 2004, violence re-erupted, however, first in the city of Gonaïves, where an anti-Aristide rebel force (the Revolutionary Artibonite Resistance Front) emerged, and then in Port-au-Prince, where armed gangs terrorized the local population and drove away the police.

Shortly after the outbreak of violence in Port-au-Prince, the United States persuaded President Aristide to go into exile in South Africa. In an attempt to secure the country and to put an end to an escalating civil conflict between Aristide's supporters and his opponents, the UN Security Council authorized a three-month multinational interim force under Chapter VII of the UN Charter.[3] U.S. marines as well as French, Canadian, and Chilean troops who were all heavily armed initially comprised the force. Yet the growing controversy over Washington's role in the Aristide affair prompted the UN to adopt a broader mandate in an effort to ensure a more balanced international presence in Haiti (Weiner and Polgree 2004).

MINUSTAH was created in April 2004 with a complex mandate that included reforming the Haitian National Police, demobilizing forces, restoring law and public order, monitoring elections, and protecting human rights (UNDPKO 2012a). The MINUSTAH force originally consisted of some 6,700 military personnel, 1,620 police officers, five hundred international civilian personnel, and one thousand local civilian staff (UNDPKO 2012b). Among the military contingents, Latin America provided almost half the personnel while other states supplied full battalions and observers (table 5.1). National peacekeeping contingents deployed all over the country in six military sectors (figure 5.1); however, over 60% of the blue helmets went to the nation's capital. As indicated in chapter 2, Brazil led the mission's military component, and it in turn annually appointed a Brazilian general as force commander.

The mission progressed slowly, resulting in criticism. Force deployment took over nine months. Logistical and strategic delays abounded. There were also complications surrounding coordination efforts between the force commander and the two deputies, who acted as special representatives to the UN secretary-general (Chagas Vianna Braga 2010, 713). Moreover, the military command of MINUSTAH struggled to impose its authority when one of the Brazilian force commanders committed suicide during the mission (BBC News 2006a).

The mission similarly faced multiple challenges in maintaining stability in the country. Between 2004 and 2007, civil unrest continued to be a serious concern, especially in Cité Soleil and Bel-Air (two of the largest slums in the

*Table 5.1.*  Top contributors to MINUSTAH as of December 30, 2010

| Country | Troops | Country | Troops |
| --- | --- | --- | --- |
| Brazil | 2,187 | Japan | 225 |
| Uruguay | 1,130 | Bolivia | 207 |
| Nepal | 1,075 | Philippines | 157 |
| Sri Lanka | 959 | Guatemala | 147 |
| Argentina | 715 | Paraguay | 131 |
| Jordan | 609 | Ecuador | 67 |
| Chile | 501 | Canada | 10 |
| Peru | 371 | USA | 9 |
| Republic of Korea | 242 | France | 2 |

*Source:* UNDPKO (2010b).

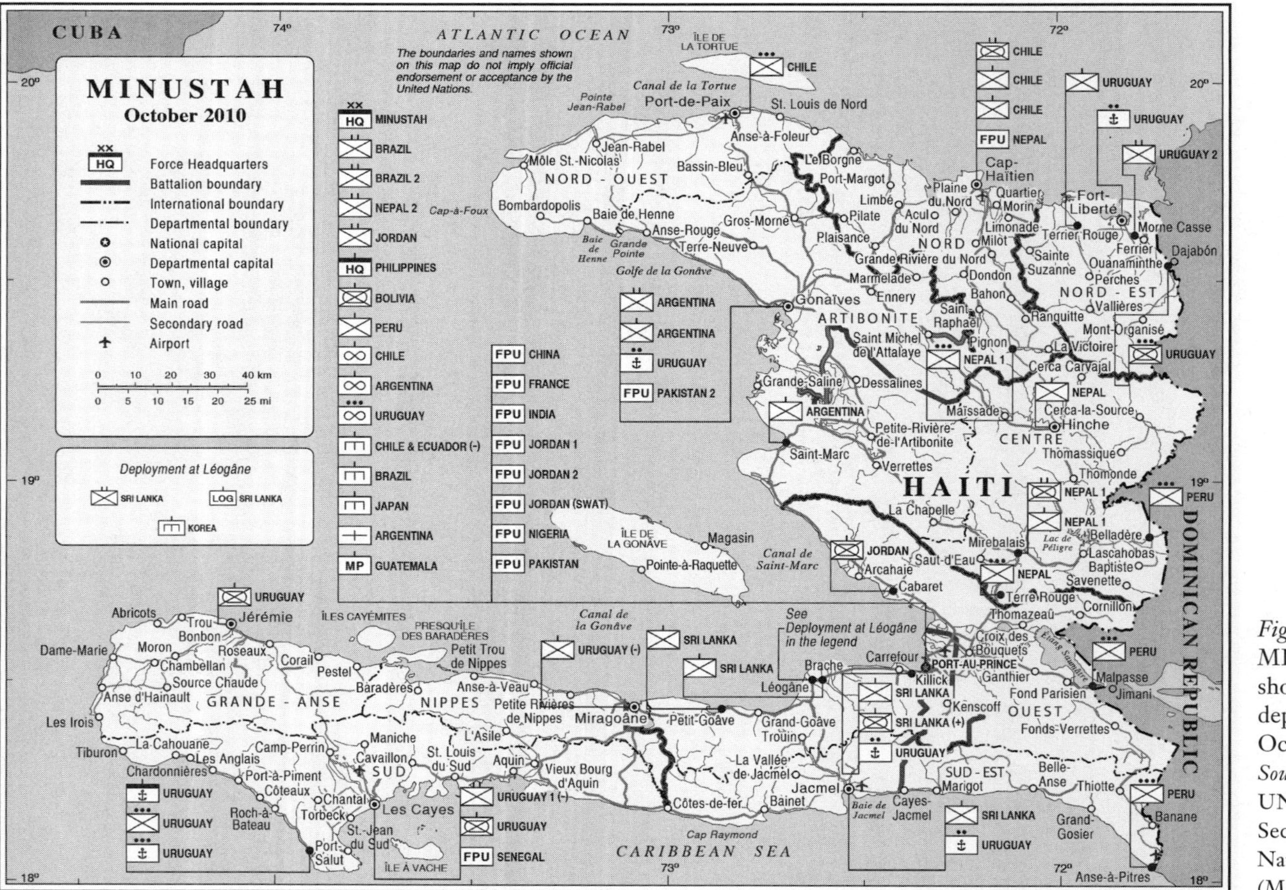


Figure 5.1.
MINUSTAH map showing force deployment, October 2010
Source: Courtesy of the UN Cartographic Section, United Nations, New York (Map No. 4224 Rev. 27)

capital), where there was a strong presence of forces loyal to Aristide and armed gangs with ties to drug trafficking.[4] These persistently high levels of instability and violence gave rise to hesitation over the timing of the country's elections. As a result, there were delays in the distribution of ballots, and elections were postponed at least five times.

In early 2010, the situation appeared to stabilize, with national elections scheduled for the fall of that year. Sadly, an earthquake destroyed the capital city and had a profound, almost-devastating impact on the UN mission. Almost a quarter of a million people died, including some one hundred UN staff members, the head of the mission, his deputy, and the police commissioner (BBC News 2011a). Hundreds of government offices—including the national palace, senate, and UN mission headquarters, Camp Charlie—were partially destroyed. Thousands of people were left without homes, and almost two million people were displaced. Millions of earthquake victims took refuge in IDP camps located in public spaces (public parks, golf courses, and churches). Close to 450,000 people were forced to leave the capital because there was no electricity or water. Elections inevitably had to be delayed, and the mission mandate adapted once again to encompass the humanitarian crisis caused by the earthquake.[5] In practical and psychological terms, the UN mission was so affected by its own losses that almost ten thousand American forces had to temporarily deploy to assist in the rescue mission; they eventually took over strategic positions, including ports and the national airport.

Almost fifteen months after the earthquake, the UN sponsored a national election. By then, a second crisis hit Haiti, this time a cholera outbreak that debilitated some 300,000 Haitians and killed over six thousand people between 2010 and 2011. To make matters worse for the UN, the disease seemingly originated from a Nepali peacekeeping camp north of the capital, which spilled raw sewage into a tributary of the Artibonite River.[6] A sexual abuse scandal involving peacekeepers also erupted in the fall of 2011, leading to yet another crisis within the mission.

MINUSTAH made a significant contribution to the postearthquake rescue effort, although the delay in organizing elections inevitably halted reconstruction efforts. The electoral process suffered constant delays and controversies. There were serious irregularities in the first round of national presidential elections in late 2010, including voter fraud, intimidation, tampered ballot boxes, and thousands of disenfranchised voters, mostly individuals who had been displaced by the earthquake (*Economist* 2010b). The second round of elections, conducted almost four months later, finally yielded a result; Michel Martelly, a former Kompa singer known as "Sweet Mickey," won after a chaotic presidential race. As all of this illustrates, the success of the mission faced challenges on several fronts. But what impact did the soldiers on the ground have? How have the troops' peacekeeping experiences affected the socialization process?

## MINUSTAH and Its Socializing Effects

### Socialization in the Argentine Contingent

Argentina joined MINUSTAH after a long, tense congressional debate about whether the country should authorize the deployment of troops to Haiti. A political compromise was ultimately reached: Argentine military forces would deploy, but not for the purposes of civil conflict resolution, policing, public security, gang control, or political order. The Argentine mandate was far more constrained than the UN's (Follietti 2005, 37–56). As a consequence, the Argentine contingent consisted of one full battalion (roughly 650 soldiers), a traveling air force hospital (thirty soldiers), and a forty-member air force crew known as UNFLIGHT (Micha 2007, 113). MINUSTAH eventually became the country's most important peacekeeping commitment in the post-financial-crisis era. In 2010, over 70% of Argentina's troop contribution to the UN system was concentrated in Haiti,[7] a reflection of the potential significance of the mission's post-2004 socializing effects on blue helmets.

An Argentine Air Force unit, UNFLIGHT, was sent to Delta Camp, near the airport in Port-au-Prince. By contrast, the Argentine battalion deployed to the port of Gonaïves in the northwest part of the country and five hours from the political capital by car. Why Gonaïves? The Haitian port was one of the few military sectors where the peacekeepers performed monitoring and observing functions, and where policing was not heavily needed. Gonaïves, a city with an estimated population of 200,000, experienced intense looting and violence in early 2004, but it stabilized almost as soon as Aristide left the country. According to a military advisor to the Argentine UN mission in New York, Gonaïves was more isolated than the capital, but it was also more politically stable:

> Gonaïves is a strategic port and there is a lot to monitor. It was there where check points and control posts were most needed. Argentine peacekeepers are much more capable of conducting monitoring tasks; we can verify if vehicles are not carrying lethal weapons, we can establish control posts and observe the

peace. The Argentine force does not conduct public security functions; we are constitutionally constrained from performing public security operations, so we must follow our legal mandate, even if we are abroad in Haiti.[8]

The peacekeeping force in Gonaïves was mostly in charge of monitoring and demobilizing the Revolutionary Artibonite Resistance Front. Unlike the gangs in Port-au-Prince, the front actually welcomed foreign peacekeepers, thus helping to ensure a relatively stable environment for the Argentine battalion.

Policymakers in Buenos Aires who were interviewed for this research suggested that Argentine soldiers did not receive formal training to conduct policing functions because they were not legally permitted to intervene in civil conflicts. To quote Marcelo Saín, an expert in defense policy in Buenos Aires, "soldiers cannot detain individuals, they cannot conduct anti-riot operations and they are prohibited from carrying rubber bullets guns of the type peacekeepers carry in Port-au-Prince."[9] Indeed, Argentina did not commit troops for general policing functions. It instead put forward some forty police personnel from the Gendarmería Nacional (National Guard), an institution subordinated to the Interior Ministry and not the military. As a result, the military's exposure to the policing and nation-building functions of MINUSTAH was limited.

Gonaïves is remote in general, but the Argentine battalion there was particularly isolated. Its relative seclusion in a rural area also meant that it required daily logistical support from Buenos Aires. The head of the Department for Peacekeeping Operations in the Ministry of Defense explained, "this is the first time that we send troops with self-sustenance capacity. We provide all inputs, from matte [tea] to toilet paper and all logistical support for our battalion. We are no longer dependent on the UN or other contingents to carry out the logistical burden."[10] Consequently, there was no intense interaction with other forces or even with international NGOs, which were largely concentrated in the political capital. The Argentine troops' most frequent interactions took place with their Uruguayan counterparts. In 2008, a hurricane devastated Gonaïves, causing intense flooding that prompted the temporary deployment of Uruguayan troops to assist their Argentine colleagues.

What did Argentine peacekeepers gain from this experience? The interviews conducted in the field identified variations between the battalion in Gonaïves and the air force unit in Delta Camp. Infantrymen, who had to satisfy the minimum requirements for deployment, predominantly comprised the battalion. They all received basic training in CAECOPAZ, and some admit the mission helped improve their language skills. As a whole, participants from the army viewed their experience with MINUSTAH positively, in part because they had been able to sustain their troops while being miles away from Buenos Aires. This is something they utterly failed to do in 1982, when the army deployed conscripts to the Malvinas/Falklands only to abandon them during the most intense portion of the conflict. For the handful of officers who commanded the battalion (forty-eight in all), the experience of leading an internationally mandated force enhanced their leadership skills. Many received promotions upon their return home (or even to their redeployment to another UN mission, in some cases). But most of the personnel that made up the battalion were noncommissioned officers. In other words, the top junior officers were no longer serving on UN peacekeeping operations, as was the case in the early 1990s.

Soldiers who were part of the battalion in 2008 also participated in an international humanitarian operation that required intense coordination with various UN partners. As a result of several consecutive seasonal hurricanes, Gonaïves suffered an enormous loss of life and property. During this time, the Argentine battalion mostly distributed food and drinking water, as well as shored up defenses near the city.[11] This type of mission helped the Argentine Army prepare soldiers for civic action operations and natural disasters at home (for which they have a limited mandate in Argentina). A policy report by Resdal, a defense think tank based in Buenos Aires, indicated that "because the Argentine battalion is deployed outside the capital in a rural area, its challenges are different from those encountered by those deployed in the capital . . . cooperation with NGOs and other UN humanitarian agencies is easier as there are less actors and thus less competition" (Avelar Giannini 2001, 29). The MINUSTAH experience probably increased the Argentine battalion's exposure to civilizing trends, but quantitative evidence of increased military professionalism is currently limited.

Comparatively speaking, it would appear that troops in Haiti were no longer receiving the same professional and individual benefits they once had in places like Cyprus, where a large number of officers served as individual observers rather than as unit members. Furthermore, even if the Argentine battalion conducted observation duties (posts and checking points), peace observation is no longer a novel activity for the army; after all, they have been conducting observation missions for two decades now. The troops were not necessarily acquiring new professional skills. In fact, it would appear that their primary motive for participating in the mission was a financial one. A lieutenant earned about $1,000 a month in Argentina, while soldiers being deployed to Haiti for a six-month rotation period earned $2,500 a month.[12]

The air force's experience at Delta Camp would appear to have a radically different impact on the socialization of these troops. The unit was entirely made up of officers who were fluent in English. For the most part, the pilots flew helicopters that provided logistical support to the Argentine battalion and the UN mission. They transported and delivered inputs for the mission, which varied from food and humanitarian supplies to election ballot boxes to VIPs. Most of them had participated in at least two, sometimes three, previous peacekeeping tours; all of them had been to Cyprus (where there was another Argentine air unit). In this case, MINUSTAH offered professional enhancements. One pilot admitted that "air force commodores and vice-commodores need at least one peacekeeping experience for promotion."[13] Similarly, most pilots acknowledged that MINUSTAH had allowed them to fly more hours than at home. According to one of the pilots interviewed in Delta Camp, "the norm is twenty five hours per trimester; here we fly roughly forty hours per trimester, so we exceed, by far, the domestic norm."[14] The frequency with which pilots needed to fly varied substantially in MINUSTAH; during elections, helicopters flew more often, as they transported ballot boxes from rural areas to the capital. Increased numbers of flights were the norm in the aftermath of the earthquake, when humanitarian needs required pilots to fly more than usual.

The MINUSTAH experience also enabled the air force to simulate contingent and natural disaster operations. Both the 2008 hurricane season and the 2010 earthquake taught pilots hard lessons about how to prepare for natural disasters. Some of those lessons learned were later applied in Chile, which was hit by an equally devastating earthquake a month later and to which Argentina provided assistance with airlifts.

As the working conditions in Haiti often proved to be more difficult than those of other missions, the pilots became well tutored in adapting as necessary. In MINUSTAH, air units mostly supported a peacebuilding and humanitarian operation; in Cyprus, the air force supported an observation mission. However, a veteran pilot in the unit remembered flying more hours in the UN Assistance Mission to Iraq and UNPROFOR than in MINUSTAH, in part because these were peace enforcement operations with no-fly zones that required more air support,[15] providing further evidence that observational and enforcement missions sometimes offer positive military professional enticements.

Contingents also interacted differently in Haiti than in other UN missions. As the Argentine, Chilean, and Uruguayan aviation units on the island were all next to one another, the pilots spent time together (interaction effects). There was social interaction, but it was no longer the positive professional experience that generated excitement about being involved in a different operational environment and with equally professional counterparts from NATO, which was the case in the 1990s.

What, if any, were the civilizing effects of MINUSTAH on the troops? In theory, there should have been more interaction between soldiers and civilians, since the mission in Haiti involved a plethora of NGOs performing humanitarian and electoral assistance, especially in Port-au-Prince. But the Argentine aviation unit had a strict curfew; pilots were required to return to their unit after completing their flight schedules, and they could not leave Delta Camp premises. Many pilots expressed frustration that they could not leave their headquarters and interact with locals as observers, as they had been able to do in Cyprus. Still, one pilot suggested that the curfew was positive because it made it easier for them to save money.[16] In any case, the result was that most civil-military interactions occurred when pilots flew civilians or UN staff. This was not the close and dependent relationship that Moskos, Williams, and Segal (2000) had in mind when he asserted that peacekeeping "civilianized" military actors delivering humanitarian aid and refugee assistance. Compared with other contingents on the ground, pilots in MINUSTAH were far more segregated from the civilian components of the mission.

## Socialization in the Brazilian Contingent

Brazil took the military lead in MINUSTAH and received a higher level of responsibility for the stability of the mission. It first deployed twelve hundred troops, but after the 2010 earthquake, it increased its peacekeeping commitment to over two thousand. The contingent included two separate units: an army brigade composed of two infantry battalions (about two thousand army troops) and a marine corps operating group (265 troops) recruited from a marine infantry battalion (Fuzileiros Navais). Brazil invested more heavily in Haiti and its capital than anywhere else. In 2010, over 95% of its UN troop contribution was concentrated in MINUSTAH, and most of its soldiers deployed to Port-au-Prince.[17] These soldiers handled the most delicate aspects of the mission, including the disarmament of groups and militias, as well as joint patrolling activities shared by MINUSTAH and the Haitian police (Diniz 2007, 105–6). Two of Brazil's battalions (BRABATT I and II) were put in charge of patrolling several areas in Port-au-Prince's most dangerous zones, including Bel-Air and Cité Soleil.

The general pattern observed among Brazilian troops in MINUSTAH is one in which service diffused professionalizing effects that were marked by heavy exposure to peacebuilding and policing functions. Much like the Argentine battalion in Gonaïves, the core of the Brazilian Army contingent in Port-au-Prince was made up of infantry soldiers. Of these, less than 20% of the army officer corps had served during a peace mission. Although soldiers had strong economic incentives to join the foreign peacekeeping mission (for every rotation at home, there were five volunteers for each available position in the battalion), their chances of moving up the ranks were limited because participation in such operations was not considered for promotion. The evaluation scheme used by the Brazilian Army did not award deployments abroad unless the officer received a special medal for UN service. If chosen, army personnel could only participate in one UN peace operation, ensuring there was no repetition and no way of building peacekeeping skills by adding deployments. Only the corps of engineers, medical staff, and interpreters repeated peacekeeping rotation tours. Language instruction was only required for those officers occupying observer posts but not troops, as "UN troops do not require language expertise."[18]

The Fuzileiros Navais, a smaller, all-volunteer, professional combat force, had a somewhat different experience. Ninety percent of these officers were exposed to at least one peacekeeping rotation tour. The navy officer corps thus benefitted from more international exposure than the army, and it valued the peacekeeping experience. That said, it is difficult to assess whether or to what extent this experience influenced their subsequent chances of promotion.

What did Brazilian peacekeepers learn from the UN mission in Haiti? It is worth mentioning that most Brazilian officers did not perceive themselves as agents of socialization but rather as socializers. Specifically, they saw MINUSTAH as a stage to display their military might and export some of their homegrown military tactics. For officers, peacekeeping was a means to put leadership skills into practice. In the words of one Brazilian blue helmet, "we are not only responsible for our own soldiers, we are responsible for the military success of the whole mission. We are not only commanding our own forces, we are now in command of an international force."[19]

In terms of social interaction with other military contingents, only a handful of officers acknowledged that they had learned something valuable from their international counterparts. Socialization with other troops was common in Port-au-Prince, with the capital divided into various military sectors that included contingents from Bangladesh, Bolivia, Jordan, Nepal, Nigeria, Paraguay (embedded within the Brazilian contingent), Sri Lanka, and Uruguay. It was a diverse group of soldiers, most of them from the developing world, but they generally had far fewer resources than Brazil. One officer confirmed that Brazil deployed its "most modern equipment and communication technology, with satellite lines, privileged mobile lines, and social media."[20] A visit to BRABATT I headquarters in Port-au-Prince confirmed that Brazil deployed large amounts of military equipment, including several kinds of armored vehicles and several types of communication technologies. They also had state-of-the-art, fully air-conditioned facilities. The base, located near Delta Camp, was almost four times larger than its neighboring battalions.[21] If anything, the Brazilian soldiers felt that other national contingents could perhaps learn something from their peacekeeping doctrine, rather than the other way around.

Some officers perceived MINUSTAH as a valuable learning experience from a logistical perspective (Jomini 2009, 29–32). Like Argentina, Brazil could deploy and logistically sustain a large force overseas in a difficult operational and cultural environment. At an institutional level, MINUSTAH was seen as a positive operational experience, as soldiers acquired field (or combat) experience that allegedly improved their professionalism. As one of the senior officers explained, "we have conducted over 6,450 patrols, more than 3,300 hours of flights, and we have covered almost 50,000 square kilometers in mechanized patrols."[22]

All officers shared the view that MINUSTAH was a hard-core security mission that resembled real war conditions. As one former peacekeeper described it, "MINUSTAH is a Chapter VII mission and we had to use force because the level of threat was high. The mission was very dangerous and risky."[23] They have internalized Haiti as the ultimate (urban) combat experience, even though MINUSTAH is not strictly a peace enforcement operation. Several officials interviewed for this research at the UNDPKO in New York described

MINUSTAH as a mission with no parties to the conflict, but in which criminals and gangs were heavily armed, could come back and reorganize, and then start riots. One official said that "the core of the problem is policing."[24]

Nevertheless, Haiti had only about ninety thousand police officers, and they were largely ineffective and required substantial human rights training. At the same time, UN member states had committed infantry rather than police officers to the mission.[25] The tasks of securing and policing Haiti were delegated mostly to military contingents, and the heavy lifting of this policing mission was put in the hands of the Brazilians. The decision to use Brazilians soldiers was logical; they had antigang training and knew how to "clean" slums. One UN civilian official admitted that Brazilian soldiers "understood that they had to clear the area from gangs and then bring development projects, like Viva Rio."[26] In fact, most members of the Brazilian contingent were first recruited from units that were originally headquartered in Rio de Janeiro, where gang violence and drug trafficking were also common.[27]

Brazilian generals were initially cautious and refrained from exercising excessive force. But in 2006, two Jordanian peacekeepers were killed in Cité Soleil. The murders prompted the UN to take a tougher stand in early 2007, when close to seven hundred Brazilian troops flooded Cité Soleil, resulting in a major gun battle known as the "siege of Cité Soleil." It was the most significant attempt to make regular, forcible entries into the area. Also, since armed gangs routinely took their kidnap victims to Cité Soleil, the Brazilian ability to penetrate the area for even a short time was seen as a sign of progress (BBC News 2006b, 2007a). Other similar operations followed suit, including one in Bel-Air, another slum in the capital. The tactics used in all these operations were similar: a large number of peacekeepers, UN police forces, and the Haitian National Police cleared the slums by hunting members of violent gangs and drug traffickers. Next came months of heavy UN patrols, in which some NGOs moved in to provide basic services to the local inhabitants. If this strategy sounds familiar, it is probably because the operations in Haiti were training grounds for the so-called pacification strategies conducted in Brazil in 2010 (chapter 3).

From the Brazilian perspective, MINUSTAH was close to successfully achieving its security mandate because their policing strategies yielded some results (*Economist* 2007b). The UN Security Council recognized their successes in 2009 when it admitted, "since the deployment of MINUSTAH, there has been an improvement in the overall security situation, as demonstrated by declining crime rates and the public's growing confidence in the Haitian National Police."[28] But the results observed in Haiti were similar to the outcomes witnessed in Brazilian *favelas* under pacification, where crime rates remained low so as long as troops stayed. Ultimately, these were only temporary improvements. Crime rates continued to fluctuate, while drug-related crimes increased. MINUSTAH was never capable of replacing military troops with police forces; Brazilian blue helmets remained for months and years after their incursions in shantytowns. Jorge Ramalho, a well-known defense scholar, found that the mission faced a dilemma common to most peacekeeping operations—there was no clear exit strategy. The stability of the country was so precarious that peacekeepers could not be removed from their posts or withdrawn from the mission.[29] Ironically, the use of Brazilian peacekeepers in public security spheres inhibited police reform in Haiti, as politicians delayed decisions or altogether failed to establish clean and fully accountable forces; instead, they relied on South American troops.

The socializing experience in Haiti could have been positive if Brazilian troops had at least learned good and acceptable international practices. After all, conventional wisdom holds that peacekeeping contributes to the diffusion of liberal norms that reshape military organizations and even individual identities. Brazilian troops replicated standard procedures and followed domestic tactics, however. In Haiti, as in Brazil, soldiers were accused of using excessive force against Aristide's supporters, locals, and student demonstrations in Port-au-Prince. Unlike Canadian or Scandinavian blue helmets, whose presence in peacebuilding missions is typically much "softer,"[30] Brazilian peacekeepers were heavily armored and relied on force when confronted with crowds.

There were serious allegations of human rights violations, specifically with regard to the incursions in Cité Soleil and Bel-Air. In one of the raids on Cité Soleil, soldiers expended twenty-two thousand rounds of ammunition over the course of a seven-hour operation, which not only included ground troops but also air support, with helicopters shooting at targets. Close to thirty people were killed, and most of the dead and wounded were found inside their homes. According to one NGO report, "these accounts charge that soldiers shot at people indiscriminately, which had devastating effects in a neighborhood where housing conditions are extremely precarious" (qtd. in Mendonça 2008).

To add insult to injury, NGOs providing medical services in poor neighborhoods, such as Doctors without Borders and the Red Cross, were not allowed to assist the wounded. In a report on human rights violations during

MINUSTAH, the Red Cross coordinator reported that "UN Soldiers prevented Red Cross vehicles from entering the zone to assist wounded children" (qtd. in Halling and Bookey 2008, 465).

The UN claimed that the military was there "only to provide cover, working with local authorities," and that "only police forces can conduct inspections and arrests."[31] Yet Brazilian troops committed multiple law enforcement functions. In a raid that was branded by the Brazilian force as Operation Cajado (Operation Silence) in the region of Belecour, in Cité Soleil, blue helmets arrested gang members and seized weapons, which were later turned in to the Haitian National Police (Informativo mensal do Batalhão Brasileiro 2007, 2). These were not exceptional operations; UN peacekeepers conducted several such large-scale military incursions between 2005 and 2010. At least seven small-scale raids took place between 2006 and 2008, in which incidents of murder and unlawful detention took place under the Brazilian peacekeeping command (Halling and Bookey 2008, 465–68).

Few of these incidents were documented or reported to UN Headquarters in New York. In response to criticism by human rights organizations denouncing these operations, MINUSTAH and Brazilian commanders justified their actions by claiming that they were combating dangerous gangs and drug traffickers in Port-au-Prince.[32]

I asked UN officials in New York if they were concerned about the implications of using Brazilian troops in Haiti, especially since so many of them relied on doctrines and strategies that have prompted numerous accusations of human rights abuses in the past.[33] One official thought that MINUSTAH was actually teaching troops good lessons on human rights, socializing them to refrain from using excessive force against civilians. In their view, the mission in Haiti differed from operations conducted by the military in Brazil because MINUSTAH was legal and legitimate. "All basic principles of consent are present in MINUSTAH: consent from the Security Council and from the René Préval government; also, the population had had enough. There was little collateral damage and domestic and international legitimacy."[34]

Reports from NGOs and lawyers nevertheless indicate that the so-called collateral damage was not minimal and that MINUSTAH's role in fact deteriorated human rights conditions. The Harvard Law Student Advocates for Human Rights and the Centro de Justiça Global in Brazil conducted one of the most comprehensive evaluations of the UN mission in Haiti in 2005, also known as the "Harvard Report." The report (Harvard Human Rights Program 2005, 8) concluded:

> Despite one of the strongest human rights mandates in the history of UN peacekeeping operations, MINUSTAH has not effectively investigated or reported human rights abuses; nor has it protected human rights advocates. Charged to train and reform the Haitian National Police, MINUSTAH instead has provided unquestioning support to police operations that have resulted in warrantless arrests and detentions, unintended civilian casualties and deliberate extrajudicial killings . . . In consequence, Haiti is ruled by guns and terror, not law.

From the outset, the UN mission lacked the necessary mechanisms to ensure accountability of its own troops. First, the chain of command inhibited transparency. Many of the violations committed by Brazilian blue helmets went unreported because force commanders were military officials from Brazil. Appointed on a yearly basis, the force commander always returned to Brasilia at the end of his one-year term, effectively creating a principal-agent challenge in which he was theoretically an agent of the UN even though his de facto obligation was to his principals in the Brazilian Army. He might have formally been in charge of the military component of the UN mission, but informally his primary objective was to protect his own. Therefore the force commander could not report or denounce Brazilian troops without jeopardizing the army's prestige and perhaps endangering his career. As a result, most violations committed by Brazilian blue helmets went unaccounted for.

Second, the UN had been unable to hold peacekeepers legally accountable. The Status of Forces Agreement governing MINUSTAH, and agreed upon by the UN and the Haitian government, allowed for civil action to proceed in Haiti only with the mission commander's approval, which was impossible. Avery (2010) considers that criminal trials are equally unlikely: "While the Brazilian civil code allows foreigners to sue in domestic courts for acts perpetrated by Brazilian citizens abroad, the costs and difficulty of bringing a case in a foreign jurisdiction are prohibitive. Brazil is also unlikely to bring criminal charges against its own soldiers on behalf of Haitian victims."

Consequently, MINUSTAH offered few incentives to modify military behavior and norms of conduct. The mandate given to the Brazilian blue helmets in Port-au-Prince did not contribute to enhancing military professional skills; in fact, it diverted military expertise to mere policing functions without proper mechanisms of accountability. Brazilian blue helmets assumed a *mão firme*, or "iron fisted," approach to peacekeeping. Brazilian soldiers simply replicated and reinforced their domestic organizational understandings and practices. This approach is certainly far from the model suggested by Moskos (1976, 10), in which peacekeeping was supposed to enhance professional skills by "deemphasizing the application of violence in order to attain viable political compromises."

How did MINUSTAH affect civilianizing trends? Brazilians have widely believed that troops on the ground integrated well with the local population in Haiti. As Kenkel (2010b, 657) describes, "the approach is based on a high level of personal contact of military contingents with the population in the area of responsibility. The essentialist notion is that warmth and close interaction is particularly Latin American and especially a Brazilian quality . . . a popular anecdote recites that, whereas Haitian ran in fear from U.S. troops during the occupations of 1994–2004, today Brazilian foot patrols are greeted with banter and open arms."

One of the most interesting civil-military initiatives that flourished during MINUSTAH was the arrival of the Brazilian NGO Viva Rio, which implemented numerous development projects in Bel-Air. Viva Rio emerged in response to the growing violence in Rio de Janeiro's *favelas*. In Brazil, Viva Rio manages various social programs related to culture, music, community outreach, and human security (small arms control, demobilization, and disarmament). Although cooperation between Viva Rio and the armed forces was limited in Rio, the organization accepted an invitation to run twin projects in Haiti. The project, Honor and Respect for Bel-Air, included programs designed to empower women, to distribute water, to collect garbage, and to organize cultural programs. Although most of these projects were run independently of the Brazilian peacekeeping contingent, others actually relied on them. Blue helmets from Brazil partnered with Viva Rio to clean water canals, to train emergency brigades in Bel-Air communities (providing first aid in cases of natural disasters), to provide goods for development projects (blankets, mattresses, stoves, etc.), and to perform patrols to protect staff members from extortions and threats from gang members.[35]

As a result, it soon became common practice to refer to Viva Rio as an example of the positive, intense synergies between civilian actors and blue helmets in Haiti. The underlying claim was that projects like Honor and Respect for Bel-Air built bridges between humanitarians and blue helmets, allowing both groups to understand their respective working cultures and practices.[36]

All of this suggests that MINUSTAH had considerable civilizing effects upon Brazilian troops. The partnership between Brazilian peacekeepers and Viva Rio was indeed an improvement from previous peacekeeping deployments. But it is the only example of positive civilizing effects available, and there is plenty of room for skepticism.

First, Honor and Respect for Bel-Air was the only project of its kind in which Brazilian peacekeepers engaged actively with the NGO community. There were no equivalent programs with other international NGOs or even with other areas outside of Bel-Air, because most Brazilian troops (infantry and non-commissioned officers) were not fluent in English or French, let alone Creole. Viva Rio became part of the mission in part to overcome the linguistic and cultural barriers that Brazilian peacekeepers faced when they interacted with international actors and locals. On the one hand, the joint venture with Viva Rio allowed Brazil to export and tropicalize its own development projects in Haiti as part of its own signaling strategy to indicate its emergence as a major power. On the other hand, Viva Rio facilitated the role of peacekeepers because the organization managed programs in Portuguese and was Brazilian in character. But the disadvantage of this approach is clear: troops cooperated only with those NGOs that shared cultural affinities to Brazil.

Second, the aggressive policing tactics used in Cité Soleil and Bel-Air created an insurmountable hurdle for Brazilians trying to work with international NGOs such as the International Committee of the Red Cross (ICRC) and Doctors without Borders. Cooperation was compromised when NGOs were denied access to the neighborhoods where military incursions took place, which might have prompted the Brazilian government to search for a local NGO in Rio de Janeiro, as no other international humanitarian organization was willing to endorse the military tactics pursued in Port-au-Prince.

Third, Brazil's forces seemed incapable of transitioning from their traditional police force roles to a humanitarian mode after the 2010 earthquake. Their inability to do so affected the relationship between civilians and the peacekeepers and limited the scope of the civil-military (CIMIC) activities implemented by the Brazilians. The catastrophic events of January 12, 2010, overwhelmed the Brazilian contingent, which lost eighteen of its members; not since World War II had Brazil lost so many soldiers. Then, nearly twelve hundred Brazilian troops were set aside and replaced by U.S. troops that led the humanitarian operation and temporarily took over the entire country for a three-month period.[37] The earthquake also had a devastating effect on locals, as it triggered a refugee crisis with millions of victims displaced in camps. It is in this context that civil-military integration was most needed, and it is where the Brazilian peacekeepers' most obvious shortcomings showed.

In September 2010, I was granted access to three different IDP camps in the Brazilian military sector of Port-au-Prince. These camps varied in size, mission, and location, and were managed by a diverse group of international NGOs with distinct working procedures. It was a small sample of the more than one thousand IDP camps in Haiti after the earthquake. But the three camps I visited represent mini case assessments of the extent to which Brazilian troops integrated with civilian components. From a research design point of view, these camps were "most likely cases" for civilianizing effects, since most IDP camps were concentrated in Port-au-Prince, where most Brazilian blue helmets deployed. Given the large presence of international NGOs in IDP camps, those forces located next to them would have had the most exposure to civil-military interactions. As Moskos, Williams, and Segal (2000, 3) argue, integration occurs where soldiers build refugee camps, assist aid workers, deliver food and medical supplies, and provide security for humanitarian organizations. In fact, my field observations indicated the opposite.

I first visited the Pétionville camp, which sat on the golf course of a former country club, next to the U.S. ambassador's residence. It was known as Camp Penn—actor Sean Penn's aid group, the J/P Haitian Relief Organization, managed it. It once housed close to fifty-five thousand displaced persons (one of the largest camps in the capital), but it had managed to relocate almost ten thousand of them to some form of permanent housing by the fall of 2010. Camp Penn was a success story, given that most IDP camps had actually grown into tent cities with more, not fewer, displaced persons.[38] The camp offered a number of services including medical support for emergencies, women, and children; garbage and housing relocation; and job assistance for men. The camp partnered with a panoply of NGOs running different service projects, including OXFAM and Save the Children. The staff included international workers, locals, and medical volunteers. Its administration had a more pragmatic view of neutrality than the ICRC, working closely with U.S. troops and even some peacekeepers. The tennis courts next to the camp were used to host the U.S. Eighty-Second Airborne Division in early 2010.

Although located in a sector safeguarded by one of the two Brazilian battalions, the camp did not provide joint programs or services in tandem with Brazilian peacekeepers. Blue helmets from Brazil conducted routine patrols (roughly three times a day) but had no cooperative endeavors with any of the NGOs, staff members, or locals in the camp. Those who conducted the patrols could only communicate in Portuguese and had no translators within their units, so they were unable to connect with international workers or locals. Furthermore, Camp Penn reported a number of incidents in which the blue helmets had used tear gas without properly investigating the situation or asking questions of any of the staff members. As one of the interviewees argued, "Brazil knows how to deploy technologically and strategically, but psychologically, they don't get it. The mission would benefit if they could assume a softer phase, less forceful and less fearful of crowds."[39]

A similar trend was witnessed in a second IDP camp, Ancien Aéroport Militaire, which housed close to forty-eight thousand displaced persons. It was run by the American Refugee Committee and, like the one in Pétionville, it partnered with multiple NGOs to distribute tents, food, water, and basic medical and emergency services. At the time of the visit, there was an attempt to implement a cash-for-work project, coordinated by the UN Development Program to hire workers to clean off rubble and debris in the streets left by the earthquake. But here, as in Pétionville, there were no joint military/NGO programs with Brazilian troops. MINUSTAH's troops were dedicated solely to public security. Although gated and with a permanent UN Police observing post at its entrance, Ancien Aéroport Militaire faced increasing security concerns. There were reports of gender-based violence such as rape, as well as minor petty crime. In this case, Brazilian units conducted motorized patrols, sometimes on their own, occasionally in the company of UN Police and the Haitian National Police. Once again, language barriers impeded communication between international police forces (mostly recruited from French-speaking countries such as Burkina Faso and Cote d'Ivoire) and the Portuguese-speaking troops from Brazil. But the responses to incidents of violence were similar to those undertaken when gangs were still the main source of threat in the capital: pepper spray, tear gas, and bullet guns. As one of the NGO staff members explained, "we are no longer threatened by kidnappings or gang-related crimes; those who have been involved in sexual assaults are not necessarily from inside the camp, so we need more community work to identify who is local and who is not. The mandate is not for a heavily armored mission."[40]

The earthquake did what the UN mission could not achieve in six years: reduce crime rates throughout the capital, not just in the slums. As 450,000 people—most of them displaced victims—left Port-au-Prince, so did gangs and criminals, at least temporarily. Although close to five thousand prisoners escaped from jail after the earthquake (creating a serious security crisis), the real threat to the mission post-2010 was posed by the IDP camps. A survey of incidents of sexual violence in IDP camps, conducted by the Center for Human Rights and Global Justice (2011, 1), found that 14% of households surveyed had experienced rape or unwanted touching. The camps were not only sites of sexual abuse and crime, but the precarious sanitation conditions within them added to the tents' vulnerability to natural disasters (hurricanes) and created an extremely vulnerable context for MINUSTAH, especially in the advent of a national election. The mission thus required a humanitarian approach, and many of the NGOs interviewed for this study thought that peacekeepers needed to assume a "softer presence" with small, concealed weapons; soft berets; and an accessible, less intimidating attitude toward locals. This was a tactical change (as opposed to a strategic one), and so it did not require a new Security Council mandate but rather a simple order from the force commander to his troops. Instead of adjusting the rules of engagement, however, the highest UN commander at the time in Haiti, General Floriano Peixoto, indicated his major concern was that gangs would reorganize and spark a turf war. In an interview he gave only a few days after the earthquake, he stated: "My understanding is that they [gangs] are trying to reorganize themselves, trying to establish a kind of kingdom for themselves inside the slums . . . To establish that, they need to fight with each other. This is what we don't want . . . The strategy is to deter, to tell them 'do not show up, because if I see you, I catch you'" (qtd. in Agence France Presse 2010). Therefore the Brazilian approach to peacekeeping remained obsessed with policing and gang control, relying heavily on force.

I then visited a third camp, known as the Tabarre Issa IDP, located on the outskirts of Port-au-Prince. It was smaller and more organized in comparison to Camp Penn and Ancien Aéroport Militaire. Tabarre Issa held around five hundred displaced people and was run by Concern Worldwide, an NGO headquartered in Europe. Its efforts focused on providing displaced people with the necessary skills (carpentry, plumbing, and construction) to build their own permanent housing within the camp. It was an innovative approach in that they deincentivized tents and short-term shelter for permanent housing. They delivered inputs (wood and tools), organized workshops, and provided the sketch plans for new houses that were hurricane and earthquake resistant, with toilets and running water. The underlying philosophy was that a self-made home creates a special kind of ownership, encouraging homeowners to care for their property and their surroundings. The camp thus aimed to develop not only property ownership but a sense of community. The Haitian government was naturally resistant to this approach because it effectively converted camps into permanent neighborhoods that required public services (electricity and water). But, surprisingly, Tabarre Issa did not have the security challenges that other camps in the capital faced. Certainly, it was much smaller, but part of their success was that weapons were not allowed inside camp premises (the zone was officially designated as a weapon-free sector). Brand-new homeowners slowly developed their own informal neighborhood associations that kept their still-unpaved streets clean and safe. Children had a safe playground area, and there was even a soccer field for leisure activities. One element was notoriously absent from this camp, however: heavily armored, patrolling peacekeeping units. The camp resided within the Brazilian military sector, and the "no weapons allowed under any circumstance" edict applied to inhabitants, workers, and peacekeepers. Since the Brazilian rules of engagement stipulated that troops be fully armed, they could not access the Tabarre Issa camp. As a result, those living inside the camp were relatively protected (and perhaps isolated) from crime, but also sheltered from violence generated by the peacekeepers. Of the three camps I visited in Haiti, Tabarre Issa had the least interaction with Brazilian soldiers but the fewest reported incidents of violence.[41]

One of the most common claims made by Brazilian officials is that their principled attitudes (neutrality and impartiality), biases against military organizations, and negative perceptions of developing nations hamper cooperation with international NGOs. Chagas Vianna Braga (2010, 715) finds that "in the field, most 'peace partners' are unwilling to operate together with a military component . . . Some, such as the ICRC, recognize that neutrality is paramount for success in their own mandates, and close cooperation with a military component that is resorting to increased force is far from neutral." However, the organizations managing these IDP camps varied in terms of their approach toward impartiality and neutrality. The camps in Pétionville and the Ancien Aéroport Militaire had operated with military agents on various initiatives and at different strategic and logistical levels. Only Tabarre Issa embraced a principled approach, yet the level of civilian integration with Brazilian troops was almost the same across these camps—minimal at best and restrained to patrolling. Therefore the absence of civil-military integration cannot be explained solely in terms of NGO biases or neutral positions.

Civil-military interactions in IDP camps were channeled through the UN Office for the Coordination of Humanitarian Affairs and the CIMIC Field Cell for MINUSTAH, an observer post within the mission. The latter's primary goals were to liaise, coordinate, and cooperate with civil actors; to convey their concerns to the headquarters; and to inform the force commander about their interactions in the field. Interestingly, Canadian and American military officers, who fulfilled the language and field experience requirements for the mission, had traditionally held most staff members of the CIMIC Field Cell. One of the Canadian officers informed me that "the cell was established following NATO CIMIC principles."[42] Whereas developing and democratizing states like Brazil contributed large units (battalions and companies), developed nations mostly provided a handful of observers who predominantly served in the CIMIC Field Cell.

Permeability between international NGOs and Brazilian blue helmets was limited, but was that the case with locals? Another piece of conventional wisdom held by Brazilian officials is that a natural connection based on cultural affinities such as soccer, music, a shared African legacy, and poverty developed between their troops and Haitians (Kipman 2009, 58–59). Thanks to this bond, Brazilian peacekeepers did try to "win the hearts and minds" of the locals upon arriving in the capital. In 2004, they organized a soccer match between Haiti's national team and Brazil's world's cup champion team, which was publically advertised as "Brazilian soccer diplomacy." The idea behind the match was that locals would give up their small weapons for tickets to the game. But the event actually encouraged weapon possession, and few gang members were willing to give up their guns (*Economist* 2004b).

Regrettably, no surveys were conducted on Haitian attitudes toward blue helmets in general or toward specific contingents. But I was able to spend half a day with one BRABATT I patrolling unit in Cité Soleil,[43] which enabled me to observe interactions between locals and blue helmets. Patrolling units clearly knew how to conduct their mission, as they had effectively mapped every street within their sector, identified the hot spots, and knew their area of deployment. But they seemed to be challenged by a familiar hurdle. Just like troops deployed at the Complexo do Alemão in Rio de Janeiro, those in Cité Soleil were greeted by wary residents. Military patrols in slums once again faced language and cultural barriers, as well as the absence of translators, all of which complicated any attempt to communicate directly with the inhabitants. But the problem of distrust in the slums stemmed directly from the rules of engagement they adopted in order to reduce risk. The military compound in Cité Soleil, which housed about one hundred soldiers (including Paraguayan-embedded troops), was heavily fortified and inaccessible to locals. The patrolling posture included heavily armored soldiers with high-ammunition weapons that were never concealed (mostly rifles), face visors, antibullet helmets, and body armors (vest, neck protectors, and knee pads). So much for the soft presence so often mentioned by international NGOs in the IDP camps.

Patrols took place roughly every three hours; the standard procedure was intended to reduce risk by assuming a "ready to fight" position. Patrols usually involved four to five vehicles, with four to six blue helmets in each. Every vehicle had one soldier with a rifle pointing to the front, while two monitored the sides and one guarded the rear with a shotgun. This procedure resembled an urban counterinsurgency operation more in tune with military missions in places like Afghanistan or Iraq, rather than a UN peacekeeping mission.

Ultimately, the heavy antiriot and military postures assumed by blue helmets inhibited any cooperative or integrated interaction with residents. The more security measures the UN undertook to protect troops and deter gangs and criminals, the more distance it created with the population it attempted to protect. The image of the Brazilian soldier as an aggressive police enforcer and not a peacekeeper spread. If anything, inhabitants from Cité Soleil appeared to be intimidated by the presence of Brazilian patrols.

As a result, Haitians became increasingly impatient with the presence of Brazilian troops. Their efforts to win the hearts and minds of locals failed time and again. Even before the tragic earthquake and cholera outbreak of 2010, Haitian politicians and activists visited the Brazilian Senate—not UN Headquarters in New York—to request the immediate removal of soldiers (Campos 2009). By 2011, the *Economist* (2011) joined human rights activists by endorsing the petition to remove troops. The civilizing effects of peacekeeping among Brazilian blue helmets were consequently limited to the Viva Rio experience. Even so, Brazilians soldiers failed to adjust to the circumstances of the mission after the earthquake. If they struggled to adapt their rules of engagement on the field (a minor logistical change), one has to wonder how this peacekeeping experience could have possibly changed individual identities, let alone military organizations. On the contrary, it would appear that peacekeeping in Haiti replicated and then reinforced policing roles, thus failing to effectively change practices, behavior, or military identities. The Brazilian socializing experience clearly diverted from the civilianizing model suggested by the Moskos, Williams, and Segal (2000) framework.

### Socialization in the Uruguayan Contingent

Uruguay's first contribution to MINUSTAH was a battalion of fifty-seven officers and five hundred soldiers, each from the three branches (Rosales 2007, 141–42). In 2006, Uruguay doubled its troop contribution by supplying an additional battalion. It also contributed a small unit of forty air force pilots in support of UNFLIGHT. In 2009, the UN assigned the Uruguayan Navy the task of safeguarding Haiti's maritime sovereignty. URUMAR (Uruguay's Maritime Peacekeeping Unit) was created with 187 marines and about twenty patrol boats to control the Haitian coasts. By 2010, with a force of over 1,130 troops, Uruguay became the second-largest troop contributor to MINUSTAH (about 14% of the entire force). By December 2010, close to 92% of Uruguay's UN blue helmets were evenly distributed between MINUSTAH and MONUSCO (UN Organization Stabilization Mission in the DRC), suggesting that Uruguayan troops were heavily socialized by the experience in Haiti and the DRC.

Uruguay provides further insight into the process of socialization because, unlike the other contingents analyzed so far, the Uruguayan troops deployed across the country in different posts. Unlike the Argentine soldiers, who concentrated in specific areas outside the capital, the Uruguayan peacekeepers were placed in and often moved around different regions. Compared with the Brazilian soldiers, who were mostly in charge of policing functions in Port-au-Prince, blue helmets from Uruguay received multimission assignments, including border control, observing posts, maritime law enforcement, and policing. The Uruguayan case best reflects the multiple and diverse socializing effects that peacekeeping generates among its agents.

Did the peacekeeping experience in Haiti have an impact on military professionalism? The answer to this question varies from one unit, service, and post to another. As in the Argentine case, the pilots in UNFLIGHT appeared to have improved their flying skills as a result of accruing more flight hours on the UN mission than they would have at home. Uruguay had forty pilots in Port-au-Prince as part of UNFLIGHT; although this was a relatively small contribution, it was significant given the size of the country's air force officer corps. In 2010, Uruguay had only 433 air force officers, meaning that almost the entire fleet of pilots had been sent to MINUSTAH, MONUSCO, or both.[44] In fact, the air force found itself in a dilemma because most of its pilots either deployed on a UN mission or had left the force to join commercial airlines as soon as they returned from their peacekeeping assignment (Infodefensa 2010). The Uruguayan Air Force encountered multiple problems in Haiti. In 2009, one of its planes crashed near the border between Haiti and the Dominican Republic, killing eleven blue helmets—six from Uruguay and five from Jordan (*El País* 2009). The accident raised concerns about the conditions of the Uruguayan fleet, which some suspected to be outdated. A routine inspection in 2010 by a UN delegation in Haiti found that 70% of Uruguay's battalion equipment was not operational (Melgar 2010). Furthermore, a number of allegations made by retired military officers indicated that the air force had inflated the number of hours flown by its pilots so that they could comply with MINUSTAH's requirements. The Ministry of Defense contended that the discrepancy was merely a mathematical confusion, as pilots reported hours in terms of civilian standards and not in military flying hours (*El País* 2009b).

A large number of noncommissioned officers were needed to ensure that the Uruguayan battalions in Haiti were also organized, but they offered few professional enticements, a limitation common among the other cases analyzed in this chapter. But the two battalions deployed in Haiti conducted different types of functions and faced different operational environments, leading to various types of socialization. One of the battalions, commonly referred to as Batallón Uruguay V, was sent to Fort Liberté in the northeast of the country, on the border between Haiti and the Dominican Republic. Uruguay's blue helmets replaced Spanish soldiers who had withdrawn from the mission in 2006, leading to the surge of Uruguayan troops in Haiti. Given its location on the border, this unit predominantly performed observation functions including border observance, control, and checkpoints. A UN force also deployed in this sector in response to a request from the Dominican government, which was concerned about the potential implications of a massive wave of immigrants from Haiti. Diplomatic relations between the two Caribbean and neighboring nations had been historically tense. Dominican soldiers had deployed to the border, and the risk of military escalation was relatively high. UN peacekeepers were sent to appease the Dominicans and to prevent an international refugee crisis from occurring in the common frontier.

Peacekeepers from Batallón Uruguay V assisted with a variety of border projects. A European Union–funded project helped build a cross-border trade bridge between the two countries. Peacekeepers then established new border posts and oversaw border security on the Haitian side; they also controlled traffic in the border bridge. Some of these tasks included elements of law enforcement, including the prevention of the illegal movement of people, drugs, and contraband. Emilio Castañeda, the UN official in charge of the northeast region of Haiti, remarked, "the country simply lacks the resources to control the more remote stretches of the frontier which remained highly permeable despite recent steps taken by the Dominican military to prevent illegal immigration" (qtd. in Trenchard 2009). So the main task assigned to the blue helmets in Fort Liberté remained securing the border, as opposed to appeasing gangs and drug traffickers in Haitian slums.

To some extent, this mission resembled a traditional peace observation, in which peacekeepers served as a neutral body, demarcating border zones and separating two parties by creating buffer zones through checkpoints. It is worth noting that not one single human rights violation or incident of sexual abuse was reported in the Fort Liberté area (as was the case in Gonaïves).

By contrast, members of Uruguay's second battalion, Batallón Conjunto Uruguay I, experienced a different form of socialization. The battalion included members of the three forces, most of which had previously served in MONUC. They were put in charge of Les Cayes and Port Salut in the southern part of the country. But this unit was often rotated and asked to support other contingents. In September 2004, Hurricane Jane swept Gonaïves, and the Argentine battalion stationed there was soon under water. Uruguay offered its help to distribute food and aid to the region (Novarese 2005). The unit then shifted from humanitarian aid to policing roles in 2006. In order to control Cité Soleil, Brazil requested reinforcements, and Uruguay quickly responded to the call for help. A group of five hundred additional Uruguayan troops participated in the siege of Cité Soleil. Uruguayan peacekeepers were also involved in the rescue operation of Jordanian blue helmets, which came under heavy fire from drug lords and pro-Aristide forces in Port-au-Prince. Following the orders of the Brazilian UN force commander, Uruguay's peacekeepers counterattacked, managing to successfully rescue the Jordanians, but not without collateral damage. Like the Brazilians, Uruguayan troops conducted a number of raids in the capital city (*El País* 2006).

Members of Batallón Conjunto Uruguay I learned some hard lessons in slum and gang control. But this experience ultimately provoked unintended consequences. MINUSTAH reintroduced policing tactics to the armed forces. According to the Uruguayan political framework, operations conducted jointly with Brazilian blue helmets had not been not legally permitted. Unlike the Brazilian military, the Uruguayan armed forces were banned from undertaking public security functions at home after the democratization process.[45] MINUSTAH was an external mission, however, justified and legalized by an international body. The UN context provided an environment that tolerated public security functions, even as such operations remained controversial in Uruguay.

The experience in Haiti had a direct impact on Uruguayan politics. In 2011, the Uruguayan government allowed one thousand soldiers to be recruited by the national police as a means of improving public safety in Montevideo. This policy stirred controversy and prompted a public debate in Congress. According to Senator Jorge Saravia of the Frente Amplio party, which controlled Congress, "I was of the view that the armed forces could perform internal peace missions, as they do in the DRC or Haiti. There, Uruguayan soldiers are complimented for providing security. They have had to disband guerrilla groups in violent contexts, without firing a shot" (qtd. in Urgente 24 2011).[46] By contrast, the opposition denounced such measures as regressive and dangerous for democratic stability. Tabaré Viera, a member of the opposing party Partido Colorado argued "while the soldiers that will join these tasks will be trained in the Police Academy, they are not prepared to do police work because that is not their role" (qtd. in Urgente 24 2011).[47] Ironically, the UN mission in Haiti provided politicians with a framework to use armed forces for public security, ultimately re-exposing some military agents to old tactics that blurred military and public security functions.

How did MINUSTAH affect navy officers? URUMAR, the naval force chosen by the UN to safeguard Haiti's coasts, acquired a different set of skills. For the Uruguayan Navy, the mission provided an opportunity to put its naval and coastal guard capabilities in practice and to project force into an area beyond Uruguay's shores, all while collaborating with the Haitian police and customs service. On its official website, the navy emphasizes that its fleet sailed more than 100,000 nautical miles, navigated more than 6,800 hours, patrolled over 5,200 times, and conducted about six hundred interdictions (Armada Nacional de la República de Uruguay 2011a, 2011b). The area of responsibility covered by URUMAR included Fort Liberté, Gonaïves, Killick in Port-au-Prince, and Port Salut and Jacmel in the south. In normal conditions, URUMAR would have been classified as a traditional maritime peacekeeping mission, in which navies engage in such activities as naval diplomacy, port management, medical evacuation, enforcement of sanctions, escort and protection of civilian vessels, and environmental programs on public beaches.[48] Naval forces in Haiti were required for other purposes, however, namely to combat drug trafficking.

The island's strategic location in the Caribbean, with more than twelve hundred miles of unprotected coastline, converted Haiti into a major transit country for cocaine and marijuana. "Haiti's under-strength and dysfunctional police force is unable to respond to the challenge . . . Haiti's tiny coast guard has only two patrol boats, 95 personnel, and no air assets" (Perito and Maly 2007). For this reason, URUMUAR was to mainly assist Haitian authorities in deterring drug trafficking, which is why it was based in the south near Jacmel and Port Salut, where drug shipments usually entered the country to be later distributed into the Dominican Republic, Puerto Rico, and Miami.

MINUSTAH never made public its official figures on drug seizures, so interdiction estimates vary from source to source. Some military experts believe that URUMAR managed to capture over 1,540 pounds of marijuana from Jamaican ships between 2004 and 2010, but estimates for cocaine seizures (the most profitable drug in the Caribbean) were difficult to find in Haiti, New York, or Uruguay (Carneiro Alvárez 2011).

While MINUSTAH enabled the navy to acquire and develop law enforcement and drug interdiction skills, it also exposed its members to some of the negative dynamics of drug trafficking. Perito and Maly (2007) remind us that drug trafficking in Haiti fostered corruption in the police, courts, and at customs. It fueled weapons trafficking and financed armed gangs. In fact, UN naval forces conducted interdiction operations in the company of the very same Haitian law enforcement agencies known for colluding with drug traffickers. Even so, the U.S. State Department indicated that the Haitian government made only modest advances in the fight against drug trafficking, as seizures remained limited and institutional corruption prevailed (U.S. State Department 2009). In this environment, it is unclear how the UN and its peacekeepers might have evaded the perverse consequences of drug-related corruption, especially since MINUSTAH had no way of enforcing or ensuring the accountability of its own troops. The UN mission in Haiti could hardly be considered an appropriate mission to reform and clean up the armed forces. Instead of shifting the military away from the traditional antidrug campaigns and internal roles, MINUSTAH squarely directed the armed forces into law enforcement and drug interdiction.

Did MINUSTAH civilianize the Uruguayan blue helmets? Once again, civilian integration with troops varied from one service and post to another. Pilots and naval officers conducted their peacekeeping missions independently of most civilian actors on the ground. UNFLIGHT and URUMAR moved medicines and food to help victims after the January earthquake, but it was an essentially logistical operation that did not entail constant interactions with NGOs or local residents. That said, ground troops in Fort Liberté were highly exposed to civilian components, especially after the 2010 earthquake. Large shipments of humanitarian aid from the Dominican Republic had to cross the northern border because the southern border was blocked for ten days due to debris on the roads. Many NGOs had to temporarily operate from the Dominican Republic because their facilities in Port-au-Prince were damaged. UN troops stationed in Fort Liberté were probably the most in demand in the north during the earthquake crisis. They were the most exposed to humanitarian activities, just by virtue of the fact that they were in charge of border traffic and immigration control. Hence civilian penetration of military structures was perhaps most visible during Haiti's natural disaster crises.

Despite being in contact with multiple humanitarian organizations, Uruguayan blue helmets became increasingly segregated from the civilian and NGO communities after abuse complaints emerged from their own military sector. Unconfirmed reports of sexual misconduct by peacekeepers first surfaced in the summer of 2011 in the south, where Uruguayan peacekeepers were based. UN and Uruguayan authorities denied any wrongdoing, but in September 2011, a one-minute mobile phone video—filmed at the UN naval base in Port Salut, where URUMAR was stationed, and then posted on the Internet— circulated that showed "several men in camouflage uniforms laughing and saying 'no problem' in Spanish as they pinned a young man down on a mattress with his hands behind his back" (Yapp 2011). The mother of the alleged victim, an eighteen-year-old resident of Port Salut, then told Haitian radio stations that Uruguayan marines had raped her son inside the UN base. The case prompted a crisis in Uruguay and Haiti, forcing President José Mujica, himself a victim of torture during the Uruguayan dictatorship, to publically apologize to the Haitian people (BBC News 2011b).

Soon after, Uruguayan authorities dismissed URUMAR's commander, and five sailors accused of the assault were withdrawn from the mission, decommissioned, and then put under military justice. An initial investigation by the UN, the Uruguayan Navy, and the Ministry of Defense determined that the complaints of alleged sexual abuse were only acts of "misconduct" (qtd. in *El Observador* 2011). The measures taken by both the UN and Uruguay's government, however, proved to be insufficient. The reports were not welcomed in Haiti, where outraged public demonstrations broke out in the streets. The angriest protests were reported in Port Salut, where residents demanded the complete withdrawal of Uruguayan blue helmets. Locals complained about the filthy conditions of the naval base. Also, women who had apparently traded sex for food with peacekeepers raised new, unconfirmed sexual abuse allegations (BBC News 2010).[49]

Mariano Fernández, the special representative of the secretary-general and head of MINUSTAH, minimized the incident and argued that the "acts of a few should not also tarnish [the image] of thousands of military, police, and civilian personnel" (qtd. in Bhatt and Grandin 2001). The problem, however, was that this incident took place in a context in which UN peacekeepers in Haiti had been consistently accused of sexual abuse. In 2007, some one hundred Sri Lankan blue helmets, about 10% of an entire brigade, were repatriated because they were exchanging small amounts of cash, food, and sometimes mobile phones for sex with underage girls (BBC News 2007b). The Uruguayan incident confirmed the belief that a culture of institutional impunity, which tolerated sexual abuse, had developed within the UN mission. The UN had been haunted by similar incidents in other missions, including MONUC, but it was incapable of punishing such behavior. Prosecution is the responsibility of the troop-lending state.[50]

In this context of institutional impunity, residents in Haiti reacted angrily to the Uruguayan contingent. The unintended consequence of this scandal was that blue helmets from Uruguay became a toxic liability for MINUSTAH. They had to be either quartered or put under strict curfews, severely restricting their interactions with locals and eventually segregating Uruguay from the overall mission, as NGOs and civilian staff also distanced themselves from the peacekeepers that once protected them (Boutellis 2011). Unfortunately, the scandal also affected the troops in Fort Liberté, as they, too, became the target of anti-MINUSTAH demonstrations. In the end, blue helmets became less intimately involved with civilians, while military practices and norms of conduct remained intact.

## Conclusion

One of the main puzzles of this book is how peacekeeping socializes blue helmets. Evidence gathered from MINUSTAH suggests that peacekeeping socializes troops in different and divergent ways. This complex mission had many components, including observation, security, and peacebuilding. Interestingly enough, blue helmets involved in observing functions experienced different professional and civilianization effects than those who performed heavy policing and public security functions. Professional and civilian integration effects varied substantially according to the type of function performed and the post conducted in the mission. My findings also indicate large variations between and within national contingents (especially among Uruguayan contingents). Ironically, the three South American states that were the most likely to converge because of their regional proximity and common foreign policy in Haiti actually diverged in their socializing experiences in MINUSTAH.

The UN mission in Haiti had vast peacebuilding mandates that included elections, law enforcement, and refugee assistance, meaning that some UN troops were delegated with heavy policing, drug interdiction, and public security responsibilities as part of their peacebuilding mandate. For troops involved in policing functions, peacekeeping did little to improve military professionalism or civilian integration. Instead, peacebuilding tasks contributed to stimulating what Stepan (1973, 50) once termed the professionalism of internal warfare: the development of "doctrines and training techniques to prevent or crush insurgent movements." As a result, these recently democratized armies became more concerned with military-political management, internal security, and political problems. Political order, law enforcement, organized crime, gang control, drug interdiction, and crowd management, to name a few, eventually became "the mission."

The troops most likely to be penetrated by civilian spheres paradoxically became segregated from the mission and less civilianized, confirming what a huge body of literature in civil-military relations has argued persuasively for decades. Overmilitarization of the civil polity can take place when military agents serve broad police roles, and civil society and police reform can be undermined when states dend regimes rely too heavily on the armed forces for security. Force and violence are more likely to occur when military agents are used to placate internal conflicts. In the final analysis, overmilitarization tends to undermine democratic consolidation and civilian control. MINUSTAH did the opposite; it overmilitarized the mission by delegating police functions to the armed forces of recently democratizing states with poor human rights records.

The multilateral framework of the UN was insufficient to guarantee accountability and ensure civilian control. Few peacekeepers were socialized to ensure that their behavior corresponded to acceptable norms. The large number of abuse cases in Haiti seems to suggest that impunity was institutionalized, as peacekeepers learned and were socialized to practices that were not always consistent with appropriate norms and standards.

Social interaction between contingents did little to enhance positive socialization processes. Troops from democratizing states involved in MINUSTAH did not interact with blue helmets from other consolidated democracies because there was no higher density of professional soldiers in Haiti. True role models were absent in the mission. Brazil's commanding position in Haiti influenced the other national troop contingents, but not in a way that was conducive to re-educating military officers. The Brazilian peacekeeping model was everything but appropriate, far from the diplomat-soldier model envisioned by the conventional wisdom. As a result, socialization did take place, but it was not always professional, progressive, civilianized, liberal, or conducive to reforming the military.

# 6

## Does Peacekeeping Help Integrate Defense and Foreign Policy?

Does peacekeeping influence foreign policy? If, as argued in chapter 1, peacekeeping can serve as a foreign policy tool by signaling international commitment, it would also appear that it can influence those who shape and formulate foreign policy. Peacekeeping participation can be consequential for military reform if it can help bring members of the foreign service into doctrinal and national defense policy debates. A qualitative expansion of the defense policy community can take place when foreign policy experts supply ideas and integrate themselves into military affairs. Here I try to answer the following questions: Does peacekeeping allow diplomats to play a larger role in national defense policies? Do foreign and defense ministries increase their interactions when soldiers deploy to UN peace missions? Is there an increased interest in defense and foreign policy matters when peacekeeping operations are authorized?

I rely on three sources of evidence to answer these questions. First, I conducted interviews with diplomats and foreign policy experts to assess the extent to which the foreign policy community inserted itself into doctrinal and defense matters. Second, I looked for indicators of defense and foreign policy integration such as the establishment of interministerial meetings, dual committees, and the appointment of attachés to military and diplomatic posts. Finally, I searched for academic and commercial publications (including books and journals) on peacekeeping published by experts on foreign policy as an indicator of how civilian ideas might have affected national doctrinal debates. If the conventional wisdom on foreign policy integration holds, we should be able to witness a broadening of the defense policy community as foreign policy experts become increasingly engaged in the decision-making process, whether by providing advice and opinions directly or by contributing to the debate through publications.

The first part of this chapter summarizes theoretical arguments about defense and foreign policy integration, especially as it applies to peacekeeping policies. The second part examines the empirical evidence from the three selected case studies.

## Arguments about Foreign and Defense Policy Integration

As noted in chapters 1 and 2, several democratizing states have deployed their soldiers to peacekeeping missions to send a signal that a seismic shift has taken place within their own political culture. Civilian leaders in transitional societies may commit themselves to UN peacekeeping not only to direct their military away from undesired roles and missions or to change their soldiers' professional self-image, but also to reduce the policy influence of military commanders by increasingly interjecting themselves into doctrinal debates. The conventional wisdom is that participation in UN peace operations can strengthen civilian control when diplomats become involved in the decision-making process. Civilian intervention by foreign policy bureaucrats can help reduce the exclusive prerogatives and reserve domains enjoyed by military establishments in democratizing states. If the military focuses on external challenges—whether of their own accord or as a result of civilian prodding— the coordination and cooperation inevitably required of politicians and generals will lead to greater integration of defense and foreign policies. Such integration in turn nudges military and diplomatic agents to work together to identify common national goals and to open up military doctrine development to civilian influence.[1]

Scholars of Latin American politics have sometimes treated peacekeeping as a confidence-building measure that enables civilian intervention and allows for transparency in decision-making procedures within military institutions (Child 1995). In this view, peace missions compel countries to reveal doctrinal preferences and defense policies, making military perspectives known to the domestic and international arena (Diamint 2001, 100). Furthermore, diplomatic engagement in peacekeeping facilitates interstate cooperation, ultimately leading to foreign policy convergence among those involved in similar UN operations (Hirst 2009, 329–57).

Conventional wisdom states that foreign policy decisions can affect doctrinal debates and facilitate civilian intervention without resulting in conflictive civil-military relations. But when can diplomats insert themselves into doctrinal and defense debates? The available literature on doctrinal change and foreign policy suggests that this can take place at various stages. The first step begins at the UN itself, where permanent representatives and diplomats participate in peacekeeping debates. Resolutions, mandates, troop requests, threat level assessments, as well as the political implications of each operation are all assessed and first negotiated in New York, providing an educational, socialized experience for diplomats interested in defense affairs.

Second, a window of opportunity emerges when domestic political leadership ponders the advantages and benefits of contributing to a peacekeeping deployment. Such consideration offers diplomats an occasion to intervene in doctrinal issues by contributing to the debate. Participation in UN missions can suddenly become an issue of public debate, linked to foreign policy aspirations. A qualitative expansion of the defense policy community can then take place; that is, a network of elite defense policy experts who are passionate about policy outcomes in that area interact regularly and attain a certain degree of access to key politicians.[2] The eventuality of a peacekeeping mission allegedly allows foreign policy experts, perhaps with limited knowledge of defense matters, to participate in a broad discussion on UN and foreign affairs. This interaction in turn permits the gradual entrance of civilian experts into defense debates.

The regularity with which civilian experts debate peacekeeping issues is key to determining their position in policy communities and even to reinforcing policy networks and coalitions. As Solingen (1998, 10) argues, once certain groups routinize debates and voice their ideas through formal and informal networks, they generate political coalitions spanning state and private political actors. In so doing, some of these networks will advocate for change and reform, questioning and challenging the traditional monopoly often exercised by active officers in the defense sector. Once diplomacy prevails politically, as a function of its size, cohesiveness, and effectiveness, its preferred strategies can become the raison d'état.

As international security debates become routine practice among diplomats and security experts, democratically elected civilians can gradually transfer some policy decisions from military organizations to diplomatic bureaucracies, where ambassadors institutionally supervise, monitor, and implement the policy in question. Commonly known as a "policy handle," it is "a way to redefine the nature of a policy decision and force change on a subordinate organization by removing the policy decision from the organization's exclusive area of expertise . . . it allows leaders to institutionalize supervision of the policy by another organization, which enables them to monitor implementation and ensure that the change takes place" (Kaufman 1994, 362). By giving precedence to geopolitical and diplomatic considerations, over and above those that are strictly military, politicians and diplomats can determine who the peacekeepers will be and when and where they will be sent abroad. In due course, this process increases the role of diplomats and civil servants in the defense sector, generating increased accountability and transparency as diplomats impose additional screening mechanisms to more closely monitor the military when they are sent abroad.[3]

How well do these arguments stand up? Did peacekeeping promote foreign and defense policy integration? Were diplomats more actively engaged in defense matters? Was policy handling the preferred strategy? Below are some answers to these questions.

## Defense and Foreign Policy Integration and Segregation: Evidence from Case Studies

### Argentina

Efforts to integrate defense and foreign policy in Argentina were only notable during the early 1990s. Subsequently, foreign and defense policies would appear to have become more segregated, especially since the deployment to MINUSTAH. Here I present evidence of how this state of affairs may have developed.

### Phase I: From Segregation to Integration, 1990–96

Between 1990 and 1996, Argentina obtained some tangible diplomatic benefits as a result of its active peacekeeping policy. It joined the Brady Plan for foreign debt relief in 1992, which provided new International Monetary Fund loans. Likewise, the Clinton administration granted Argentina the status of major non-NATO ally in recognition of its peacekeeping contribution, which made it possible to buy outmoded equipment from NATO states, to participate in interoperability exercises, and to obtain credit to buy military gear for UN peace operations (*International Herald Tribune* 1994).[4] Peacekeeping effectively enabled the Menem administration to realign the country's foreign policy with that of the United States (Gerschenson 2001, 16).

The most interesting diplomatic development occurred within Argentina's own borders, however, as the foreign policy establishment became increasingly relevant in peacekeeping affairs. The country had historically always been involved in UN security debates, occupying a nonpermanent member position on six occasions, a record exceeded in Latin America by Brazil alone. But such engagement was interrupted during the dictatorship when the junta, fearing human rights accusations, abstained from participating in UN Security Council meetings (Zawels 2000). When democratic rule returned to Argentina, diplomats were eager to put a new foreign policy in practice.[5] Argentina actively sought a seat in the fifteen-nation UN Security Council. Over a thirteen-year period from 1987 to 2000, Argentina served as a nonpermanent member of the council on three occasions (1987–88, 1994–95, and 1999–2000). On average, Argentine diplomats were reappointed to the council every three years.

The country's engagement in UN affairs offered the Cancillería (Ministry of Foreign Affairs) an invaluable opportunity to involve diplomats in high-level international talks. They negotiated key UN resolutions and mandates at a time when demands for peacekeeping were increasing. Argentine diplomats were thus exposed to international security debates at the same time as they discussed troop requests, analyzed military conditions for deployment, and served in various peacekeeping committees. This unusual attention to UN affairs also thrust the Ministry of Foreign Affairs into the national spotlight. Ambassador Fernando Enrique Petrella, former secretary of state for foreign affairs and former head of the Argentine permanent mission in the UN, said: "Peacekeeping had a beneficial side-effect on our foreign policy. We wanted to be a leading country; that was our goal and it was successful."[6]

Under the leadership of Minister Guido di Tella, diplomats in the Cancillería were more absorbed by UN politics and peacekeeping than any other foreign policy area except the North American bureau. At the peak of Argentina's peacekeeping participation, between 1994 and 1996, the Argentine mission to the UN had a staff of almost twenty members of the foreign service, including three ambassadors, three ministers, and a plethora of counselors and secretaries.[7] It was one of the largest UN missions among developing states. Slowly but surely, diplomats developed professional expertise in international security and peacekeeping issues as they became socialized by and exposed to UN dynamics. Gradually, the Ministry of Foreign Affairs began to win unprecedented influence in the realm of security because it was "staffed by a highly trained, politically savvy team of specialists" (Pion-Berlin 1998, 86).

The Argentine political leadership eventually removed some policy decisions from the exclusive area of military organizations and transferred powers to diplomatic bureaucracies. Policy-handling strategies were implemented when a group of influential Foreign Service members occupied key positions in the defense ministry. During the Menem administration, the defense establishment had an unusually strong presence of diplomatic officials within its ranks (Diamint 1997, 38). Ambassador Oscar Camilión, a diplomat and former foreign affairs minister during the dictatorship, became Menem's second minister of defense in 1993. Norden (1995, 333) explains that "immediately prior to taking over as Minister of Defense, Camilión had worked as the UN envoy to Cyprus. Camilión's trajectory thus coincided perfectly with the government's new internationalism."

Civilian monitoring mechanisms improved when the foreign ministry used its network of embassies to gather information about the field and to supervise peacekeepers in the mission. Soldiers deployed to places where Argentina had diplomatic missions, which in turn facilitated cooperation between the defense and foreign policy establishment in the field. Ambassadors had clear instructions to pay constant visits to Argentine troops in peace missions.[8] There was a symbolic component in this policy, as diplomats showed respect, political support, and encouragement to soldiers to enhance their morale. But ambassadors also supervised deployments and made sure that the mission was taking place as diplomats in New York and Buenos Aries intended.

Diplomats in the defense ministry introduced working procedures similar to those practiced in the foreign ministry. Interministerial working groups between defense and foreign affairs ministries coordinated the use of military power abroad. Through these regular meetings, a certain degree of cooperation and tolerance developed between some military officers and diplomats. To ensure that defense and foreign policies were in tune and synchronized, the Ministry of Defense appointed liaison officers and military attachés in the UN mission in New York. These officers provided diplomats with a direct link to military organizations and an additional source of information to make sure that the decisions were being implemented as stipulated. A deputy military advisor to the Argentine UN mission described, "our mission is to coordinate and provide logistics to the decisions made by our leaders with regards to foreign policy."[9]

In due course, participation in UN peacekeeping gave diplomats the capacity to decide when the country would contribute to a UN peace operation and how many peacekeepers it would send abroad. The foreign ministry thus won an uncontested position in which no other ministry could compete for influence over external affairs. Minister Guillermo Lucotti, head of the UN peacekeeping department in the Cancillería, explained that "peacekeeping may have important military components, but in Argentina, the Ministry of Foreign Affairs is in charge of the political and technical dimensions of all peace missions. We set up the criteria for participation and the chain of command originates from this office."[10]

The military did not resist or reject the role of diplomats in the defense sector, which is somewhat puzzling for an institution that contested most civilian policies. For the most part, the military tolerated civilian intervention and cooperated with diplomats. One navy captain explained it this way: "Dialoguing with the foreign ministry was easy. Analogous to the military profession, diplomats have training, degree, hierarchy and international exposure."[11]

Bureaucratic relations were cordial in part because diplomats became the military's best political allies. One of the foreign ministry's main responsibilities included lobbying and pressuring the Ministry of Economics to release funds for peace operations. Hence the armed forces were more than happy to have a political organization fighting for their cause. For years, the military had been isolated from the political process and incapable of preventing budget cuts because it lacked political support. In peacekeeping matters, however, the Ministry of Foreign Affairs was the military's best political ally.

Pion-Berlin (1997, 152) argues that the Ministry of Foreign Affairs went "beyond its legal mandate, trespassing on ground that should normally have been reserved for the Ministry of Defense. Nothing in the Constitution or Law of Ministries specifically allows it to represent the nation's interests in security or defense affairs, although it may do so in a host of other areas." This process eventually shifted power and resources from military to diplomatic organizations. By relying on policy-handling strategies, the Menem administration almost gave the foreign ministry a monopoly on international security issues, which in turn enabled civilians to supervise decisions regarding troop deployments abroad (Fraga 2000, 1–4). Policy-handling strategies strengthened civilian control by introducing some degree of diplomatic monitoring and an additional layer of bureaucratic checks and balances. Interministerial working groups, liaison officers, and ambassadorial visits to the mission required military personnel to inform and report to civilian authorities about peacekeeping and logistics.

Nevertheless, diplomatic intervention into defense policies also had some negative effects. In 2001, Carlos Menem; Domingo Cavallo, a former minister of economics; Oscar Camilión; General Martin Balza, the army's joint chief of staff; and Emilio Cárdenas, a former ambassador to the UN, all faced accusations of illegally shipping and selling Argentine weapons in defiance of UN weapons embargoes to Croatia and Ecuador at a time when Argentina was participating in peace missions. A house arrest order was placed, and all politicians involved were put under investigation. But a federal Argentine court dropped all charges in 2003, allowing Menem to run for a third presidential term (Krauss 2001a, 2001b; Mirodan 2003; *La Nación* 2003; *Washington Post* 2003). Menem bypassed the congressional committees that were supposed to authorize and supervise the deployment of forces abroad. Political bribery was rife in Argentina; Congress rarely properly checked the act of delegating policy implementation and policymaking power to bureaus. According to Linz and Stepan (1996, 210), "the fear of a coup or a breakdown of democracy is increasingly receding but those have been replaced by fears about the degradation and emptying of democracy." Not surprisingly, most Argentines believe that Menem's administration abdicated political responsibility and control.

Notwithstanding the limitations of diplomatic intervention in defense matters, a debate regarding the role of the armed forces in peacekeeping operations contributed positively to increasing civilian expertise in military affairs. Scholars, diplomats, journalists, and politicians began to discuss troop deployments as part of the country's foreign policy. This dialogue facilitated the establishment of policy networks and the expansion of defense policy communities that challenged doctrinal thinking and favored cooperative policies with the UN and the United States. Experts and scholars who were not originally knowledgeable in defense matters but who had a level of expertise in diplomacy publicly debated important military issues as a consequence.

Particularly important was the role played by CARI, an institute analogous to the U.S. Council on Foreign Relations. An independent, national, and nonpartisan center for scholars dedicated to producing information to better understand Argentina's foreign policy choices, CARI's members include diplomats, journalists, retired and active military officers, and scholars.[12] Many civilians, including elite experts and scholars in foreign policy, debated and analyzed Argentina's peacekeeping policies in several conferences and seminars organized by CARI. Between 1993 and 1999, CARI conducted a wide range of studies and conferences on Argentina and the UN. It produced articles and books on peacekeeping issues and made concrete policy recommendations for the government (CARI 1997, 1999). CARI's policy recommendations had a direct influence on national policy, and some of CARI's members eventually attained a certain degree of access to key politicians, in the process influencing the decision-making process of Argentine military affairs. Scholars and fellows at CARI such as Carlos Escudé and Andrés Fontana served as foreign policy and security advisors for Minister di Tella in the Ministry of Foreign Affairs.[13]

Menem certainly did not independently determine that Argentina's defense policy had to be restructured toward a nonconfrontational internationalism. His knowledge of international security issues was limited when he first took office, so his reliance on his policy advisors was no doubt considerable. It appears that, for the first time, the inclusion of outside policy expertise resulted in civilian scholars participating in defense and security policy debates. To a certain extent, peacekeeping policies served as a conduit between scholars and practitioners, establishing policy networks and enabling civilians to enter defense and doctrinal debates. As a consequence, peacekeeping forced a qualitative expansion of the defense policy community.

A considerable amount of academic literature on peace missions appeared during this period, reflecting the extent to which peacekeeping shaped security policy debates beyond the confines of the military establishment. I identified over thirty publications on Argentina's peacekeeping contributions by civilians, including books, articles, and working papers published between 1993 and 2001.[14] On the surface, this volume of publications may seem limited compared with the large number of articles available in military journals like *Revista Militar*. There are no more than fifteen civilian authors, mostly diplomats, scholars of international relations, and military experts. Some of their writings are heavily descriptive, but others (particularly those cited in this work) make interesting analytical contributions. Because military authors once exclusively dominated Argentine security studies, however, the mere surfacing of civilian-led publications on military affairs would appear to represent a radical and welcome change. More academic publications on peacekeeping in the Southern Cone of South America have emerged from Argentina than any other country. Some Argentine civilian experts even authored articles in military journals, suggesting that there was a minimum degree of acceptance of civilian defense views within the military establishment.[15] The extent to which these publications were actively read—and by whom—remains a matter of debate.

### Phase II: From Integration to Segregation, 2004–11

In chapter 2, I described how Argentina gradually withdrew from the peacekeeping circuit as a result of a severe financial crisis. In 2004, when the country contributed troops to UN peacekeeping operations again, the process of foreign and defense policy integration witnessed in the first phase was almost completely reversed, as the Ministry of Defense regained full control of all peacekeeping policies.

How and why did the Ministry of Defense regain influence, and why did the diplomatic establishment lose relative control of defense policy? Four factors explain this outcome. First, peacekeeping issues reflected Menem's personal views and were thus limited to his administration. As one policy analyst described it, "peacekeeping was part of a government's policy, but not a state policy."[16] Few of the measures described in the previous section, such as the interministerial meetings and working groups, were properly institutionalized or formalized in the Argentine decision-making process. Therefore efforts to integrate foreign and defense policy ceased when Menem left power.

Second, MINUSTAH created serious rifts within the foreign policy establishment. Scholars and foreign policy analysts who once recognized peacekeeping as a means of asserting foreign policy aspirations diverged in both academic and public policy discussions, notably on how to proceed in Haiti.[17] These divisions were particularly evident during congressional debates over whether to authorize the deployment of troops. President Néstor Kirchner's government did not simply receive *carte blanche* approval from Congress. A group of left-leaning political coalitions within the House of Representatives perceived the UN mission in Haiti as a foreign intervention subsidized by U.S. interests and opposed peacekeeping initiatives there (Follietti 2005). In the end, there was strong dissent and fragmentation among civilians.

Third, whereas peacekeeping during the first phase generated academic interest from a wide range of foreign policy experts, in the latter phase, interest waned. After the onset of the 2001 crisis, only a handful of books on peacekeeping were published in Argentina, and fora such as CARI lost their prominence as a center of innovating thinking on civil-military relations.[18] Resdal, or the Security and Defense Network of Latin America, was the lone exception. This

Buenos Aires–based think tank on defense policy and military affairs closely followed the events in MINUSTAH. It even commissioned a report on gender issues in Latin American peacekeeping troops (Avelar Giannini 2011). But academic interest in peacekeeping remained relatively limited, and the defense policy community ceased to expand.

Fourth, the defense ministry became more organized, bureaucratized, and self-contained, relying less on diplomats and recruiting its own cadres of officials. MINUSTAH provided an opportunity for the defense establishment to practice its own foreign policy independent from the foreign service. In 2007, Nilda Garré, President Nestor Kirchner's defense minister, created the position of deputy secretary for external relations within her own ministry, permitting the defense ministry to slowly re-establish its relevance in foreign affairs by reassuming control of all external military missions, including peacekeeping operations, the appointment of military attachés in embassies, and other regional and bilateral military-to-military initiatives. Garré then established and formalized the Department for Peacekeeping Operations, a unit supervised by the deputy secretary for external relations, which implements peacekeeping policies in tandem with the joint chief of staff. Garré was then in a position to nominate a member of her own staff as Argentine ambassador to Haiti, first Ernesto López and then Vázquez Ocampo, both of whom had served as deputy secretaries for external relations in the defense ministry. Gradually, the Ministry of Defense increased its leverage in peacekeeping matters and its influence in foreign policy, especially in places where Argentina deployed troops for UN missions.

Many perceived the "comeback" of Argentina's defense and military establishment as an inevitable component of the democratization process. Several members of the foreign policy establishment believed that the Ministry of Foreign Affairs had accomplished its mission, leaving an important institutional legacy in Argentina's defense policy. According to one diplomat, "our role in the 1990s triggered a constructive dialogue and thinking about defense policy. To date, civilian control is an *acquis*; there are few remnants of the dictatorship."[19]

On the one hand, the bureaucratization of the defense ministry was necessary to effectively institutionalize civilian control. For years after the transition, the Ministry of Defense was considered to be merely a symbolic political institution; its reform in 2006–7 attempted to give teeth to its institutional apparatus.[20] On the other hand, military officials no longer dominated the country's defense establishment, since mostly civilians staffed the defense ministry. As Alfredo Forti, deputy secretary for external relations in 2009, described it, "the Ministry of Foreign Affairs has learned that the Ministry of Defense is not the same as the military; we are civilians too. This is the new context, in which we are just first among equals."[21]

While the foreign ministry was involved in the initial decision to deploy troops into Haiti, it eventually lost policy control over peacekeeping issues. In fact, a 2006 defense decree, which gave the joint chief of staff the power to purchase and reimburse, effectively released the foreign service from its lobbying responsibility to raise funds for peacekeeping. One diplomat conceded: "We finally got rid of that issue, it was hard enough to fund our embassies during the crisis, can you imagine how difficult it was to procure for peacekeeping while negotiating with the economists at the Ministry of Finances!"[22] Surely enough, the defense establishment gradually became more autonomous, relying less on diplomats for funding.

Gaps in terms of policy and practice inevitably arose between the defense establishment and the foreign service. For some diplomats, the government's position in MINUSTAH lacked a "grand strategic" dimension. During the Menem administration, peacekeeping helped realign and shift Argentina's self-image. By contrast, Kirchner sought to achieve more reserved and limited foreign policy goals through MINUSTAH to focus on enhancing Argentina's defense cooperation with its neighbors, especially influential Brazil and Chile. As a result, many diplomats believed that the government's peacekeeping strategy lacked diplomatic clout.[23]

### Brazil

The Brazilian case contrasts with that of Argentina. Foreign and defense policy integration has been both conditional and limited. Here I provide evidence of how peacekeeping first segregated foreign and defense policies in the early 1990s and then integrated them in the post-2004 phase. In this case, however, integration would appear to be the product of military activism in foreign policy debates.

*Phase I: Foreign and Defense Policy Segregation, 1986–2003*

Brazil is Latin America's most active player in the UN system. Since 1946, this South American country has been a UN Security Council member ten times (1946–47, 1951–52, 1954–55, 1963–64, 1967–68, 1988–89, 1993–94, 1998–99,

2004–5, and 2010–11), more than any other nonpermanent state member with the exception of Japan. But while Brazilian diplomats have enjoyed a privileged position in the foreign policy establishment, there is little evidence to suggest that they have been able to increase their overall influence and policy leverage in defense and military affairs. In fact, from 1988 to 2003 the peacekeeping decision-making process was shared but never fully controlled by foreign policy bureaucrats. Leading journalist at *Estado de São Paulo* Carlos Antonio Pereira explained, "the army does not have a voice or a vote in foreign policy issues, but they certainly have the last word if they do not want to commit troops . . . Sure, they will never openly express their rejection, but they will elaborate other arguments in order not to go."[24] When the UN requested Brazilian troops for a peacekeeping force in Namibia in 1991, Brazil refused, saying that the army was unprepared and that the government lacked the necessary resources for such venture. Itamaraty was favorable to such engagement, but the army opposed it (Hudson 1997).

Peacekeeping required intensive domestic and intragovernment negotiations. One diplomat explained in an interview that troop deployments overseas required congressional authority, executive initiative, military consent, and economic approval from the Ministry of Economics.[25] Itamaraty hence did not originally perceive large UN deployments as an opportunity to insert itself into broader defense debates; in fact, it avoided them, instead preferring to maintain low levels of peacekeeping engagement—mostly observers—which did not require congressional authorization or intense negotiations with the military.

In this phase, there was a tacitly agreed-to division of labor between soldiers and diplomats. Itamaraty abstained from interfering in national security debates so long as the military refrained from meddling in Brazil's foreign policy. Once a peacekeeping deployment was authorized, Itamaraty assumed a hands-off position and allowed the army to implement policies. From a national perspective, peacekeeping was a matter of concern for the president and the armed forces themselves.

Shiguenoli Miyamoto, a security policy expert, considered that relations between soldiers and diplomats were path dependent and influenced by historical legacies. As he argued during the dictatorship, the armed forces delegated international trade issues to Itamaraty, while security policies continued to be managed by the military. "This had an impact in post-dictatorial Brazil, because Itamaraty did not have security experts within its ranks, although there were important exceptions."[26] Journalists like Carlos Antonio Pereira agreed that Itamaraty's strength lay in economic and trade policies, while international security was secondary for its organizational purposes.[27]

Nowhere was this division of labor more explicit than in Brazil's peacekeeping policy from 1988 to 2003. Itamaraty had a rather conservative and principled approach toward UN peace missions (often referred to as the "old school" or orthodox school of diplomacy). Brazil did not support resolutions involving UN coercive interventions and opposed the arms embargo in the former Yugoslavia, the UN intervention in Rwanda, and the intervention in Haiti in 1994. In all three instances, Brazil followed a principled and legalistic approach based on international public law and peaceful resolution (Herz and Wrobel 2002). In maintaining its reluctance to endorse military intervention, however, the foreign ministry failed to broaden the scope and domain of Brazil's international security policies by including military issues as part of its agenda. Therefore peacekeeping did not trigger a comprehensive national debate about the country's international security policies. In contrast to the Argentine case in the same historical phase, diplomats never challenged the nature of Brazil's defense policies.

Despite the deployment of a relatively large number of Brazilian soldiers to UN missions in Africa and Asia—Angola, Mozambique, and East Timor— there was scarce civilian literature published in Brazil on peacekeeping issues.[28] From a scholarly perspective, few Brazilian institutions showed any interest in peacekeeping affairs. The Núcleo de Estudos Estratégicos, or Strategic Studies Center, at the State University of Campinas and the Group of Strategic Studies at the Federal University of Rio de Janeiro—all leading research centers on strategic affairs—did not offer courses, lectures, or seminars on peacekeeping. A few individual scholars expressed an interest in military topics and conducted personal research on security studies. In twelve personal interviews conducted in Brazil, foreign policy experts recognized that the scope and domain of the defense policy community was limited. Professor Eliézer Rizzo de Oliviera explained that "public opinion is not mobilized and politicians, including Congressmen, are not interested because there are other national priorities."[29] Professor Leticia Pinhero, a Brazilian foreign policy expert, considered that Brazil had "an impressive combative foreign policy discourse, but [that] its actions do not always follow the rhetoric."[30] In her view,

Itamaraty was receptive to ideas generated by academics, but rarely put into practice policies that limited its flexibility and liberty or were perceived as too radical for the establishment.

It would hence appear that the Brazilian foreign ministry's activism in UN affairs and peacekeeping did not initially generate changes in defense policy. The presence of diplomats neither contested nor shaped the defense establishment. During the initial wave of democratization in Brazil, the military effectively resisted civilian attempts to intervene in defense matters. In fact, there was an absence of a unified, civilian-led defense ministry until 2000, when President Fernando Henrique Cardoso was finally able to appoint a civilian as head of the defense sector. From 1985 to 1999—when Brazil deployed the largest number of troops to the UN—the service commanders, and particularly the army, were in control of the implementation process. The country's defense and foreign policies thus effectively remained segregated and bureaucratically distinct.

### Phase II: From Defense Policy Segregation to Integration in the Field, 2004–11

The administration of President Luiz Inácio Lula da Silva gave peacekeeping a new impetus in 2004 with MINUSTAH. This troop commitment eventually became the country's largest foreign military deployment since World War II and initiated a new phase in Brazil's peacekeeping trajectory. Under him, Brazil used its foreign policy to signal certain international commitments and to proactively market itself as an emerging power.

Yet, as Cason and Power (2009, 117–40) point out, though Brazil's international relations policy caught the attention of the media, it has not necessarily prompted deconstruction of the country's foreign policy. Instead, evidence suggests that Lula's peacekeeping strategy modified the process by which policy decisions were made and achieved some level of foreign and defense policy integration.

Brazil witnessed an essentially progressive erosion of the traditional dominance of Itamaraty in foreign policy making, while new actors such as Congress, NGOs, and other governmental agencies emerged. For Cason and Power (2009, 119–24), this erosion was partly a consequence of democratization and of increased executive diplomacy, whereby the president dominated and set the foreign policy agenda. Lula gradually became his own foreign minister as he managed and centralized the decision-making process. One diplomat explained, "foreign policy follows Lula's lead, but his strategy is too ambitious and can sometimes overstretch our institutional capacity."[31] Lula diverged from previous democratic administrations in that he used Brazil's military might to accomplish foreign policy objectives in UN peacekeeping operations. The armed forces were no longer a supplemental or reinforcing instrument of Brazil's foreign policy; instead, they were a key component of the country's new global strategy. By establishing this arrangement, however, Lula allowed the military to regain some of its past policy relevance. As Brazil increased its peacekeeping presence, the military improved its policy leverage over the country's international agenda.

This does not mean that Lula abdicated efforts to integrate foreign and defense policy. He tried to bring the military closer to the foreign policy establishment, but it ultimately backfired. In 2003, he appointed Ambassador José Viegas as Brazil's defense minister. Viegas was raised in a military family, but he was a career diplomat who served as ambassador to Moscow and negotiated Brazil's entrance to the nuclear nonproliferation regime in 1994. His appointment raised expectations about rising levels of cooperation between soldiers and diplomats. But these prospects appeared to be ill fated when, in 2004, Ambassador Viegas was forced to resign after the publication of photographs of a nude man who had been allegedly tortured and murdered by the military during the dictatorship. The army's response to the photos—its public affairs office issued a statement justifying military rule as a "legitimate response to Communist-inspired violence"—incited a scandal that led to Viegas's forced resignation. The Lula government punished Viegas for the photos, not the army commander. Viegas, the diplomat, then left the post denouncing "the persistence of authoritarian thinking in the armed forces" (*Economist* 2004c).

His replacement, Waldir Pires, was also sacked in 2007 after two fatal airline disasters caused chaos in Brazil's busiest airport in San Paulo, which at the time the military controlled (Barrionuevo 2007). Pires's resignation prompted Lula to blame his defense minister—not his commanders—for the crisis as a whole. Both incidents illustrated that the Brazilian armed forces, while accepting democracy, had not fully adapted to civilian intervention and continued to resist attempts to fully integrate their defense goals with foreign policy and civilian imperatives.

In view of the military's resistance to civilian and even diplomatic intervention, Lula changed tack. By 2007, he surrounded himself with a group of foreign and defense policy experts drawn predominantly from outside the diplomatic establishment. In the defense sector, Lula appointed Nelson Jobim, a former minister of justice and president of the Supreme Court under Cardoso, to implement reforms in the aviation sector and to negotiate with the armed forces. Previously secret diplomatic documents released by WikiLeaks and made public in *Folha de São Paulo* (2010b) revealed that U.S. diplomats identified Jobim as a moderate, pro-military politician who bureaucratically opposed to the orthodox diplomatic establishment. Jobim's relations with the armed forces were in fact much more fluid, and he tended to shy away from confrontation. To some extent he was the archetypical political manager of defense policy; politically adroit, he had a close relationship with the president, knew the political system, kept the military out of the front pages of newspapers, knew how to manage a public administration, and had no previous experience or knowledge of military affairs.[32] He was exactly the type of manager the armed forces preferred to work with—not an intrusive bureaucrat from a competing organization who probably knew too much already as far as they were concerned.

Similarly, Lula's top foreign affairs advisor, Marco Aurelio Garcia, was recruited not from Itamaraty but from the rank and file of Lula's Workers' Party. Credited for designing Brazil's political strategy in Haiti, "Garcia was there to find a way to restore the political process and increase the pace of reconstruction. It was decided that the first step was to establish the logistical and political conditions necessary for the scheduled 2005 election to go ahead" (Biato 2011, 195).

In addition to surrounding himself with an entourage of independent defense and foreign policy advisors, Lula created the Ministry of Strategy and Long-Term Planning to address Brazil's long-term domestic and international goals. The president appointed Roberto Mangabeira Unger, a philosopher and Harvard law professor, to chair this new office in 2007. Unger, who once taught U.S. President Barack Obama, was appropriately nicknamed the "minister of ideas" because he was assigned to "think" about Brazil's future (Gallego Díaz and Arias 2009). As the minister of ideas, Unger was in charge of planning Lula's national defense strategy. He proposed to broaden the concept of conscription, suggesting that the military serve as a vehicle for the promotion and implementation of innovative technology to run navy power submarines on nuclear energy and to create a domestic arms industry. He was also credited with forcing the Lula administration to reassess the army's role in a postdemocratic era, in which projecting military power abroad would be necessary to accomplish full power status (*Economist* 2009b).

A number of international initiatives on military cooperation came directly from the president's office and from his entourage of ministers and advisors. The peacekeeping strategy was just one of many mechanisms designed to signal military power projection. In 2008, Jobim convened the defense ministers of the region to a meeting in Brasilia to create the Defense Council of the Union of South American Nations. The council included the nine South American states involved in MINUSTAH and had the explicit purpose of strengthening regional defense and military cooperation (Mendelson Forman 2011). Many saw it as a Brazilian attempt to establish a successor institution for the inter-American system and as a means of limiting Washington's power in the region (Sánchez 2008). Ultimately, all these initiatives instituted what might be termed as "military diplomacy" in Brazil, in which the defense establishment made international security coordination efforts, but without conventional diplomatic involvement of Itamaraty. None of these ideas was new; the military had already envisioned this long-term view for Brazil during the dictatorship.[33] What was surprising, however, was that most of these ideas were resuscitated under a civilian and democratic leadership.

Interestingly enough, the ideas and policies advocated by this group of "outsiders" facilitated the slow return of the military into the decision-making arena. Under Lula, the goal was no longer to exclude or restrain the military's sphere of influence (policy handling), but to integrate them into Brazilian statecraft. Foreign and defense policy integration was achieved by including the military sector in the process and by managing the decision-making process from the top.

As the leading troop-lending country in command of MINUSTAH, Brazil relied on direct input and feedback from the armed forces. In this context, the army appointed the UN force commander, whose role was ultimately to reinforce that of the service commanders. These officials then linked peacekeeping to exposing Brazil's military competence on an international level. For Brazilian military experts, a force that can deploy its soldiers abroad can equally mobilize them to counter a threat from a nearby enemy (Cunha Velloso 2002). Consequently, military thinking coincided with Lula's view of peacekeeping.

Lula's strategy—to use military force to accomplish foreign policy goals—yielded some interesting results in terms of defense and foreign policy integration. Diplomats and commanders interacted intensely with each other in Haiti. There was a concerted effort from the presidency to ensure that Brazil would lead the UN mission politically and militarily. To this end, the presidency made efforts to guarantee control as Brazil controlled nearly every key diplomatic and military position in the mission. Brazilian nationals held all strategic positions, from the UN deputy head of the mission and the force commander to the OAS representative in Haiti. The team was diplomatically supported by Brazil's embassy in Port-au-Prince, which brought social, cultural, and economic aid projects of its own to implement in tandem with Viva Rio. MINUSTAH developed civil-military synergies and policy integration as diplomats, soldiers, and even a Brazilian NGO exchanged information and interacted with each other.

The unusually high levels of integration between diplomats and commanders in Haiti nevertheless did not affect the relationship between Itamaraty and the armed forces at the strategic level in the headquarters. Jorge Ramalho, a civilian expert on defense policy, argued: "In MINUSTAH there is integration in the field, not so at the strategic and doctrinal level, in Brasilia. We still need more joint efforts to emulate what has been done in the field."[34] Back in Brasilia, the working procedures remained relatively segregated. Joint working groups, interministerial meetings, and dual appointments were not routine but sporadic. Interministerial meetings were often convened by the executive, or by Aurelio's and Unger's initiative. It was a top-down decision-making process led by the executive branch with little direct feedback from the diplomatic establishment. Similarly, with the exception of the Brazilian mission at UN Headquarters in New York, there were no formal liaisons between the ministries of defense and foreign affairs. It is not to say that diplomats were completely excluded from the decision-making process, but the role of Itamaraty was constrained to providing diplomatic support in Haiti and in New York. This diplomatic activism, in both the UN mission and the field, did not appear to influence defense policy directly.

Although soldiers and diplomats were much more in tune in the field, bureaucratic disputes did emerge in the political capital. Most Brazilian diplomats considered their country's engagement in Haiti as part of a multidimensional, reconstruction-oriented mission and were hesitant to accept that Chapter VII of the UN Charter, involving the use of force, was part of the mandate. Director for UN Affairs at Itamaraty Gilda Motta Santos Neves found that "Brazil was in the Security Council as a non-permanent member in 2004, and accepted and approved the mission with the understanding that a new multidimensional mission would be later approved involving political, human rights, and the consolidation of all political institutions. The 2004 resolution was only a temporary, emergency, multidimensional force. It was to last three to four months."[35] By contrast, the military had no qualms dealing with a Chapter VII–mandated peace operation on the Caribbean island and, as shown in chapter 5, to some extent they used force liberally.[36] MINUSTAH eventually created a disconnection between defense and external relations, which could only be bridged through executive intervention (Albuquerque Lima and Figueiredo Lins 2007).

Furthermore, Lula's strategy did not facilitate civilian or diplomatic intervention in defense matters. Peacekeeping did not substantially improve the institutional capacity of the Ministry of Defense, which remained weak throughout Lula's administration.[37] In 2009, when field research was conducted in Brasilia, peacekeeping policies were managed by the Ministry's Department of Logistics, with the term "logistics" implying that its function was merely operational, not strategic. All other aspects—including training, doctrine, troop recruitment, and force contribution—were reserved for the services. In Brazil's defense establishment, civilians and diplomats generally continued to represent a minor component of the operational side of peacekeeping. Defense and policy integration was achieved in the field because the armed forces were given a strategic place in the decision-making process, which the executive branch and not the diplomatic establishment centralized and implemented.

Interestingly, Lula's active foreign policy triggered a renewed interest in international and security affairs from the foreign policy community, evidenced by the increasing number of books, articles, and publications on peacekeeping published between 2004 and 2011.[38] Brazil's involvement in UN missions suddenly became an issue of academic debate, a reflection of the country's foreign policy aspirations. It provided an opportunity for a small cohort of foreign policy experts to discuss defense issues from a foreign policy perspective. The interest in peacekeeping went beyond the academic world, as NGOs such as Viva Rio became intimately involved in MINUSTAH and even organized workshops on civil-military relations in peacebuilding operations.[39]

There was also significant expansion in security- and defense-related academic programs. The Institute of International Studies at the Pontifical Catholic University of Rio de Janeiro took the lead by offering postgraduate courses on humanitarian missions with links to peacekeeping operations. Some new research programs sprung up, such as the Strategic Studies Group jointly run by Fluminense Federal University and the Federal University of Rio de Janeiro. Most of these programs focused on international relations and analyzed peacekeeping matters in the context of the so-called emerging power debate. While the network of foreign policy experts remained small (an elite minority), a qualitative expansion of the defense policy community did occur slowly. Nevertheless, it had limited influence on the defense establishment. No foreign policy scholar served as advisor to the president, as was clearly the case in Argentina.

In the Brazilian case, peacekeeping has facilitated civil-military coordination between soldiers and diplomats in the field, but only by increasing the role of the armed forces in the decision-making process. Diplomats complement the military, but they have limited influence in defense matters, even as Brazil has increased its UN involvement and troop commitment.

### Uruguay

Chapter 2 identified two distinct periods in Uruguay's peacekeeping history: 1992–2000 and 2002–11. Although the country engaged in a variety of missions in this period, those missions did not appear to help integration of foreign and defense policy. In Uruguay, peacekeeping is not a diplomatic or foreign policy mission but a military endeavor. As described in chapter 3, the core of the decision-making process resides in the National Defense Council and in SINOMAPA, which coordinates peacekeeping policies in which the regular attendees are the service commanders. The system does little to empower the Ministry of Foreign Affairs, which can neither convene nor veto decisions, even though it must appoint a representative when invited to do so. There are no interministerial meetings, dual appointments, or liaison officials. The decision-making process is essentially an affair between the executive branch and the service commanders.

True, the system is currently being reformed with the approved National Defense Act of 2010 (yet to be enacted), which will eventually disband the council and appoint a joint chief of staff who will in turn report to the defense minister, not the commanders. In 2011, President Mujica announced his readiness to allow the judiciary to process as many as eighty human rights abuse cases that were pending investigation (Reuters 2011).

In spite of these recent reforms, however, the Uruguayan case is intriguing because two decades of massive UN peacekeeping deployments seemingly failed to empower diplomats or to change the underlying relationship between soldiers and civilians. In 2003, when field research was conducted in Montevideo, I searched for possible policy areas in which diplomats might have had some degree of policy leverage. It was a daunting task because international signaling was not a motivating factor behind Uruguay's peacekeeping commitment. Simply put, foreign policy motivations were completely absent from the decision-making process. Unlike Argentina and Brazil, Uruguay participated only one time in the UN Security Council as a nonpermanent member (1965–66). One Uruguayan diplomat gave the following explanation: "we are a small country that does not have strategic interests abroad. Being in the Security Council exposes state-members to enormous international pressures."[40]

To coordinate peacekeeping policies in New York, the president similarly appointed three active military officers (one for each service) as military attachés in the UN mission. The attachés did not report to the Ministry of Foreign Affairs but to the Ministry of Defense. They advised SINOMAPA and traveled to each of the different peace operations, gathering information from the field about the level of threat to the mission and the political conditions for deployment. The attachés served as liaison officers between the Ministry of Defense and UNDPKO, developing links and contacts between military organizations and the UN system. The attachés devoted more time to developing their expertise on peacekeeping matters than any other civil servant in the Uruguayan mission to the UN. Ultimately, they and the commanders became key to assessing the conditions for deployment.[41] The system effectively guaranteed the centralization of the decision-making process within the Ministry of Defense, mostly staffed by military officers.[42] Moreover, the information gathered by its agents was rarely debriefed or diffused to other civilian-led bureaucracies such as diplomats. Diplomatic input at the UN mission level in New York was nonexistent.

Furthermore, there was no concrete correlation between Uruguay's foreign policy and its peacekeeping strategy. Peacekeepers deployed to countries with which Uruguay had no diplomatic or bilateral relations and in regions that were beyond its national interests, including Afghanistan, Angola, Cambodia, Côte d'Ivoire, the DRC, East Timor, Haiti, India, Liberia, Mozambique, Pakistan, and Rwanda, to name a few. Uruguay did not even have embassies in many of these countries. Interviews conducted in New York with Uruguayan diplomats revealed that foreign trade and economic interests were not the prime factors motivating Uruguay's active peacekeeping engagement in Africa. As Ambassador Felipe Paolillo, the Uruguayan representative to the

UN, explained in 2003, "there are countries that see Africa as an important international market. We believe the continent has an economic potential, but that is not our immediate goal. We are there for solidarity and we are a neutral party."[43]

The one policy area in which the Ministry of Foreign Affairs could have exerted more influence was in the $2 \times 9$ coordination mechanism of Latin American peacekeepers, which gathered two deputy ministries of foreign affairs and defense from all nine South American states involved in MINUSTAH (Diamint 2007; Marconedes de Souza Neto 2009). As mentioned in chapter 2, the purpose of this group was to enhance cooperation and coordination efforts within Latin American contingents in Haiti. The policy input of the Uruguayan foreign ministry was ultimately limited, however, in part because there was no Uruguayan embassy in Haiti. Uruguay's contribution to Haiti was entirely military—troops and water treatment plants managed by the Army Corps of Engineers. The armed forces clearly controlled Uruguay's peacekeeping agenda, and they determined the criteria for participation.

The problem resided in the presidency, which had delegated peacekeeping matters to its commanders, not its ambassadors. The primary responsibility for peacekeeping operations lay in civilian hands. Even the left-oriented administration of President Tabaré Vázquez (2005–10) followed peacekeeping policies similar to those implemented by the previous moderate and pro-military administrations of Jorge Battle (2000–2005), Julio María Sanguinetti (1985–90 and 1995–2000), and Luis Alberto Lacalle (1990–95). In all these cases, peacekeeping was never implemented as a policy-handling strategy aimed at eroding the military's decision-making authority.

Not only was the country's peacekeeping strategy devoid of diplomatic input and policy handling, it also caused a serious rift between the country's defense and foreign affairs establishments. The fracture emerged in 2003 when Uruguayan peacekeepers proved unable to halt the looting and killing of civilians in the eastern region of the DRC. Joel Rosenberg (2003), a journalist from Uruguayan newspaper *El País*, described the situation as "mission impossible" and "hell on earth." The UN Security Council called an emergency meeting to analyze MONUC and consequently changed the mission's mandate from Chapter VI (peace observing) to Chapter VII (peace enforcement), effectively giving Uruguayan soldiers the authority to use force to protect civilians (Barringer 2003). The transformation of the UN mandate did not prompt a parliamentary debate in Montevideo, but the country's legislators and its diplomats were extremely concerned about the developments in the DRC. Some members of the foreign service opposed Uruguay's engagement in MONUC, as they believed that the mission violated the principle of nonintervention in internal affairs. "MONUC is now in clear contradiction with our diplomatic tradition, based on non-violence and peaceful resolution. We are now intervening in Congo's internal affairs and we are no longer an impartial party," one diplomat explained.[44] Likewise, opposition legislators like Representative José A. Bayardi, president of the Defense Committee in the House, argued that it was inherently problematic to send troops to the DRC without taking the political ramifications into account. "Even if there are important military professional lessons to be learned from peacekeeping, we are not an occupying force and DRC poses challenges for our foreign policy. We are also worried for their lives. We want our soldiers to come back alive."[45]

The Ministry of Defense and the army's general staff had a different take on the issue, however. In their view, pulling troops out of MONUC posed a major financial challenge for Uruguay, as thousands of soldiers would have stopped receiving payments for peacekeeping. As Colonel Álvaro Picabea, the director of peacekeeping operations in the army's general staff, explained: "Peacekeeping provides jobs that are needed when the country is facing its worst economic crisis."[46] The armed forces therefore justified the presence of two thousand peacekeepers in MONUC on economic grounds and, despite the misgivings of the Ministry of Foreign Affairs, the troops ultimately remained integral the mission.

In 2004, Uruguay experienced a second rupture with MINUSTAH when Congress authorized the executive branch and the armed forces to join Argentina, Brazil, and Chile in Haiti. For diplomats in the Cancillería, the timing of this mission was far from fortuitous. Zurbriggen (2005, 85–109), a foreign policy expert, found that the mission in Haiti imposed the same challenges and political dilemmas as the mission in the DRC: the fear of militarizing peacekeeping while overriding the country's diplomatic principles. Moreover, the deployment took place precisely when its neighbor on the other side of the Río de la Plata—Argentina—began proceedings against Uruguay at the International Court of Justice, which froze diplomatic bilateral relations. Argentine authorities alleged that their Uruguayan neighbors had violated international public law by allowing the construction of pulp mills across the border. It was yet another indication that UN troop commitment decisions were being made irrespective of Uruguay's diplomatic agenda in the region.

The final blow to Uruguay came in the form of the aforementioned accusations of sexual abuse against five Uruguayan peacekeepers in Haiti. The incident damaged Uruguay's external image. Uruguayan authorities had convened a long-planned meeting in Montevideo of the $2 \times 9$ mechanism in September 2011 to discuss the future of the UN mission in Haiti. The crisis over the Uruguayan peacekeepers, however, diverted the talks and prompted the foreign minister to announce a gradual withdrawal of troops (MercoPress 2011b). The accusations of sexual abuse had clearly embarrassed the Uruguayan diplomatic establishment and further alienated the country's soldiers from its diplomats.

If peacekeeping did not empower diplomats, did it attract the attention of the academic community? Unlike in Argentina and Brazil, where a relatively small defense policy community eventually emerged in tandem with UN troop commitments, in Uruguay, civilians rarely discussed or debated peacekeeping matters. This is a surprising finding for a county with almost one peacekeeper for every 280 citizens, the largest per-capita peacekeeping contribution in the world. In theory, almost every Uruguayan inhabitant knew or was in direct contact with at least one blue helmet. In practice, however, there was little knowledge of peacekeeping. Lack of civilian expertise cannot be attributed to poor education levels, because Uruguay has the highest literacy indicators in South America. Experts on Latin American civil-military relations refer to this phenomenon in terms of attention deficits; that is, a widespread disinterest in defense policy and a general lack of concern for the "development of plans and processes designed to provide for the oversight, organization, training and deployment, and funding of the armed forces" (Pion-Berlin and Trinkunas 2007, 77).

When field research was conducted in 2003, there were virtually no civilian academic programs dedicated to war and peace studies. One notable exception was the Southern Cone Observatory for the Study of Defense Policies and Armed Forces at Republic University, the nation's largest public higher education institution in Montevideo. The observatory distributed a weekly bulletin of defense news electronically through a blog.[47] But it had no formal teaching programs or research projects on peacekeeping. As a result, the civilian defense community was poorly institutionalized.

Conversely, the Ministry of Defense established its own center, the Center for Higher National Studies, in 1992. It offered graduate courses in security and strategic studies to uniformed students and civilians. The instructors were all active military officers. By decree its director had to be an active general who appointed all full-time and part-time faculty members.[48] The staff at the Center for Higher National Studies certainly had expertise on peacekeeping issues and was well trained to organize panel discussions on UN operations. But this organization could not be considered as an independent think tank because it was directly managed by the military.

The available literature on peacekeeping issues published inside Uruguay revealed the extent to which there are enormous information asymmetries between soldiers and civilians. As expected, most of the information on peace missions—books, journal articles, and reports—was produced or funded by the armed forces. The Military Center, an institution dedicated to the analysis of military history and culture, published two major publications on peacekeeping (Cabrera 1994a; De León 1996). Military journals also addressed the topic in numerous articles. *El Soldado*, the most widely read military magazine in Uruguay, published over 115 articles on peacekeeping between 1992 and 2002—mostly authored by former blue helmets. Similarly, at least seven articles were published in *Revista del Ejército*, the army's official journal.

During the same time period, only three articles and book chapters authored by civilians addressed the issue of Uruguay's UN peacekeeping participation (Fuentes 1997; González 2002; López Chirico 1999). Commercial or academic publishers did not produce a single book or major volume on the matter. The country's involvement in MINUSTAH in 2004–5 did not incite increased academic interest in UN peace missions, either. I was able to retrieve three articles authored by Uruguayan scholars on peacekeeping in the post-2004 period. Of these three articles, only one was published in Uruguay. The rest appeared in foreign journals. Most of these publications criticized Uruguay's participation in Haiti and raised concerns about of the apparent incongruence between the mission and the country's foreign policy goals (Gonnet Ibarra and Hernández Nilson 2007; Peláez 2007; Zurbriggen 2005).

Uruguay appears to reflect a third model of defense and foreign policy interaction in peacekeeping operations. In this case, the exclusion and segregation of the foreign policy establishment, in which diplomats have had virtually no incidence on defense or deployment decisions in the field or at the strategic level, characterize the decision-making process. Civilian leaders could have used peacekeeping to induce change in defense policy, but they have yet to assert sufficient influence over policymakers to do so. Either as a result of civilian neglect or delegation, peacekeeping in Uruguay is an essentially military mission. In turn, UN peace operations became militarized, not only failing to induce defense reforms but also decreasing civilian incidence in doctrinal debates.

## Conclusion

Can peacekeeping help democratizing states better integrate their defense and foreign policies? The findings suggest that participation in UN peace operations can empower diplomats and force doctrinal change as much as it can strengthen commanders and eventually exclude ambassadors from decision-making processes. In other words, there was no homogenous model of foreign and defense policy integration; peacekeeping exercised varying and divergent effects between and among democratizing and UN troop-contributing states. Table 6.1 shows that increased engagements in UN peace missions led to varying levels of policy integration and segregation, with at least four possible outcomes: (1) complete foreign and defense policy integration, with the inclusion of foreign policy bureaucrats and the expansion of defense policy communities (quadrant 1, Argentina under President Menem); (2) integration of foreign policy experts in peacekeeping, though their input was limited, and

*Table 6.1.*   Comparison of defense and foreign
policy integration

|  | Defense Policy Expansion | Community Retrenchment |
|---|---|---|
| Foreign policy bureaucrats<br><br>Inclusion | Quadrant 1<br>Argentina Phase I<br>(Menem) | Quadrant 2<br>Brazil Phase I (Mello and Cardoso)<br>Argentina Phase II (Kirchner) |
| Exclusion | Quadrant 3<br>Brazil Phase II<br>(Lula) | Quadrant 4<br>Argentina Phase II (Kirchner)<br>Uruguay Phases I and II |

defense policy communities did grow (quadrant 3, Brazil under President Lula); (3) semisegregation, with some diplomatic input in peacekeeping but no expanded role for defense policy communities (quadrant 2, Brazil pre-2004 and Argentina post-2004); and (4) complete segregation, with no role for diplomats or defense policy communities (quadrant 4, Uruguay). These findings clearly contradict the conventional wisdom that peacekeeping will bring together diplomats and soldiers, enabling a civil-military cooperative environment conducive to reform and transparency. If this was the case, then states should have converged toward quadrant 1, whereby diplomats and policy communities become actively engaged in the decision-making process. The evidence also disputes liberal claims about international institutions, which often argue that states engaged in similar international organizations will increasingly have domestic practices and policies that converge. The pattern observed in the three case studies suggests the opposite: increased interaction in UN-mandated peace operations actually magnified civil-military differences (Sotomayor 2010b).

The South American states that have increasingly participated in joint peacekeeping missions (those most likely to experience convergence) diverged in terms of integration. The decision-making processes in Argentina, Brazil, and Uruguay could not be more different in the pre- and post-MINUSTAH deployments. Moreover, Uruguay, the largest UN troop contributor, has progressively segregated the diplomatic establishment and polarized the decision-making process. The fact that it exposed more troops to missions overseas does not seem to affect integration efforts. Likewise, with the exception of Argentina under Menem, the trend is to reinforce military diplomacy, where the defense establishment gradually assumes larger international roles independent from the foreign affairs ministries. In other words, in some democratizing states, peacekeeping has allowed the armed forces to become international actors in their own right.

Why such variation among states engaged in peacekeeping? A comparison of the two most similar cases of integration—Argentina under Menem and Brazil under Lula—reveals some interesting answers. Although Lula and Menem ruled their countries during different periods and had dissimilar political ideologies, they in fact had a great deal in common. Both were leaders who assumed active roles as foreign policy makers and centralized the decision-making process in the executive branch. Similarly, the two statesmen perceived peacekeeping as a tool with which to transform not only the military, but the overall identity and international alignment of their respective countries, providing the critical juncture with which to link defense and foreign policy—the possibility of "shaping and shaking" foreign policy implied a transformation of defense policy. The defense policies of Uruguay clearly lacked this foreign policy dimension, and its leaders failed to connect military contributions with diplomatic goals.

Lula and Menem had something else in common: both achieved integration by politically managing the armed forces. As a result, they did not fully institutionalize the decision-making process. To some extent, both leaders achieved some degree of control, mostly by co-opting the military to political and foreign policy imperatives. In Huntington's (1957, 80–97) civil-military relations model, using the military to achieve foreign policy goals is conceptualized as "subjective" control; that is, the simplest way of minimizing military power by maximizing the power of particular political groups (foreign policy bureaucrats in Argentina and party advisors in Brazil). This model may explain why these countries' integration policies have been relatively short lived and limited to specific administrations. Under it, integration can be reversed, which is why Huntington had strong reservations about using subjective control to manage military establishments. The Menem legacy clearly did not survive the Kirchner test, and Lula's executive policy might not be replicated in future Brazilian administrations.

Although Lula and Menem were lucky enough to have a consolidated foreign service at their disposal (something that Uruguay lacked), they integrated foreign and defense policies in different ways, suggesting that there can be many paths toward foreign and defense policy coordination. On the one hand, the Menem model gave diplomats key strategic positions in the defense establishment, leading to policy handling and Menem's considerable reliance on a core group of diplomats and the empowerment of the foreign policy establishment. On the other hand, the Lula model positioned the armed forces as the centerpiece of the peacekeeping strategy, effectively increasing their role in foreign affairs and inciting defense or military diplomacy. The impact of both models differed considerably in terms of defense policy supervision, monitoring, implementation, and doctrinal change. Integration forced organizational change and military reform only in Argentina and only under Menem. The case is unique, making it difficult to generalize the potential positive contributions of peacekeeping on the country's civil-military reform efforts.

The Argentine case is also worth noting because the country went from integration to semisegregation in less than a decade. It is one of the few countries in Latin America that has institutionalized some level of civilian control, which prevented the Ministry of Defense from working as a surrogate or addendum institution of foreign affairs. Ironically, the process by which defense institutions were strengthened during the Kirchner years eventually led to the undoing of the integration process accomplished by the Menem administration. Oddly enough, Argentina's foreign and defense policies are now less integrated than a decade ago, although the country has managed to increase civilian incidence in defense matters.

Finally, peacekeeping would appear to have had a negative effect on civil-military policy integration in Uruguay. Civilians in Uruguay emerged from the democratization process with a policy leverage advantage. Yet two decades of sizable peacekeeping deployments has neither empowered diplomats nor increased civilian intervention in defense policies. Diplomats and soldiers rarely cooperate with each other and often advocate for different policies. The absence of civilian interest in peacekeeping and defense affairs (attention deficits) is consequential. Political authorities have implicitly ceded space and passed on opportunities to exert more influence over peacekeeping policies. Most politicians have embraced the conventional wisdom, expecting that peacekeeping would induce internal reform of the armed forces. It would appear, however, that military organizations rarely evolve without some form of civilian intervention, of which there has been virtually none.

# Conclusion

*Theory and Policy Implications of the UN Peacekeeping System's Divergent Effects*

Former UN Secretary-General Dag Hammarskjöld, who in 1961 died tragically in a plane crash in the liberated Congo while managing a peacekeeping mission there, famously said that "peacekeeping is not a job for soldiers, but only soldiers can do it." Over the years, this famous quotation has become a cliché for describing the UN's dependence on military staff. While the UN would prefer not to rely on the armed forces to maintain, build, and enforce a diplomatically negotiated peace, the fact is that blue helmets recruited from various military institutions have increasingly assumed the responsibility of conducting peacekeeping operations. Since the early 1990s, a growing number of peacekeepers, mostly from newly democratizing states, have been drafted. Despite developments in the role armed forces play in peacekeeping operations, we know little about how such engagements actually affect soldiers, especially those from democratizing societies.

In an effort to shed light on this issue, I have sought to answer three empirical questions. Does peacekeeping change military organizations? Does peacekeeping socialize blue helmets? Can peacekeeping help integrate defense and foreign policies in democratizing states? The conventional wisdom on peacekeeping sustains that peacekeeping participation can (1) induce a doctrinal change in military organizations, (2) socialize troops to adopt new professional and democratic norms, and (3) improve civil-military relations by enhancing cooperation between soldiers and diplomats. A focused comparison of various South American cases provides fertile ground for testing these arguments. Each country's peacekeeping trajectory has exhibited anomalies and diverged significantly from the rest. The differences defy determinism and suggest that the impact of peacekeeping on different policy communities is not one-dimensional, unidirectional, or homogenous. The empirical cases in fact suggest substantial intraregional and within-case variations. UN peacekeeping changed military organizations in some cases but not in others. Participation in various kinds of UN operations socialized soldiers in different ways, with varying consequences, some of which were unintended. Finally, in some countries, peacekeeping facilitated foreign and defense policy integration as much as it contributed to segregating soldiers and diplomats in other states. The main contribution of this book lies not in its conclusion—that peacekeeping generates divergent effects—but rather in its explanation of how and why these divergent outcomes occurred. "Case studies remain much stronger at assessing whether and how a variable mattered to the outcome than at assessing how much it mattered" (George and Bennett 2004, 25).

To conclude, I recapitulate general findings and explore why peacekeeping may generate such distinct effects in different countries' policy communities. In theoretical terms, these findings matter because they indicate how domestic structures and institutional factors within the UN peacekeeping system can cause divergent effects in different countries. I finish by discussing what the policy implications may be for peacekeeping practitioners.

## Empirical Findings and Theoretical Implications

Each case study displayed multiple and divergent effects, and I subsequently categorize them according to their impact on how peacekeeping is organized, as well as how socialization and decision-making processes occur. I then discuss what caused each of these effects, and how they relate to international relations and civil-military relations theories.

### Institutional and Divergent Effects

All three countries reflected the shortcomings of conventional international relations approaches. Neorealist and neoliberal perspectives offer limited answers to questions about why states deploy soldiers to UN peace operations and the consequences such decisions can have on peacekeepers. On the one hand, conventional realist factors—national security interests, balance of power, and even regional influence—cannot properly explain the peacekeeping trajectories of the selected case studies. This book began with an empirical and puzzling finding: A large number of democratizing states known as "Third Wave to democracy countries" became increasingly involved in UN peacekeeping operations. Although the motivations to participate in UN peace operations vary from case to case, democratizing nations have essentially committed themselves to peacekeeping operations for three reasons: international signaling, domestic reform, and monetary incentives. Chapter 1 described how democratization provides an initial impetus for states to join international institutions, especially because democratizing states can find it difficult to make credible international commitments and to implement reforms on their own. Peacekeeping may be a tool with which to manage these shortcomings, as it declares to the world that a state has radically changed and requires international support to continue its domestic reforms. This finding runs contrary to realist expectations, because states do not typically seek international institutions to modify or alter their interests and behavior. As Mearsheimer (1994, 5) once famously argued, "the notion that institutions can serve as conduits for taming state behavior only clouds the 'realism' necessary for rational decision making."

On the other hand, from both liberal and realist perspectives, it is difficult to explain the varying effects of peacekeeping participation on democratizing states. In spite of their increased involvement in UN peacekeeping, democratizing states have reacted differently to such international engagements. The evidence emerging from the case studies yielded the following results:

1.  Peacekeeping seemingly contributed to reforms and modified the role as well as the traditional inward-looking doctrine and training procedures of the Argentine forces. Participation in UN peace operations similarly and substantially changed the mission and the orientation of the Uruguayan armed forces, but it failed to modify military doctrine and training. In Brazil, peacekeeping neither modified doctrine nor changed the military's traditional mission.

2.  Peacekeeping appeared to make it difficult for junior officers in Argentina to organize internal rebellions, as they constantly served on UN missions in far-off destinations.

3.  Engagement in UN operations contributed to strengthening the Argentine defense ministry, but it reinforced the role of army commanders in Brazil and Uruguay. The military ironically remained in control of peacekeeping policies in countries with the largest UN deployments.

4.  In 2004, all three countries participated in MINUSTAH. Although troops deployed to the same mission, the socializing effects of that

mission were disparate. In Brazil, MINUSTAH essentially served as a training ground for pacification strategies, reinforcing inward-looking doctrines practiced in the country's slums and urban settings. In Uruguay, peacekeeping resuscitated old counterinsurgency and public security operations as they were once practiced before the transition to democracy. In Argentina, MINUSTAH exposed soldiers to traditional observing and monitoring missions.

5. A handful of officers gained additional professional experiences, including promotion and military skills, in UN observation and peace enforcement missions. But the concrete, professional gains of officers engaged in peacebuilding missions were few and far between. In recent years, peacekeeping units (brigades, battalions, and companies) have been composed of a substantial number of noncommissioned officers, for which peace operations offer few or no professional enticements.

6. A handful of peace observers in MINUSTAH performing CIMIC activities fully integrated with civilian components (civilianizing effects) as they interacted with civilians and international NGOs. Nevertheless, peacekeepers engaged in policing functions became increasingly segregated from those civilian components because they often relied on abusive force to control crowds and public unrest.

7. Peacekeeping contributed to increased foreign and defense policy integration in Argentina during the Menem administration and in Brazil during the Lula administration, but it seemingly failed to improve civil-military cooperation between soldiers and diplomats in Uruguay.

8. The countries took multiple trajectories toward policy integration. In Argentina, peacekeeping enabled the foreign policy establishment to gain policy influence and decision-making power. Conversely, Brazil achieved integration by increasing the role of the armed forces in foreign affairs and peacekeeping policy making.

As disparate as these results appear to be, the cases collectively indicated that international institutions—in this case the UN—had a significant effect on domestic politics (the so-called second image reverse effect). But these findings are inconsistent with both neorealist and liberal expectations. From a neorealist perspective, international institutions exercise minimal influence on state behavior, play an insignificant role in the security realm, and only matter in settings in which there is no opposition to state interests (Mearsheimer 1994, 16). Nevertheless, peacekeeping participation in the three democratizing states appeared to have significant and largely unintended consequences in military policy, an area in which realists expect few, if any, behavioral changes. Realists dismiss this finding by indicating that the case studies predominantly involve small, developing, third world states. Thucydides (2005, 56) famously argued in "The Melian Dialogue," however, that the "strong do what they can and the weak suffer what they must."

One cannot easily dismiss the effects of UN peacekeeping on the policy communities in the two regional powers of Argentina and Brazil. Peacekeeping by Argentina helped redefine its international identity while structurally changing its civil-military relations. In Brazil, peacekeeping failed to reform the armed forces, but it did help redefine the country's status as a so-called emerging power. More importantly, UN peacekeeping missions provided a valuable point of reference and source of learning for their own public security operations. The Uruguayan military reacquired public security functions and learned a tremendous amount through their collaboration with the Brazilian Army as they sought to apply antigang tactics and to counter drug trafficking in Haiti. In other words, international peacekeeping shaped state and military behavior.

This study provides little or no support for liberal and institutional theories of international relations. Democratizing states might be tempted to seek legitimacy through international institutions, but the assumption that multilateral organizations like the UN will inevitably restrict the power of special interest factions, protect individual rights, and improve the quality of democratic deliberation is questionable (Keohane, Macedo, and Moravcsik 2009). With the exception of Argentina, participation in UN peacekeeping operations contributed to mostly illiberal and nondemocratic causes. The increased involvement of Brazil and Uruguay in multilateral peace operations did not restrict the power of their militaries. It did not improve transparency and accountability, empower civilians, persuade the armed forces to democratize or to acquiesce, or fully reorient officers away from their interest in domestic politics. From a national perspective, it would appear that peacekeeping was important for all the wrong reasons: it provided additional resources and justifications for the military to avoid modernization and downsizing in Uruguay, it increased the role of military commanders, and it militarized peacekeeping policies in

Brazil. Uruguayan peacekeepers, who were the most heavily exposed and so-cialized to institutionalized peacekeeping, were ironically the least likely to reform their armed forces. With the exception of Argentina in the 1990s, it would appear that peacekeeping did not generate the same positive, demo-cratizing effects that NATO once exercised on its own members in southern or central Europe.

Neoliberal approaches contend that, as states become members of interna-tional organizations, their domestic policies tend to converge. That is, as states interact in international organizations and become accustomed to interna-tional norms, their practices and domestic policies gradually become aligned. According to this logic, there should be significant policy divergence between members and nonmembers of an international organization (Martin and Sim-mons 1998, 753). The peacekeeping trajectories described in this book suggest the contrary. Peacekeeping clearly had divergent effects upon the foreign and defense policies of the three countries even as they all gradually participated in joint peacekeeping operations. If anything, participation in UN peace opera-tions increased the differences in the policy trajectories of these South Ameri-can states, with Argentina moving further toward democratic civil-military integration, while Brazil and Uruguay retained more traditional undemocratic practices. This finding is intriguing, especially for countries that share similar geographic, cultural, and political conditions and that are members of the same international organizations, such as Mercosur.

If liberal and realist explanations were applicable to peacekeeping issues, they should have been able to explain the overwhelming majority of cases with ease, and with high levels of confidence and parsimony. However, these conventional international relations arguments could not be easily confirmed, even in the best circumstances of having relatively powerful states engaged in common re-gional integration processes, with large joint peacekeeping deployments and similar underlying democratizing conditions. Eckstein (1975, 94–137) argues that the failure of a theory to explain a "most likely" case obviously undermines our confidence in the theory itself.

The main theoretical paradigms available in the field of international rela-tions do not adequately explain why institutions have varying effects on their members, highlighting the need for a clearer analytical framework that takes into account institutional variations and examines their impact in greater depth. We must seek alternative domestic perspectives in order to establish why peacekeeping has had such a variety of effects upon military reform in democratizing UN troop-lending states. On the basis of this analysis, I seek to answer these questions here.

## Military Organizations and Decision Makers

Does peacekeeping change military organizations? Many democratizing states face the challenge of shaping and redefining roles and missions for the armed forces. The prevailing, conventional view is that civilians are better able to tether the military when it focuses on foreign engagements. Existing studies of civil-military relations have argued that civilian control is best achieved when the military performs outward-oriented missions. As argued above, peacekeeping promises exactly the type of reform that democratizing leaders often seek: an external shift in the focus of military organizations.

Unfortunately, these findings were inconsistent. Peacekeeping contributed to modifying the traditional inward-looking orientation and doctrine of the military only in Argentina under the Menem administration. Increasing international peacekeeping engagements by Brazilian and Uruguayan troops did not appear to produce similar results. All countries established peacekeeping training centers, but few implemented organizational changes in training, education, recruitment, or logistical affairs. Blue helmets from Brazil were trained like soldiers deployed in the Amazon or the slums of Rio de Janeiro. Uruguayan peacekeepers continued to receive training for counterinsurgency operations.

From an organizational perspective, it is not surprising that peacekeeping is unlikely to change the armed forces. Posen (1984, 58) has argued that military organizations often develop preferred ways of doing things and tend to resist changes and interference: "Because military organizations seek independence from civilian authority in order to reduce the uncertainties of combat . . . soldiers will avoid including political criteria in their military doctrine if such criteria interfere with strictly instrumental military logic." In most cases, military organizations adapted their homegrown doctrines to peacekeeping while avoiding the implementation of fundamental changes in how they relate to civilians. Peacekeeping did not compel the armed forces to modify their traditional inward-looking doctrines; instead, peacekeeping training packages all included policing, gang and crowd control, public security, antidrug initiatives, and urban counterinsurgency skills, suggesting that military organizations do not change simply because they engage in international affairs.

It appears that a critical juncture must induce doctrinal change. The fact that Argentina's armed forces lost the Falklands/Malvinas War a decade before the country became engaged in peacekeeping is significant, as it no doubt prompted the country's military organizations to seek alternative doctrines before risking a defeat. This may go a long way toward explaining why the Argentine military emerged from the transition to democracy far weaker than its Brazilian and Uruguayan counterparts.

But organizational theory can only partially explain Argentina's relative success in civilianizing its military organizations through peacekeeping. While Brazil and Uruguay had not experienced military defeats, their civilians emerged from the transition to democracy with varying levels of policy leverage and influence. Argentine civilian leaders were the only ones to seize this opportunity to induce organizational change. From a comparative perspective, the Argentine and Uruguayan cases were most similar. In both instances, it appears that civilians had a clear political advantage vis-à-vis the military and could have potentially changed their organizations if they had persevered. In Uruguay, however, civilians merely delegated peacekeeping functions to the armed forces, and then failed to supervise and monitor their decision-making processes. Civilians in Argentina did the opposite; they made decisions and subsequently delegated authority to rival bureaucratic institutions, keeping peacekeeping doctrine and training beyond the purview of military commanders. Civilians' positions in the institutional hierarchy, and how they use them, would hence help determine the root of the difference between the Argentine case and the others.

When civilian leaders are in a position to make a policy choice, the short- and long-term implications of how they use this opportunity are significant. Civilian leaders who actively managed and controlled the decision-making process—such as Menem in Argentina—were far more successful in inducing change than those who simply delegated peacekeeping functions without engaging in police patrols to determine what was happening inside the military establishment. In Brazil and Uruguay, civilian leaders neglected peacekeeping policies over the long run, generating attention deficits and ultimately overlooking the importance of maintaining civilian control of the armed forces. To some extent, those leaders expected that peacekeeping would automatically compel the military to reform without having to interfere directly in their doctrinal affairs. Political leaders gradually abdicated political control of peacekeeping policies, seemingly without realizing that they risked compromising their power. This finding is consistent with principal-agent arguments, which focus on the various forms of delegation and monitoring that civilian leaders are likely to embrace in order to improve accountability (Feaver 2003). In other words, two conditions impeded peacekeeping from encouraging further organizational reforms: military organizations' resistance to change and neglectful civilians.

## Positive and Negative Socialization

Does peacekeeping socialize troops? My research suggests that peacekeeping missions do appear to encourage the socialization of blue helmets. However, determining precisely how this process evolves is a much more complicated affair. The conventional wisdom is that participation in UN peacekeeping missions professionalizes the armed forces by developing their skill sets while enabling a high level of integration with civil society. Moskos's (1976) constabulary framework best synthesizes the model, which de-emphasizes the application of violence in order to attain viable political compromises in the mission. As the qualitative evidence in chapters 4 and 5 makes clear, however, only one case approximates the constabulary model: Argentina in the 1990s. The other cases—including Argentina post-2004—report mixed or negative results of professionalism and civilian integration. In other words, socialization in peacekeeping did not converge in the constabulary model. Why were Argentine troops successfully socialized in the 1990s while the others were not?

Two factors appear to explain this variation. First, Argentina's peacekeeping approach selectively exposed its soldiers to specific types of UN operations. The constabulary model was first proposed at a time when the UN was exclusively conducting observation missions in which troops were not heavily armed and consent from belligerents was a given. Today, the UN conducts a broad spectrum of operations ranging from observation and peacebuilding to peace enforcement. In this context, professional and even civilian integration dynamics vary depending on the type of mission being performed. A closer examination of Argentina's engagement in UN operations in the 1990s reflects this variation. For instance, a policy that predominantly involved sending blue helmets to observation and peace enforcement operations had a significant professional impact on Argentine soldiers. In places like Cyprus, Iraq, and even the former Yugoslavia, Argentine peacekeepers acquired new diplomatic and military skills, which eventually enhanced the professional careers of a selected group of young army officers. In these missions, soldiers learned something new about their own profession, such as how to negotiate and monitor international truces (most evident in Cyprus) or how to enforce embargos and no-fly zones (in the former Yugoslavia and Iraq).

Second, this experience was reinforcement that, in UN observation and enforcement operations, Argentine peacekeepers interacted and socialized with fellow troops from democracies that were already consolidated (mostly NATO members). Such interaction provided recently induced troops with a positive model or reference point from which they witnessed and then often emulated the practices of their fellow blue helmets. A selection bias appeared evident in the Argentine case, as peacekeepers participated in missions into which they were more likely to be inducted and socialized by professional soldiers from consolidated democracies.

Conversely, peacekeepers from Brazil and Uruguay served in peacebuilding missions in Angola, Cambodia, and the DRC, where soldiers essentially performed security and policing functions that bore greater resemblance to their traditional, inward-looking missions at home. At best, peacebuilding missions replicated the operational environments in which the soldiers had been traditionally trained for decades. They did not necessarily develop diplomatic or highly specialized military skills; instead, the most important skills were policing and public security ones. Soldiers from Brazil and Uruguay had fewer opportunities to interact with blue helmets from consolidated democracies because they predominantly performed observational and enforcement operations.

This study also showed that current peacekeeping deployments differ from the Argentine model of the 1990s. To begin, the peacekeeping units from democratizing states mostly consist of noncommissioned officers who receive little or no specialized language instruction before their deployment. These are no longer the *crème de la crème* members of the junior officer corps, whom Argentina deployed during its initial peacekeeping trajectory. Fewer consolidated democracies are committing troops to UN operations, prompting a different type of interaction in the field, because newly inducted troops now have fewer opportunities to interact with highly specialized professional soldiers. Peacekeeping has become a predominantly third world affair. It is not to say that peacekeeping has become a second- or third-rate phenomenon, but troops now largely come from developing states and not from consolidated democracies. Furthermore, observation missions are almost extinct, and an increasing number of peacebuilding and peace enforcement operations now dominate the UN agenda.

In this environment, blue helmets are increasingly engaging in peacebuilding missions and playing more significant policing roles. Chapter 5 described the unintended consequences of this policy during MINUSTAH, where soldiers perform multiple law enforcement and public security functions. Peacebuilding and peace enforcement encourage what Stepan (1973, 50) once termed "the professionalism of internal warfare," which emphasizes doctrines and training techniques aimed at preventing and crushing crowds, gangs, drug lords, and rebels. Professionalizing warfare approximates the police-soldier model more than the soldier-diplomat and corporate manager model envisioned by Moskos. It seems that, for some peacekeepers, peacebuilding involves the type of functions for which they have traditionally been trained and from which civilian reformers want to wean them. It is therefore not surprising that training programs run by military organizations continue to emphasize law enforcement and public security functions, which is exactly what the UN appears to mandate in its peacebuilding missions.

I also identified variations with regard to the so-called civilian integration or civilianizing effects of peacekeeping missions. According to the conventional wisdom, military organizations should experience a profound transformation as a result of peacekeeping (thus becoming increasingly integrated into civilian structures when troops build refugee camps), provide humanitarian services, and deliver food and medical supplies (Moskos, Williams, and Segal 2000, 1). The available evidence suggests that such transformation is most likely to occur in peacebuilding missions, in which blue helmets tend to work closely with civilians and NGOs. As a result of the peacekeeping mission, for instance, soldiers from Brazil developed a new working relationship with a Brazilian NGO—Viva Rio—in MINUSTAH. But this is not an indicator of organizational change or civilian integration in itself. Integration varies substantially in accordance with the post and function being performed. CIMIC officers, who operate as observers, develop a much closer relationship with civilian actors than troops or units that merely conduct policing or patrolling functions. Moreover, segregation between military and civilian actors can emerge in settings in which the belligerent parties do not give their consent and in which peacekeepers assume significant law enforcement duties. Intense policing techniques such as raids and gang or crowd control inevitably create civil-military gaps and conflict. The indiscriminate use of police force as applied in places like the DRC and Haiti generates mistrust with locals and complicates coordination efforts with international NGOs. Likewise, the absence of language skills and poor training in humanitarian affairs, common among democratizing troops, creates linguistic and cultural obstacles to civil-military integration. Peacekeepers are more likely to integrate with civilian components when there is consent, when police force is constrained, and when adequate training has been provided. Troops from democratizing states rarely meet these conditions.

Evidence from this field research also identified something new about the logic of socialization in international institutions. Analysis of military sociology and constructivism has focused on positive socialization, including the conditions required for agents to acquire appropriate behavioral norms—increased professionalism, civil-military integration, and other democratic-reinforcing identities. This study suggests that such socialization is certainly plausible in peacekeeping, as demonstrated by the Argentine case study. But we cannot easily rule out the possibility that the opposite occurs; that is, that actors are exposed to illiberal norms, are encouraged to adopt inappropriate practices, and are persuaded to engage in serious acts of misconduct. Because peacekeeping has become so complex, multifaceted, and conducted in so many different environments, its effects inevitably vary in terms of their persuasiveness and social influence. In other words, we cannot assume that positive socialization will automatically occur when soldiers are involved in UN peacekeeping.

Delivering peace can be a messy affair. MINUSTAH clearly showcased that scandals, natural disasters, and a lack of accountability can tarnish a mission's reputation. The UN has an inherent institutional weakness: it cannot monitor, punish, prosecute, or hold its peacekeepers accountable for serious acts of misconduct. As a result, the UN constitutes an environment in which forceful and sexual abuse can occur. Such practices have become pervasive in peacebuilding operations, including those in Haiti, the DRC, and Sudan. This institutional context can give rise to negative socialization and can diffuse illiberal and praetorian practices. Biases and liberal assumptions about the logic of socialization in peacekeeping should therefore be avoided. Kowert and Legro (1996, 485–86) argue in a critical review of constructivism, "a related bias in the study of norms is the 'good norms' problem. Analysts tend to focus on those issues that are normatively desirable, e.g., the spread of democracy, the rise of human rights, the integration of world society, and prohibition against the use of force. Yet undesirable norms are equally possible . . . These issues too deserve attention from the emerging sociological approach." I have tried to rectify this shortcoming in the literature by examining how peacekeeping can improve professionalism and integration in some environments, while eroding military skills and promoting segregation in a different set of circumstances.

Much of the socialization literature infers that military officers are passive agents of social interaction, frequently overlooking that soldiers can effectively resist international persuasion. This study demonstrates that soldiers bring to UN missions preexisting values, understandings, and organizational biases that are difficult to change through international peacekeeping alone. Brazilian peacekeepers in Haiti brought their own homegrown, antigang practices to the mission and then refined them in the Haitian slums. They also brought their own NGOs, which then adapted, or "tropicalized," to MINUSTAH conditions. In this case, peacekeeping did not modify practices and identities; it reinforced preexisting norms and forms of behavior among national contingents. Krebs (2004, 85–124) suggested that military identities are often the result of what the uniformed officer brings into her own environment, and some offers have strong preexisting values and beliefs that are largely intact when socialization occurs.

## Foreign Defense Policy Integration and Segregation

Can peacekeeping integrate defense and foreign policies? There is no simple answer to this question, but there is a clear need for democratizing states to establish effective means of improving civil-military relations. Democratic consolidation cannot be achieved without greater cooperation between civilians and soldiers. Poor civil-military relations impede democracy and are obstacles to successful peacekeeping missions. That peacekeeping involves as much diplomacy as military force is promising for recently democratizing states. Most believe that strategic deployment decisions are largely civilian, and that the military in the field mostly implement diplomatic preserves and logistical issues. In practice, however, ambassadors and commanders interact on multiple levels. I identified at least four distinct pathways of civil-military interaction in UN peace missions: (1) integration at the strategic level, (2) integration in the field, (3) semi-integration with minimum diplomatic input, and (4) complete segregation. The dearth of cases in each category makes it difficult to reach strong conclusions about the effects of peacekeeping participation on integration efforts, however.

The results of the fieldwork revealed significant variations between and within cases. Increasing engagement by Argentina and Brazil in UN peace-keeping missions created significant opportunities for defense and foreign policy integration. The cooperation between military and diplomatic actors in both countries did not clearly correlate with the extent of their regional influence or their joint integration effort, Mercosur. Under the Menem administration in the 1990s, Argentina fully integrated its defense and foreign policy objectives, almost fifteen years before Brazil achieved similar levels of integration in Haiti during Lula's presidential term in 2004. Moreover, the two states' pathways to integration could not have been more different. The Argentine model empowered the foreign policy establishment by delegating decision-making authority on peacekeeping issues to the Ministry of Foreign Affairs. Conversely, the Brazilian model strengthened its military services by granting them full access (and veto power) to the decision-making process. In hierarchical terms, Brazilian commanders were either on a par with their diplomatic counterparts or else had more significant decision-making powers. Furthermore, Argentina went from full integration in the 1990s to semi-integration in the post-2004 era, suggesting that integration dynamics can sometimes regress over time. Brazil, by contrast, experienced a progressive cycle of civil-military policy integration as it went from semi-integration to civil-military integration in the field, but not at headquarters. These cases never converged or overlapped. Nevertheless, the two countries did witness a qualitative expansion of the defense policy community, as foreign policy experts developed an interest in military issues stemming directly from their commitment to UN peacekeeping.

The case of Uruguay—one of the top-ten UN troop-lending countries—is quite different. Segregation took hold as diplomats and soldiers drifted apart. Interministerial cooperation never came to fruition, and defense policy moved away from foreign policy objectives. Civilians remained apathetic and uninterested in peacekeeping and defense issues, even with large UN deployments. It fell short of the ideal integration model because military officers formulated and implemented policies independent of foreign policy considerations. In Uruguay, peacekeeping did not promote an environment that was conducive to cooperative civil-military relations.

It is in the choices made by civilian leaders that Argentina and Brazil differ from Uruguay in integrating civil-military affairs. Countries that achieved some level of foreign and defense policy integration had political leaders—Menem and Lula—who conceived of peacekeeping as a policy tool with which to transform not only the military but also foreign policy. In contrast, leaders who engaged their countries in peacekeeping for economic reasons, such as alleviating military budgets, found it increasingly difficult to link defense with foreign policy. In other words, countries that pursued peacekeeping as part of an international signaling strategy were more likely to integrate policies than those primarily motivated by economic enticements.

## Policy Implications and the Future of Peacekeeping

This concluding section addresses the issue of how to translate insights into policy strategies. We have learned how peacekeeping affects soldiers. Now, what can be done with what we know? George (1993) and Solingen (2008, 289) suggest that causal and theoretical analysis is often more capable of conceptualizing and framing questions than of formulating detailed policy plans. This study does not make detailed policy recommendations, but it does put forward a number of ideas and preliminary steps that are worth applying in the policy arena.

Domestic variables—including military organizations, civilian leaders, and institutional/diplomatic capacity—evidently diffuse and tame many of the effects described in this volume. The degree of democratic consolidation varies from case to case, also leading to different policy outcomes. Given how difficult it is for military organizations to change on their own and how civilians can neglect defense policy, the incentives for change could well come from the institution that employs the blue helmets. The UN could implement changes within its own peacekeeping system by modifying the incentive structure, which is mostly based on monetary reimbursements and per diems. One way of changing the incentive structure is to have the UN take ownership of training programs and assume a much more active role in defining peacekeeping doctrine—absent civilian leaders willing to manage those issues on their own. The proliferation of peacekeeping training programs and the flexible system in which member states can prepare and train their own troops for peacekeeping have not flourished. Military organizations have trained troops according to their own standards, which has led to variations in levels of professionalism and, on occasion, to poor performance in the field. Quality and homogenizing standards are needed. The UN could start by certifying training centers that implement changes and apply good standards (inclusion of civilian instructors, training in humanitarian law, language instruction, etc.) while decertifying those that continue to rely on outdated, perverse peacekeeping doctrines. Reputational costs—prestige or the fear of being decertified—might compel democratizing states and resistant military organizations to implement desired changes.

Another policy that probably requires a fundamental shift in the UN system is the use of military troops for law enforcement and public security functions. If policing is necessary to bring stability, law, and order in peacebuilding and enforcement missions, then the UN might be better off recruiting police forces trained for that specific purpose. The idea that democratizing states can undertake policing functions with military personnel merely because they have the training and skills to conduct those missions is a recipe for disaster. Such a policy does little to reform the armed forces and instead replicates inward-looking doctrines, reinforces existing practices, and erodes the quality of peace the UN is trying to deliver. No matter how well trained, resourceful, or experienced the military can be, it will never be—or conduct itself as—a police force. The history and legacy of these democratizing states speak for themselves. Collateral damage inevitably occurred when soldiers performed broad law enforcement functions during the dictatorial era. Sending members of these previously authoritarian institutions overseas to perform exactly the same policing tasks does not reduce the potential perils of military abuse. These troops will evidently require a different type of socializing experience if they are to be properly changed. Policing is not one of them.

Another fundamental change in the UN peacekeeping system—one that is greatly needed but politically sensitive—involves the issue of internal accountability. Member states might be resistant to giving the UN greater authority to investigate and severely punish troops when they misbehave on a mission. But the absence of "sticks" with which to enforce discipline in the field, and the weak system of internal oversight, provides an environment that enables abuse and can produce unintended consequences for socialization. If the UN cannot prosecute its own blue helmets for legal and political reasons, it can at least ensure that appropriate agents are in charge of its own peace operations. For instance, the policy of appointing mission force commanders from the largest troop contributor nation is defective. As the MINUSTAH case clearly demonstrated, it effectively delegates authority to the military agent, who in turn responds to his own military organization and not to the UN. The force commander thus has strong incentives to hide information and to engage in shirking when his own troops misbehave.[1] Appointing force commanders with no vested interests in the mission is one way of ensuring institutional loyalty to the mission and to UN principles. The role of the force commander should be to serve as a gatekeeper and to pull fire alarms when things go wrong in the mission. This might induce the armed forces to adopt international standards, leading perhaps to small organizational changes in the field.

The current system encourages developing and democratizing states to make troop contributions, but it can also be helpful to provide them with incentives for developed democracies to join peace missions. As described in chapter 1, the financial incentives of peacekeeping sometimes allow national governments and individuals to use UN compensation to support national budgets and salaries. This trend has allowed the UN to address the demand for peacekeeping by recruiting soldiers from developing states (who may need money) without having to send American or western European soldiers into peace missions. Consolidated democracies must make greater contributions, not just because they share the responsibility of maintaining the peace, but also because their participation reinforces the socializing experience for democratizing states already involved in peacekeeping.

Redesigned training programs and workshops need to address the so-called attention deficit problem in peacekeeping. One of the significant barriers to military reform is the lack of civilian policymakers with expertise in military matters. Perhaps the central policy prescription of this project is that, although participation in UN peace operations remains important for socializing militaries, it will have little success if not supplemented with programs that reach out to civilians, who also need to develop defense and peacekeeping expertise. The assumption that peacekeeping will reform the military if politicians leave matters of war and peace in the hands of soldiers is dubious. Programs and policies need to be designed with a view to educating, empowering, and strengthening civilians, which involves training more career diplomats and members of civil society in security affairs so that they can be engaged in peacekeeping and war-making issues. I have not argued that military views are necessarily incompatible with civilian perspectives, but as the French statesman George S. Clemenceau once said, "war is too important to be left to the generals." If this adage is valid when it comes to war, it is even more compelling for keeping the peace, which under normal conditions tends to be the purview of politicians and diplomats, not generals.

Finally, the framework proposed here provides a road map to examine the impact of peacekeeping on civil-military relations in other regions. It reflects the situation in most South American states and has reasonable likelihood to persist in other cases. As indicated in chapter 1, this framework can be tested in a large pull of democratizing countries. South Africa's peacekeeping contribution has been linked to both its post-Apartheid transformation and its new regional leadership role in Africa, providing strong incentives for foreign and defense policy integration (and perhaps resembling Argentina or Brazil in many variables). The South African experience may contrast with that of Ghana or Nigeria; both are large peacekeeping contributors and recently democratizing states still facing serious civil-military challenges (and perhaps resembling Uruguay). In South Asia, Pakistan's sizeable UN troop deployments—according to the UN, ranking first—should provide ample evidence of the role of peacekeeping in a country that has continuously struggled with democracy and civilian control. Other countries worth exploring include some of the world's largest democratizing states that have also recently increased their peacekeeping commitment, including Turkey, Egypt, and Indonesia. In Latin America, states like Bolivia, Chile, Paraguay, and Peru have also joined the South American bandwagon in Haiti, which could make them interesting case studies. Even former peacekeeping recipient states like El Salvador and Guatemala are now engaging their previously praetorian armies in UN missions.[2]

A note of caution is in order. My prime goal is an analytical one, aiming to enhance our understanding of why democratizing states deploy troops to UN missions and what effects such decisions have on their behavior. The argument elaborated here is probabilistic at best and not deterministic, as with most arguments in the social sciences. Soldiers involved in UN policing functions may in fact be effectively reformed. The armed forces may change on their own accord, without civilian intrusion in peacekeeping affairs. Civil-military cooperation may well flourish in UN peace missions without specific diplomatic efforts to achieve this end. All these instances could prove that my argument is falsifiable and subject to empirical refutation. This is a healthy scientific attribute; theoretical problems arise not when the theory is falsifiable, but when it is not. Regarding nuclear proliferation trajectories, Solingen (2008, 286) argues, "even if one finds this approach reasonably persuasive in explaining the past, it does not necessarily follow that it will also apply in the future." Indeed, the dynamics of national self-interest can change, modifying the conditions under which states might be willing to continue supplying troops for UN operations.

# Notes

INTRODUCTION: Myths and Realities of Peacekeepers
in Democratic Transition

1. The increasing involvement of European, Canadian, and even American troops in peacekeeping during the Cold War era fostered a growing debate regarding the feelings and attitudes of military personnel toward peace assignments. Students interested in this field have at their disposal statistics, data, surveys, and research designs arguing both in favor and against the participation of military personnel in such missions. See Miller (1997), Moskos (1976), Moskos, Williams, and Segal (2000), Segal and Segal (1993), Segal and Tiggle (1997), Sorensen (1992), Weinberger (2002), and Williams (1998).

2. For a discussion on military roles, see Desch (1999) and Hunter (1999).

3. See Posen (1984).

4. I follow the theoretical insights of Pion-Berlin and Arceneaux (2000) with regard to the role of civilians in crafting missions.

5. For a detailed analysis of South America's engagement in UN peacekeeping operations, see Kenkel (2010a) and Sotomayor (2010a).

6. I follow George and Bennett's (2004, 203–32) use of process tracing as a research method.

7. On the role of time horizons and time sequences, see Pierson (2003).

8. On how different global and regional organizations perform peacekeeping, see Barnett (1995).

9. In 1995, for instance, Argentina, Brazil, Chile, and the United States (also known as the 1942 Rio Protocol guarantors) provided a peacekeeping framework to settle a territorial dispute between Ecuador and Peru. See Herz and Pontes Nogueira (2002).

10. For a typology of peace operations, see Boutros-Ghali (1992), Doyle (1998, 2001), Doyle and Sambanis (2000), and Pirnie and Simons (1996).

11. On peacebuilding operations and their multiple functions, see Demurenko and Nikitin (1997, 6).

12. For a broader discussion of defense reform, see Bruneau and Trinkunas (2008).

13. There are, of course, notable exceptions, including Agüero (1995), Bruneau and Trinkunas (2008), Desch (1999), Pevehouse (2002a), and Whitehead (1996).

14. One of the few studies available on unintended consequences in peacekeeping operations is Aoi, de Conic, and Thakur (2007).

15. Two projects that have recently focused on institutional variation include Acharaya and Johnston (2007) and Koremenos, Lipson, and Snidal (2001).

CHAPTER 1: Why Do Democratizing States Participate in Peacekeeping?

1. For a review of this literature, see Andersson (2002), Bobrow and Boyer (1997), Daniel and Caraher (2006), Neack (1995), and Regan (1998).

2. See Findlay (1996, 1).

3. For a discussion on international diffusion, contagion, and the demonstration effects of democratization, see Whitehead (1996).

4. For an analysis of the larger context of possible motivations and rationales for participation in peace operations, see Bellamy and Williams (2013).

5. For a discussion on how international institutions help shape collective identities, see Risse-Kappen (1996, 357–99).

6. This falls within the second image reversed framework, which analyzes how international factors—military intervention, international economic trends, and the anarchic nature of the international system—affect domestic political outcomes. See Gourevitch (1978).

7. The concept of national security doctrine has often been used interchangeably with that of policing, which refers to the common domestic or internal roles performed by the armed forces in developing and authoritarian countries. For the purposes of this book, however, the two terms are considered separately, as they refer to different types of roles under different types of regimes. A national security doctrine, as developed by Rouquié (1978) and Stepan (1971), refers to a much broader military interest in domestic affairs, which covers not only policing but also social and economic dynamics; that is, preventing labor unions from mobilizing or impeding students and peasants from politically demonstrating by directly intervening in national development projects. By contrast, policing roles refers more narrowly to the adoption and use of military models, methods, concepts, doctrines, procedures, and personnel in police activities and thus giving a military character to public safety questions (i.e., drug trafficking or law enforcement). National security doctrines bourgeoned in South America's authoritarian regimes; policing roles by contrast can prevail among democratic and democratizing states. On the military's policing roles, see Sotomayor (2013) and Zavarucha (2000).

8. Marcella (1994) also makes this argument.

9. Data on peacekeeping expenditures were obtained from interviews at the Department for Peacekeeping Operations, United Nations, New York, September 15, 2010.

10. Budgetary cuts may vary depending on the type of transition to democracy experienced by every state. See, for instance, Acuña and Smith (1994).

11. For an insightful analysis of military contestation, see Jaskoski (2012).

12. For a discussion on peacekeeping monetary incentives, see Norden (1995) and Palá (1998).


CHAPTER 2: What Is the Evidence from South America?

1. See UN Security Council, Resolution 661, "The Situation between Iraq and Kuwait," August 6, 1990; Resolution 665, "Iraq-Kuwait," August 25, 1990; Resolution 669, "Iraq-Kuwait," September 24, 1990; Resolution 670, "Iraq-Kuwait," September 25, 1990.

2. On Argentina's extensive role in peacekeeping between 1992 and 1996, see Etchegaray (2001), Lagorio (1998), Norden (1995), and Palá (1998).

3. Author interview with Andrés Fontana, former foreign policy advisor to Minister Guido di Tello and current director of graduate studies, Belgrano University, Buenos Aires, February 12, 2002.

4. The expression "carnal relations with Washington" was coined by Guido di Tella, minister of foreign affairs of Argentina from 1991 to 1999. See Gerschenson (2001).

5. For a thorough description of Argentina's defense reform after 1988, see Acuña and Smith (1994, 199–240), Agüero (1992, 160–61), Norden (1996b), and Pion-Berlin (2001, 154–55).

6. On the Argentine-Brazilian rapprochement, see Carasales (1997); Escudé and Fontana (1998, 51–70); Redick, Carsales, and Wrobel (1995); Resende-Santos (2002); and Sotomayor (2004, 29–60).

7. On military trials in Argentina, see Norden (1996a), Sancinetti (1988), and Stepan (1988b, 317–43).

8. Polls designed by Edgardo Catterberg show that 37% of Argentines believed that Alfonsín did a good job in improving civil-military relations; 21% said he had done a fair job, 21% voiced dissatisfaction, and 12% expressed no opinion on his role in this area. The data are replicated in Linz and Stepan (1996, 194). See also Zagorski (1994, 426).

9. On military insubordination in Argentina, see Fraga (1991), López (1988), Norden (1996a, 151–53), and Pion-Berlin and López (1992, 84–85).

10. For data on defense budget reduction in Argentina, see Fraga (1988), Gargiulo (1988, 109), Hunter (1999), International Institute for Strategic Studies (1998–2001), Moneta and López (1985), and Pion-Berlin (1997).

11. Data on salaries were obtained from Palá (1998, 138) and from author interviews with government officials at the Peacekeeping Department, Joint Chief of Staff, Ministry of Defense, Buenos Aires, February 23, 2002.

12. Data on peacekeeping expenditures were obtained from interviews with senior diplomats who requested anonymity, Palacio de San Martín, Ministry of Foreign Affairs, Buenos Aires, February 19, 2002, and with Colonel Alfredo Berner, peacekeeping director, Joint Chief of Staff, Ministry of Defense, Buenos Aires, February 23, 2002.

13. On Argentina's debt with the UN, see EFE (2003).

14. See Llenderrozas (2006) and Micha (2005, 109–29). For an analysis of congressional debates in Argentina regarding peacekeeping deployments, see Follietti (2005).

15. Author phone interview with Rut Diamint, defense policy expert and former defense advisor to José Pampuro, Argentine Ministry of Defense, September 14, 2008.

16. For a historical review of Brazil's UN peacekeeping participation, see Campos Tarrisse da Fontoura (1999) and Sena Cardoso (1998).

17. For an analysis of Brazil's relative isolation from the UN systems, see Ubiraci (2000, 91).

18. On OAS peacekeeping missions, see Fortna (1993). On Brazil's role in OAS peace missions, see Sena Cardoso (1998, 36).

19. On Brazil's transition to democracy, see Hunter (1997) and Stepan (1988a).

20. There is an abundant literature on Brazil's aspiration to permanently join the UN Security Council. See, for instance, Amorim (1995), Arraes (2005), Pereira and Filho (1998), Sussumu Fujita (1996), and Vargas Garcia (1994).

21. On Brazil's position vis-à-vis peace enforcement missions, see Herz and Wrobel (2002, 255–318) and Taylor (1997, 1–32).

22. For an analysis of Collor de Mello's and Cardoso's foreign policy, see Cruz, Cavalcante and Pedone (1993) and Lampreira (1998, 5–17).

23. On Brazil's view of regionalism, see Soares de Lima (1996, 2000).

24. On the role of budget and defense expenditure cuts, see Hunter (1994, 1997).

25. For an analysis of the National Defense Plan, see Rizzo de Oliveira (1998).

26. See Weiner and Polgree (2004). For a general overview of the peacekeeping mission in Haiti, see Kretchik (2007, 8–34).

27. There is an abundance of literature on Brazil's role in MINUSTAH. See, for instance, Chagas Vianna Braga (2010), Diniz (2005), Leone Pepe and Mathias (2005), Marconedes de Souza Neto (2009, 2010), and Seitenfus (2008).

28. See *Economist* (2009a). For a conceptual discussion of Brazil as an emerging power in peacekeeping, see Kenkel (2010b).

29. See, for example, Costa Vaz (2004), Hristoulas and Herz (2005), and Lampreira (1995).

30. On Brazil's domestic debate regarding peacekeeping, see Vassoler-Froelich (2007, 5–9).

31. On the legacies of the Uruguayan dictatorship and human rights violations, see Barahona de Brito (1997, 38–66), Caetano and Rilla (1987), Gillespie (1991, 50–76), Perelli (1990, 39–54), and Stepan (1988b, 325).

32. On the transition to democracy in Uruguay, see Gillespie (1991, 128–238) and González (1993, 88–128).

33. It is worth noting that the country experienced bloody urban guerrilla and counterinsurgency warfare in the 1960s and 70s. The Tupamaros, a radical Uruguayan guerrilla movement, ceased to be a threat to the country in large part because the army relied on mass arrests, torture, and large cordon-and-search operations. See López Chirico (1985) and Rial (1986).

34. On the legacies of the transition to democracy in Uruguay, see Perelli (1990, 39–54).

35. Author interview with Dr. Mariano Brito Checchi, rector of the Universidad de Montevideo and former minister of defense between 1990 and 1993, Montevideo, August 27, 2003.

36. On Venezuela's failed attempt to participate in UN peace missions and the attempted coup organized by Hugo Chávez, see Romero (1998, 151–66).

37. Author interview with Ambassador Pablo Sader, general director for political affairs and former deputy ambassador to the UN in 1991–93, Ministry of Foreign Affairs, Montevideo, August 18, 2003.

38. Author interviews with former peacekeepers conducted at the army's General Staff Office and at the navy's Peacekeeping Operations Directorate, Montevideo, August 5 and 20, 2003.

39. Author interview with Dr. Mariano Brito Checchi, August 27, 2003.

40. Author interview with Colonel Raúl Gloodtdofsky, military attaché at the Permanent Mission of Uruguay to the United Nations, New York, July 3, 2003. Author interview with Colonel Álvaro Picabea, director of peacekeeping operations, School of Peacekeeping Operations, General Staff Office, Uruguayan Army, Montevideo, August 5, 2003.

41. According to the data available from UNDPKO (2010a), Brazil, Uruguay, Nepal, Argentina, Jordan, and Chile are the largest troop-lending countries in MINUSTAH.

42. On policy diffusion, see Simmons and Elkins (2003).

43. On the Argentine-Uruguay paper mills dispute, see *Economist* (2007a).

44. Author interview with Colonel Álvaro Picabea, August 5, 2003.

CHAPTER 3: Does Peacekeeping Reform Military Organizations?

1. I follow the theoretical insights of Pion-Berlin and Arceneaux (2000) and Posen (1984).

2. For critics of the literature on professionalism, see Cohen (2002), Feaver (2003), and Finer (1962).

3. Author interview with Major Carlos Solcín, head of the Education and Doctrine Department, CAECOPAZ, Campo de Mayo, Buenos Aires, February 18, 2002.

4. Author interview with Colonel Jorge López Parravicini, general director of CAECOPAZ, Buenos Aires, December 6, 2003.

5. For a discussion of Argentina's peacekeeping training doctrine, see Socín and Campos Dugone (1999).

6. On the Scandinavian peacekeeping doctrine, see Jakobsen (2003) and Leeds (2001).

7. Author interview with psychologist María Isabel Muzco, CAECOPAZ, Buenos Aires, February 18, 2002.

8. For a discussion of Argentina's peacekeeping strategy and its effects on military training and civil-military relations, see Lagorio (1998), Norden (1995), Palá (1998), and Worboys (2007).

9. On how old military tactics survived in postdemocratic Argentina, see Pairone (2004).

10. Author interview with a senior diplomat who requested anonymity, Ministry of Defense, Buenos Aires, February 20, 2002.

11. Author interview with Colonel Ricardo Etchegaray, deputy military advisor, Permanent Mission of Argentina to the United Nations, New York, December 5, 2001.

12. Author interview with Colonel Alfredo Berner, director of peacekeeping operations, joint chief of staff, Ministry of Defense, Buenos Aires, February 23, 2002.

13. Ibid.

14. Author interview with Dr. Rosendo Fraga, director of the Centro de Estudios Unión para la Nueva Mayoría, Buenos Aires, March 19, 2002.

15. Author interview with Elsa Llenderrozas, advisor to the secretary of military affairs, Ministry of Defense, Buenos Aires, February 19, 2003.

16. Visit to CAECOPAZ and author interview with Captain Fernando Barroso Visco, Department of Education, CAECOPAZ, Buenos Aires, July 23, 2009.

17. Author interview with Luciana Micha, Department of Peace Operations, Argentina's Defense Ministry, Buenos Aires, July 22, 2009.

18. On the role of the Advanced War School, see Miyamoto (1988) and Stepan (1973).

19. See, for instance, Carneiro (1996), Gomes de Sousa (1994), Mattos (1994), and Rego (1995).

20. Author interview with Colonel Wençeslão, director of the Department of Peacekeeping, Brazilian Army, Brasilia, April 29, 2002.

21. Author visit to the Department of Peacekeeping, Brazilian Army, Brasilia, April 29, 2002.

22. Author interview with Colonel Wençeslão, April 29, 2002.

23. Author interview with General Benedito Leonel, former head of the army's Joint Chief of Staff and former military adviser to the Brazilian permanent mission in the United Nations, Brasilia, May 1, 2002.

24. On how the transition to democracy failed to reform the military, see de Rizzo de Oliveira (1994) and Zavarucha (1998).

25. Author interview with Luis A. Bitencourt, director of the Brazil Project, Woodrow Wilson International Center for Scholars, Washington, DC, December 12, 2001.

26. Author interview with Professor Celso Castro, Universidade Gétulo Vargas, Rio de Janeiro, Brazil, May 5, 2002. See also Guedes da Costa (2001).

27. For a discussion of civil-military relations in Brazil during the posttransition period, see Hunter (1997), Martins Filho (2000), Martins Filho and Zirker (2000), and Rizzo de Oliveira and Alves Soares (2000).

28. For an analysis of military resistance to the Ministry of Defense, see Castro and D'Araujo (2001) and Zavarucha (2006).

29. Author interview with an instructor of the Corpo de Fuzileiros Navais who requested anonymity, Centro de Instrução Almirante Sylvio de Camargo, Ilha do Governador, Rio de Janeiro, Brazil, June 12, 2009.

30. A portion of this book was published by Brazil's leading newspaper, *Folha de São Paulo* (2010a).

31. Personal translation.

32. Exercise conducted during the First Seminar on Peace Operations Pro-Defesa, organized at the Escola de Operaçôes de Paz, Ilha do Governador, Rio de Janeiro, Brazil, November 16–17, 2009.

33. For a brief description of Brazil's pacification strategy, see Isacson (2011).

34. See also Soares and Kraul (2010).

35. Author interview with Colonel Roberto Urrutice, subdirector of the School of Peacekeeping Operations at the School of the Arms and Services, Uruguayan Army, Montevideo, August 8, 2003.

36. See www.ejercito.mil.uy/conozca.htm.

37. For Uruguay's force strength and commitment to peacekeeping, see González (2010, 284–91).

38. Author interview with General Hebert F. Figoli, general director of the Center of High National Studies, Montevideo, August 11, 2003.

39. Author interview with Colonel Raúl Gloodtdofsky, military attaché to Uruguay's permanent mission to the United Nations, New York, July 3, 2003; author interview with Ambassador Pablo Sader, general director for political affairs and former deputy ambassador to the United Nations in 1991–93, Uruguayan Ministry of Foreign Affairs, Montevideo, August 18, 2003. See also Ulery (2005, 39).

40. See Jane's Sentinel Security Assessment–South America (2003) and U.S. Arms Control and Disarmament Agency (2000).

41. Author interview with Colonel Álvaro Picabea, director of peacekeeping operations, School of Peacekeeping Operations, General Staff Office, Uruguayan Army, Montevideo, August 5, 2003.

42. Author visit to Major Juan Sosa Machado Peacekeeping Operations School in the army's School of Arms and Services, Camino Maldonado, Montevideo, August 8, 2003. I am grateful to the directing staff for providing me access.

43. Author interview with Colonel Pablo Pintos, director of the Peacekeeping Operations School, Camino Maldonado, Montevideo, August 8, 2003.

44. Author interview with a former Uruguayan civil servant at a UN peacekeeping operation who requested anonymity, Montevideo, August 22, 2003.

45. Uruguay has a very low rate of mortality in UN peacekeeping. In total, fourteen officers have died in different peace operations, about 0.08% of all peacekeepers.

46. For a critical view of Uruguay's peacekeeping participation, see López Chirico (1999, 276–79).

47. Author interview with a government official at the Office of International Human Rights at the Ministry of Foreign Affairs and former civil servant at a UN peacekeeping operation who requested anonymity, Montevideo, August 22, 2003.

48. On peacekeeping accountability, see Hampson and Kihara-Hunt (2007) and Kent (2007).

49. On the National Defense Act in Uruguay, see González (2010, 293).

50. Pion-Berlin and Arceneaux (2000: 428–34) reached a similar conclusion in their study of military missions and civilian control in South America.

51. This is consistent with the argument that service rivalries strengthen civilian control as they enable civilian leaders to exploit internal cleavages and rivalries between the forces as a means of eroding military influence. See Betts (1991), Feaver (2003), Huntington (1961), and Trinkunas (2005).

CHAPTER 4: How Does Peacekeeping Socialize the
Military in South America?

1. On why young officers tend to be more outspoken, see Bumiller (2007).

2. UN Security Council, Resolution 619, "Iraq-Islamic Republic of Iran," August 9, 1988.

3. UN Security Council, Resolution 693, "El Salvador," May 20, 1991; Resolution 797, "Mozambique," December 16, 1992.

4. Author interview with a former blue helmet who participated in Mozambique, Argentine Army, Buenos Aires, February 27, 2003.

5. See UN Security Council, Resolution 713, "Operation Joint Endeavor," September 25, 1991.

6. UN Security Council, Resolution 687, "Iraq-Kuwait," April 3, 1991; Resolution 688, "Iraq," April 5, 1991.

7. On the background conditions of UNIKOM, see UNDPKO (2003).

8. On the background conditions of UNMIH, see UNDPKO (2012a, 2012b).

9. Author interview with a former Argentine peacekeeper deployed to UNIKOM, Argentine Air Force, Buenos Aires, March 12, 2002.

10. Author interview with an air force officer, Argentine Air Force, Buenos Aires, February 27, 2002.

11. Author interview with a former participant in UNPROFOR, Argentine Army, Buenos Aires, February 17, 2002.

12. Author interview with Lieutenant Colonel Carlos Pérez Aquino, Argentine Army, Buenos Aires, February 27, 2003.

13. Ibid.

14. Personal translation.

15. Author interview, CAECOPAZ, Buenos Aires, February 18, 2002.

16. Author interview, Joint Chief of Staff, Ministry of Defense, Buenos Aires, February 23, 2002.

17. Author interview, Department of Peacekeeping Operations in Development, Argentine Joint Chief of Staff, Ministry of Defense, Buenos Aires, February 23, 2002.

18. Corporatism, expertise, and a sense of responsibility are the key components of military professionalism (Huntington 1957, 7–18).

19. Author interview, Military Institute of Engineering, Rio de Janeiro, Brazil, May 15, 2002.

20. Personal translation.

21. Author interview with army officers, Brazilian Army, Brasilia, April 29, 2002.

22. Ibid.

23. Ibid.; interviews with navy officers, Brazilian Navy, Rio de Janeiro, Brazil, May 13, 2002.

24. Author interview, Brazilian Army, Brasilia, April 30, 2002.

25. Author interview, Brazilian Navy, Rio de Janeiro, Brazil, May 13, 2002.

26. A large number of soldiers have participated in the multinational force operation in Sinai, which is not under the UN mandate, although it is often classified as an observational operation.

27. Personal translation. For more accounts of Uruguayan soldiers in UNMOGIP, see De León (1996).

28. Author interview with General Hebert F. Figoli, general director of Centro de Altos Estudios Nacionales, Montevideo, August 11, 2003.

29. Author interview with retired Lieutenant Colonel Denis P. Lacassy, former peacekeeper in Mozambique, Montevideo, August 21, 2003.

30. Author interview with Colonel Roberto Urrutice, subdirector of the School of Peacekeeping Operations at the School of the Arms and Services, Uruguayan Army, Montevideo, August 8, 2003.

31. Most analysts of peacebuilding missions consider Mozambique a success; see, for instance, Howard (2008, 179–224) and Jett (1999, 61–73).

32. Until 2003, Uruguayan peacekeepers experienced a low rate of mortality in UN peacekeeping operations. In total, thirteen officers died in different peace operations. See Comando General del Ejército (2003).

33. Author interview, School of Peacekeeping Operations at the School of the Arms and Services, Uruguayan Army, Montevideo, August 8, 2003.

34. For a vivid description of the chaos in the Democratic Republic of Congo, see Maharaj and Masciarelli (2003, 3).

35. Personal translation.

36. Author interview with General Figoli, August 11, 2003.

37. Author interview with Colonel Álvaro Picabea, director of peacekeeping operations, School of Peacekeeping Operations, General Staff Office, Uruguayan Army, Montevideo, August 5, 2003.

38. Author interview with Colonel Arquímedes Cabrera, former force commander in Cambodia and Congo, CALEN, Montevideo, August 11, 2003.

39. Personal translation.

40. For a critical analysis of civil-military relations in peacekeeping operations, see Williams (1998, 1–93).

41. On the issue of how trust affects civil-military operations, see Egnell (2009).

CHAPTER 5: How Does Peacekeeping Socialize the Military in Haiti?

1. For the mandate of the mission, see UN Security Council, Resolution 1542, "Haiti," April 30, 2004.

2. For a general overview of the peacekeeping mission in Haiti, see Heine and Thompson (2011) and Kretchik (2007, 8–34).

3. For the mandate of the mission, see UN Security Council, Resolution 1529, "Haiti," February 29, 2004.

4. For detailed information on the evolution of the mission, see UN Security Council, Report 302, "Report of the Security Council Mission to Haiti," May 6, 2005; Report 175, "Report of the Security Council Mission to Haiti," April 3, 2009.

5. MINUSTAH had to adjust its mandate to accommodate for the new humanitarian crisis. The number of troops increased from six thousand to 8,940 soldiers; see UN Security Council, Resolution 1908, "Haiti," January 19, 2010.

6. For an analysis of the possible causes of the cholera outbreak in Haiti, see Piarroux et al. (2011). For a critical review of the UN response to the cholera crisis, see *New York Times* (2011). For the UN's official position on the cholera crisis, see UNDPKO (2010d).

7. For data on Argentina's peacekeeping commitment in 2010, see UNDPKO (2010c).

8. Author interview, Argentine Mission to the UN, New York, September 14, 2010.

9. Author interview, Ezeiza International Airport, Buenos Aires, July 21, 2009.

10. Author interview, Luciana Micha, director, Department of Peacekeeping Operations, Ministry of Defense, Buenos Aires, July 22, 2009.

11. According to a 2009 report, "the 2008 hurricanes contributed to damages worth 15% of Haiti's gross domestic product (GDP) at a time when the Government is facing a 47% decline in budget support." See *Environment News Service* 2009; UN Security Council, Report 175, April 3, 2009.

12. Author interview, Argentine Mission to the UN, New York, September 14, 2010.

13. Author interview, Argentine Aviation Unit, Delta Camp, Port-au-Prince, September 22, 2010.

14. Ibid.

15. Ibid.

16. Ibid.

17. Data on Brazil's peacekeeping commitment were obtained from UNDPKO (2010c).

18. Author interview, Logistics Department, Ministry of Defense, Brasilia, June 18, 2009.

19. Author interview with military assistant to MINUSTAH force commander, Camp Delta, MINUSTAH, Port-au-Prince, September 21, 2010.

20. Author interview with Brazilian blue helmet, BRABATT I, Brazil's MINUSTAH headquarters, Port-au-Prince, September 24, 2010.

21. Author visit to BRABATT I, Brazil's MINUSTAH headquarters, Port-au-Prince, September 24, 2010.

22. Official presentation offered during author visit to BRABATT I, Brazil's MINUSTAH headquarters, Port-au-Prince, September 24, 2010.

23. Author interview with a former member of the Brazilian contingent in MINUSTAH, Office of Military Affairs, UNDPKO, UN Headquarters, New York, September 13, 2010.

24. Author interview with UN official, UNDPKO, UN Headquarters, New York, September 15, 2010.

25. Author interview with UN official, UN Police Division, UN Headquarters, September 15, 2010.

26. Author interview UN official, Office for Political Affairs, UNDPKO, UN Headquarters, September 15, 2010.

27. For an analysis of the military's role in law enforcement missions in Brazil, see Zavarucha (2003).

28. UN Security Council, Report 175, April 3, 2009.

29. Author interview, Rio Branco Institute, Brasilia, June 17, 2009.

30. For an analysis of the Scandinavian approach to peacekeeping, see Jakobsen (2003).

31. Author interview, UNDPKO, UN Headquarters, New York, September 14, 2010.

32. For the UN mission's response to criticisms, see UN Security Council, Report 302, May 6, 2005; Report 175, April 3, 2009.

33. According to Human Rights Watch (2009), troops in Rio de Janeiro and São Paulo routinely resort to lethal force, often committing extrajudicial executions and exacerbating violence in both states.

34. Author interview with UN official, Office of Political Affairs, UNDPKO, UN Headquarters, New York, September 15, 2010.

35. Author interview with volunteer for Viva Rio, Rio de Janeiro, Brazil, June 11, 2009.

36. For a positive assessment of the partnership between Viva Rio and the military, see Chagas Vianna Braga (2010, 717–20) and Santos Cruz (2009).

37. Brazil and France complained when U.S. military aircraft were given priority at Port-au-Prince's airport, forcing many non-U.S. flights to divert to the Dominican Republic; see Carroll and Nasaw (2010).

38. For a journalistic report of this IDP camp, see Heller (2011).

39. Author interview with NGO staff, Pétionville camp, Port-au-Prince, September 23, 2010.

40. Author interview with NGO staff, Ancien Aéroport Militaire camp, Port-au-Prince, September 23, 2010.

41. Author visit to Tabarre Issa camp, Port-au-Prince, September 23, 2010.

42. Author interview with staff member, U-9 CIMIC Field Cell, Camp Delta, Port-au-Prince, September 22. 2010.

43. Official visit to BRABATT I and Cité Soleil, Port-au-Prince, September 24, 2010.

44. For the total size of the force by service, see Resdal (2010, 289).

45. According to organic law of the armed forces No. 14.157-05/03/1974, which was modified in 1986 after the democratization process, "the armed forces are fundamentally engaged in defending the honor, independence and peace of the republic, its territorial integrity, its constitution and its laws, and must always act under the supreme command of the president of the republic, in agreement with the minister respectively, in accordance with the provisions of Article 168, paragraph 2, of the constitution" (personal translation).

46. Personal translation.

47. Personal translation.

48. For an analysis of UN maritime peacekeeping operations, see Pugh (1994).

49. For a detailed recount of events, see Amy Goodman's *Democracy Now* interview with Ansel Herz, an independent journalist in Haiti (in Goodman 2011).

50. For an analysis of sexual abuse cases in previous UN missions, see Cain, Postlewait, and Thomson (2004) and Fleshman (2005).

## CHAPTER 6: Does Peacekeeping Help Integrate Defense and Foreign Policy?

1. For arguments on integration and segregation, see Sotomayor (2010a).

2. On defense policy communities, see Zisk (1993, 21–22).

3. This is consistent with Peter Feaver's argument about agency and accountability; see Feaver (2003, 54–95).

4. For an analysis of Argentina's strategic interests in requesting NATO membership, see Escudé and Fontana (1998).

5. For an analysis of Argentina's foreign policy during the posttransition to democracy, see Diamint (1995), Norden (1996b), Norden and Russell (2002), and Tulchin (1988).

6. Author interview, Buenos Aires, March 12, 2002.

7. Author interview with Dr. Pedro Gillone, diplomat and member of the Instituto del Servicio Exterior de la Nación, Buenos Aires, February 27, 2002.

8. Author interviews with Minister Guillermo Lucotti, director of peacekeeping operations, Ministry of Foreign Affairs, Buenos Aires, March 4, 2002, and Dr. Pedro Gillone, diplomat, Instituto del Servicio Exterior Nacional, Buenos Aires, February 27, 2002.

9. Author interview, Permanent Mission of Argentina to the United Nations, New York, December 17, 2001.

10. Author interview with Minister Guillermo Lucotti, March 4, 2002.

11. Author interview, navy chief of staff, Buenos Aires, February 20, 2002.

12. Author interview with Federico Merke, member of the Consejo Argentino para las Relaciones Internacionales, Buenos Aires, February 15, 2002.

13. Author interviews with Carlos Escudé, scholar and former foreign policy advisor to Minister Guido de Tella, Buenos Aires, January 29, 2002, and Andrés Fontana, director of graduate studies, former foreign policy advisor to the presidency, Universidad de Belgrano, Buenos Aires, February 12, 2002.

14. A representative sample of this literature includes: Arredondo (2001), Cárdenas (1993), Comité Nacional de la República Argentina (1995), Diamint (1992, 1995), Fontana (1993, 1994, 1998, 2001), Fraga (1991, 1996a, 1996b, 1999, 2000, 2001), Grossi (1999, 2000), Lavopa and Hekimián (1993), Moritán (1993), Saín (1999), and Zawels (1998, 1999).

15. I was able to retrieve at least three articles by civilian experts published in military journals, including Cárdenas (1999), Castro (1994), and Fraga (1994).

16. Author interview with Marcelo Saín, military analyst and security expert, Buenos Aires, July 21, 2009.

17. For two opposing perspectives on Argentina's role in MINUSTAH, see Tibiletti (2004) and Tokatlian (2004).

18. A sample of books published on peacekeeping and peacebuilding in Argentina include Hirst (2009) and Serbin (2007).

19. Author interview, Ministry of Foreign Affairs, Buenos Aires, July 24, 2009.

20. I wish to thank Marcelo Saín, Elsa Llenderozas, and Marcela Donadio for sharing their insights and ideas on the institutionalization of defense policy in Argentina. The ideas developed here came as a result of numerous conversations during a field trip to Buenos Aires, July 20–22, 2009.

21. Author interview, Buenos Aires, July 22, 2009.

22. Author interview, Ministry of Foreign Affairs, Buenos Aires, July 24, 2009.

23. Author interview with a member of the Argentine foreign service who requested anonymity, Buenos Aires, July 24, 2009.

24. Author interview, São Paulo, Brazil, April 18, 2002.

25. Author interview with Santiago Irazabal Mourão, counselor at the Brazilian Permanent Mission to the United Nations, New York, December 11, 2001.

26. Author interview, Department of International Relations and Nucleus of Strategic Studies, University of Campinas, Campinas, Brazil, April 15, 2002.

27. Author interview, São Paulo, Brazil, April 18, 2002.

28. I wish to thank Professor Mônica Herz for granting me access to the Documentation Center in the Institute of International Relations at the Pontifical Catholic University of Rio de Janeiro, which compiled data on publications. The literature on peacekeeping issues published in Brazil during this period include Araujo (1995, 1996), Brigagão (1999), Campos Tarrisse da Fontoura (1999), Cannabrava (1996), Guedes da Costa (1998b), Herz and Pontes Nogueira (2002), Proença (2002), and Sena Cardoso (1998).

29. Author interview, Strategic Studies Center, Campinas University, Campinas, Brazil, April 15, 2002.

30. Author interview, Department of International Relations, Pontifical University of Rio de Janeiro, Rio de Janeiro, Brazil, April 22, 2002.

31. Author interview with a member of the Brazilian foreign service who requested anonymity, Itamaraty, Brasilia, June 16, 2009.

32. On the political management of the military in Latin America, including Brazil, see Pion-Berlin (2005).

33. On the origins and development of military and geopolitical thinking in Brazil, see Child (1985, 34–41) and Resende-Santos (2007, 240–95).

34. Author interview, University of Brasilia, Brasilia, June 17, 2009.

35. Twentieth Extraordinary Senate Hearing, Foreign Affairs and Defense Commission, 53th. Congress, Brasilia, June 17, 2009 (personal translation).

36. I thank Professors Jorge Ramalho and Kai Michael Kenkel for exposing me to the varying and diverse positions held by different military and diplomatic actors in Brazil through the seminar they organized with the Escola de Operações de Paz, Seminar on Peace Operations Pro-Defesa, Ilha do Governador, Rio de Janeiro, Brazil, November 16–17, 2009. The views presented here are those of the author and do not represent positions held by either Ramalho or Kenkel.

37. Author visit to the Logistics Department, Ministry of Defense, Brasilia, June 18, 2009.

38. A representative sample of this literature includes Almeida Pinto, Ramalho da Rocha, and Pinho da Silva (2004), Breda dos Santos (2002), Brigagão and Proença (2004, 2006), Cavalcante (2010), Cruz Aguilar (2005), Diniz (2006), Jaguaribe (2005), Marconedes de Souza Neto (2009), Penna Filho (2004), Soares Alsina (2009), and Souza (2009). I thank Danilo Marcondes de Souza Neto for his assistance in collecting this literature.

39. For instance, Viva Rio convened an international workshop on Revisiting Borders between Civilians and Military: Security and Development in Post-Conflict Situations in United Nations Peace Operations, Rio de Janeiro, Brazil, August 3, 2009.

40. Author interview with Uruguayan Ministry of Foreign Affairs, Montevideo, August 18, 2003.

41. Author interview with military staff at the Permanent Mission of Uruguay to the United Nations, New York, July 3, 2003.

42. Pion-Berlin (1997) found that 91.4% of all employees in the ministry were military, 7.8% were retired officers, and only 0.8% were civilians. With regard to leadership positions (advisors and head of departments), 85.5% were military, 11.3% were retired officers, and only 3.2% were civilians. See Pion-Berlin (1997, 184).

43. Author interview, Permanent Mission of Uruguay to the United Nations, New York, June 17, 2003.

44. Author interview with a Uruguayan diplomat who requested anonymity, Ministry of Foreign Affairs, Montevideo, August 22, 2003 (personal translation).

45. Author interview, Uruguay's House of Deputies, Montevideo, August 21, 2003.

46. Author interview, School of Peacekeeping Operations, School of the Arms and Services, Uruguayan Army, Montevideo, August 8, 2003.

47. I thank Professor Julián González, director of the observatory, for granting me access to its weekly bulletin. For access to the observatory's blog, see http://www.observadefensa.blogspot.com/.

48. Pion-Berlin (1997, 186) reported the same finding.

### CONCLUSION: Theory and Policy Implications of the UN Peacekeeping System's Divergent Effects

1. Shirking is a deviant form of behavior in civil-military relations that is defined as "when the military, whether through laziness, insolence, or preventable incompetence, does not do what the civilian has requested, or not in the way the civilians wanted, or in such a way as to undermine the ability of the civilian to make future decisions" (Feaver 1998, 409–10).

2. Bellamy and Williams (2013) offer multiple case studies to explore the relationship between motivation for participation in UN peace operations and domestic variables, including civil-military relations.

# Bibliography


Abraszewski, Andrzej T., Richard V. Hennes, Boris P. Krasulin, and Khalil Issa Othman. 1995. *Military Component of United Nations Peacekeeping Operations.* Geneva: United Nations. http://www.docstoc.com/docs/29564926/MILITARY-COMPO-NENT-OF-UNITED-NATIONS-PEACE-KEEPING-OPERATIONS.

Acharaya, Amitav, and Alastair Iain Johnston, eds. 2007. *Crafting Cooperation: Regional International Institutions in Comparative Perspective.* New York: Oxford University Press.

Acuña, Carlos H., and William C. Smith. 1994. "The Politics of Arms Production and the Arms Race among the New Democracies of Argentina, Brazil, and Chile." In *Security, Democracy, and Development in U.S.–Latin American Relations,* ed. Lars Schoultz, William C. Smith, and Augusto Vargas, 199–236. Miami, FL: North-South Center Press.

Agence France Presse. 2010. "Fears of Gang Wars Grow after Haiti Quake." *Taipei Times,* February 17. http://www.taipeitimes.com/News/world/archives/2010/02/17/2003466057.

Agüero, Felipe. 1992. "The Military and the Limits of Democratization in South America." In *Issues in Democratic Consolidation: The New South American Democracies in Comparative Perspective,* ed. Scott Mainwaring, Guillermo O'Donnell, and J. Samuel Valenzuela, 153–98. South Bend, IN: University of Notre Dame Press.

———. 1995. *Soldiers, Civilians, and Democracy: Post-Franco Spain in Comparative Perspective.* Baltimore: Johns Hopkins University Press.

Aguilar, Sérgio Luis. 2002. "As forças de paz do Brasil: Balanço." In *Brasil e o Mundo: Novas Visôes,* ed. Clóvis Brigagâo and Domício Proença Júnior, 363–446. Rio de Janeiro: Francisco Alves and Konrad Adenauer Stiftung.

Ahmed, Salman, Paul Keating, and Ugo Salinas. 2007. "Shaping the Future of UN Peace Operations: Is There a Doctrine in the House?" *Cambridge Review of International Affairs* 20 (1): 1–28.

Albuquerque Lima, Gisele Lennon de e Figueiredo Lins. 2007. "A (des)articulação entre o Ministério da Defesa e o Ministério das Relações Exteriores na MINUS-TAH." MA diss., Political Science Department, Federal University of Pernambuco, Recife, Brazil.

Almeida Pinto, J. R. de, A. J. Ramalho da Rocha, and R. Doring Pinho da Silva, eds. 2004. *Reflexões sobre defesa e segurança: Uma estrategia para o Brasil.* Brasilia: Ministry of Defense.

Amorim, Celso. 1995. "O Brasil e o Conselho de Segurança das Nações Unidas." *Política Externa* 3 (4): 3–15.

Andersson, Andreas. 2002. "Commitment to UN Interventions." *Cooperation and Conflict: Journal of the Nordic International Studies Association* 37 (4): 363–86.

Angelero, Coronel Carlos O. 2008. "Origen de las plantas potabilizadoras compactas y transportable." *Revista El Soldado* (November 2008). www.ingenierosmilitares.org .uy/cronicas/Cronica21.htm.

Aoi, Chiyuki, Cedric de Coninc, and Ramesh Thakur, eds. 2007. *Unintended Consequences of Peacekeeping Operations.* New York: United Nations University Press.

Araujo, Braz. 1995. *Estratégia no Novo Cenário Mundial: Anais do I Encontro Nacional de Estudos Estratégicos.* São Paulo, Brazil: Núcleo de Análise Interdisciplinar de Políticas e Estratégias da Universidade de São Paulo.

———. 1996. *Estratégia No Novo Cenário Mundial: Anais do II Encontro Nacional de Estudos Estratégicos.* São Paulo, Brazil: Núcleo de Análise Interdisciplinar de Políticas e Estratégias da Universidade de São Paulo.

Armada Nacional de la República de Uruguay. 2011a. "La Armada Nacional y las Misiones de Paz." Montevideo. http://www.armada.mil.uy/armada-misiones-de -paz.html.

———. 2011b. "La Armada Nacional y su participación en el Contingente Naval de Haití." Montevideo. http://www.armada.mil.uy/comar/repar/Noticias/contingente _haiti/contingente_haiti.html.

Armendáriz, Alberto. 2011. "Brasil: El Ejército como 'Pacificador.'" *Reforma*, July 18. www.reforma.com/enfoque/articulo/616/1230709.

Arraes, Virgílio Caixeta. 2005. "O Brasil e o Conselho de Segurança das Nações Unidas: Dos anos 90 a 2002." *Revista Brasileira de Política Internacional* 48 (2): 152–68.

Arredondo, Ricardo. 2001. "Intervención humanitaria: El uso de la fuerza como mecanismo de protección a los derechos humanos. Lineamientos para una posición Argentina." *Documentos de Trabajo del Instituto del Servicio Exterior de la Nación.* Buenos Aires: Ministerio de Relaciones Exteriores, Comercio Internacional y Culto de la República Argentina.

Autesserre, Séverine. 2010. *The Trouble with the Congo: Local Violence and the Failure of International Peacebuilding.* New York: Cambridge University Press.

Avelar Giannini, Renata. 2011. "In the Crossroads: Haiti, MINUSTAH, and the International Community." Final Report Field Work in Haiti. Resdal, Buenos Aires.

Avery, Thomas. 2010. "Missed Opportunities in Haiti: A Peacekeeping Mission Sparks Protest." *Human Rights Brief*, November 16. http://hrbrief.org/2010/11/missed -opportunities-in-haiti-a-peacekeeping-mission-sparks-protest/.

Balza, Martín Antonio. 1994. "El Ejército Argentino y las misiones de paz." *Revista del suboficial* 75 (611): 6–7.

Barahona de Brito, Alexandra. 1997. *Human Rights and Democratization in Latin America: Uruguay and Chile.* New York: Oxford University Press.

Barnes, Taylor. 2010. "Brazil Launches Peacekeeping Force in the *Favelas.*" *Miami Herald*, December 23. http://www.offnews.info/verArticulo.php?contenidoID=26790.

Barnett, Michael N. 1995. "Partners in Peace? The UN, Regional Organizations, and Peacekeeping." *Review of International Studies* 21 (4): 411–33.

Barringer, Felicity. 2003. "Security Council Votes to Dispatch Peacekeepers in Congo." *New York Times*, May 30. http://www.nytimes.com/2003/05/31/world/security-council -votes-to-dispatch-peacekeepers-to-the-congo.html.

Barrionuevo, Alexei. 2007. "Defense Minister Is Replaced as Brazil's Air Crisis Grows." *New York Times*, July 25. http://www.nytimes.com/2007/07/26/world/americas /26brazil.html?_r=0.

———. 2010. "After Operation, Rio's Forces Greeted by Wariness." *New York Times*, December 9. http://www.nytimes.com/2010/12/10/world/americas/10brazil.html? _r=1&ref=america.

BBC News. 2006a. "Haiti UN Mission Chief Found Dead." January 8. http://news.bbc .co.uk/2/hi/americas/4590700.stm.

———. 2006b. "Two UN Soldiers Killed in Haiti." January 18. http://news.bbc.co.uk /2/hi/americas/4622772.stm.

———. 2007a. "UN Troops Flood into Haiti Slum." February 11. http://www.bbc.co .uk/caribbean/news/story/2007/02/070211_unhaiti.shtml.

———. 2007b. "Sri Lanka Troops 'Abused Haitians.'" November 2. http://news.bbc. co.uk/2/hi/south_asia/7075866.stm.

———. 2010. "Haiti Protester Shot Dead by UN Peacekeepers." November 16. http:// www.bbc.co.uk/news/world-latin-america-11761941.

———. 2011a. "Haiti Quake Death Toll Rises to 230,000." February 11. http://news .bbc.co.uk/2/hi/8507531.stm.

———. 2011b. "Uruguayan Peacekeepers in Haiti Accused of Abuse." September 4. http://www.bbc.co.uk/news/world-latin-america-14783538.

Bearce, David H., and Stacy Bondanella. 2007. "Intergovernmental Organizations, Socialization, and Member-State Interest Convergence." *International Organization* 61 (3): 703–33.

Bellamy, Alex J., and Paul D. Williams, eds. 2013. *Providing Peacekeepers: The Politics, Challenges, and Future of United Nations Peacekeeping Contributions*. New York: Oxford University Press.

Besio, Félix. 2008. "The National Debate on Defense: Uruguay." In *A Comparative Atlas of Defense in Latin America*, 280–91. Buenos Aires: Resdal.

Betts, Richard K. 1991. *Soldiers, Statesmen, and Cold War Crises*. New York: Columbia University Press.

Bhatt, Keane, and Greg Grandin. 2011. "The Nation: Why The U.N. Troops Should Leave Haiti." *National Public Radio*, September 29. http://www.npr.org/2011/09/29 /140914125/the-nation-why-the-u-n-should-leave-haiti.

Biato, Marcel. 2011. "Brazil's Mission in Haiti." In *Fixing Haiti: MINUSTAH and Beyond*, ed. Jorge Heine and Andrew S. Thompson, 191–204. New York: United Nations University Press.

Bobrow, Davis, and Mark A. Boyer. 1997. "Maintaining System Stability: Contributions to Peacekeeping Operations." *Journal of Conflict Resolution* 41 (6): 723–48.

Borges, João Marcelo, and Renato Couto Gomes. 2004. "Notas Sobre as Missões de Paz da ONU." In *Panorama Brasileiro de Paz e Segurança*, ed. Clóvis Brigagão and Domício Proença Júnior, 303–28. Rio de Janeiro: Konrad Adenauer-Stiftung and Editora Hucitec.

Boutellis, Arthur. 2011. "Cholera, Haiti and MINUSTAH: What Implications for Peacekeeping?" International Peace Institute, January 11. http://www.ipacademy .org/news/comment-a-analysis/211-cholera-haiti-and-minustah-what-implications -for-peacekeeping.html.

Boutros-Ghali, Boutros. 1992. *An Agenda for Peace.* New York: United Nations.

Breda dos Santos, Norma. 2002. "A dimensão multilateral da política externa brasileira: Perfil da produção bibliográfica." *Revista Brasileira de Política Internacional* 45 (2): 26–45.

Brigagão, Clóvis. 1999. "Prevenir, Manter e Construir à Paz: Novos Desafios à Segurança Internacional." In *O Brasil e as Novas Dimensões da Segurança Internacional,* ed. Gilberto Dupas and Tullo Vigevani, 117–29. São Paulo, Brazil: Editora Alfa-Omega and FAPESP.

Brigagão, Clóvis, and Domício Proença, eds. 2004. *Panorama Brasileiro de Paz e Segurança.* São Paulo, Brazil: Hucitec.

———. 2006. *O Brasil e os Novos Conflitos Internacionais.* Rio de Janeiro: Gramma.

Bruneau, Thomas, and Harold Trinkunas. 2008. "Global Trends and Their Impact on Civil-Military Relations." In *Global Politics of Defense Reform,* ed. Thomas Bruneau and Harold Trinkunas, 3–19. New York: Palgrave Macmillan.

Bumiller, Elisabeth. 2007. "At an Army School for Officers, Blunt Talk about Iraq." *New York Times,* October 14. http://www.nytimes.com/2007/10/14/us/14army.html ?pagewanted=all.

Cabrera, Arquímides. 1994a. *Operación Camboya: Batallón Uruguay, Primer Contingente.* Montevideo: Centro Militar.

———. 1994b. "Un Contacto en la Selva de Camboya." *El Soldado* 18 (138): 56–57.

Caetano, Gerardo, and José Rilla. 1987. *Breve Historia de la Dictadura.* Montevideo: Ediciones Banda Oriental.

Cain, Kenneth, Heidi Postlewait, and Andrew Thomson. 2004. *Emergency Sex and Other Desperate Measures: A True Story from Hell on Earth.* New York: Miramax.

Campos, Marcela. 2009. "No Senado, haitianos pedem que missão liderada pelo Brasil acabe." *Folha de São Paulo,* June 16. http://www1.folha.uol.com.br/folha/mundo /ult94u582350.shtml.

Campos Tarrisse da Fontoura, Paulo Roberto. 1999. *O Brasil e as Operações de Manutenção da Paz das Nações Unidas.* Brasilia: Instituto Rio Branco-Fundação Alexandre de Gusmão-Itamaraty, Ministry of Foreign Affairs.

Cannabrava, Ivan. 1996. "O Brasil e as operações de manutenção da paz." *Política Externa* 5 (3): 93–105.

Carasales, Julio César. 1997. *De Rivales a Socios: El proceso de cooperación nuclear entre Argentina y Brasil.* Buenos Aires: Grupo Editorial Latinoamericano.

Cárdenas, Emilio. 1993. "La Argentina y las Naciones Unidas." *COMUNITAS: Revista Argentina de las Relaciones Internacionales* 1 (4): 9–12.

———. 1999. "Las Naciones Unidas y los llamados 'conflictos internos.'" *Revista Militar* 748: 18–24.

CARI. Consejo Argentino para las Relaciones Internacionales. 1997. *Fuerzas para el Mantenimiento de la Paz.* Buenos Aires: CARI.

———. 1999. *Cuadernos de Lecciones Aprendidas: Las Fuerzas Armadas y de Seguridad argentinas en las Misiones de paz.* Buenos Aires: CARI.

Carneiro, Flávio. 1996. "O Brasil e as Operações de Paz em Angola-Experiências e Ensinamentos." Rio de Janeiro: Escola de Comando e Estado-Maior do Exercito.

Carneiro Alvárez, Verónica. 2001. "Uruguayan Navy in MINUSTAH, beyond the Scandal." *Milpages,* September 28. http://www.milpages.com/blog/5900.

Carroll, Rory, and Daniel Nasaw. 2010. "US Accused of Annexing Airport as Squabbling Hinders Aid Effort in Haiti." *Guardian*, January 17. http://www.guardian.co.uk/world/2010/jan/17/us-accused-aid-effort-haiti.

Cason, Jeffrey W., and Timothy Power. 2009. "Presidentialization, Pluralization, and the Rollback of Itamaraty: Explaining Change in Brazilian Foreign Policy Making in the Cardoso-Lula Era." *International Political Science Review* 30 (2): 117–40.

Castro, Celso, and Maria Celina D'Araujo, eds. 2001. *Militares e política na Nova República*. Rio de Janeiro: Fundação Getulio Vargas.

Castro, Jorge. 1994. "El Poder Militar: Un instrumento esencial de la política exterior." *Revista del suboficial* 75 (611): 48.

Cavalcante, Fernando. 2010. "Rendering Peacekeeping Instrumental? The Brazilian Approach to United Nations Peacekeeping during the Lula da Silva Years (2003–2010)." *Revista Brasileira de Política Internacional* 53 (2): 142–59.

Cavalieri, Marco Antonio. 1998. Moçambique: Uma Missão de Paz. *Revista do Exército Brasileiro* 135 (1): 27–36.

Center for Human Rights and Global Justice. 2011. "Sexual Violence in Haiti's IDP Camps: Results of a Household Survey." New York: New York University School of Law. http://ijdh.org/wordpress/wp-content/uploads/2011/03/CHRGJ-Haiti-Sexual-Violence-March-2011.pdf.

Chagas Vianna Braga, Carlos. 2010. "MINUSTAH and the Security Environment in Haiti: Brazil and South American Cooperation in the Field." *International Peacekeeping* 17 (5): 711–22.

Checkel, Jeffrey T, ed. 2005. "International Institutions and Socialization in Europe: Introduction and Framework." *International Organization* 59 (3): 801–26.

———. 2007. *International Institutions and Socialization in Europe*. New York: Cambridge University Press.

Child, Jack. 1985. *Geopolitics and Conflict in South America: Quarrels among Neighbors*. New York: Praeger.

———. 1995. "Guns and Roses." *Hemisphere* 6 (3): 1–4.

Cohen, Eliot A. 2002. *Supreme Command: Soldiers, Statesmen, and Leadership in Wartime*. New York: Free Press.

Comando General del Ejército. 2003. *Ejército Nacional: Desde 1811 al servicio de la patria, desde 1935 al servicio de la paz mundial*. Montevideo: Comando Nacional del Ejército.

Comité Nacional de la República Argentina. 1995. *Contribuciones Argentinas a las Naciones Unidas*. Buenos Aires: Ministerio de Relaciones Exteriores y Culto de la República de la Argentina.

Corn, Tony. 2009. "From War Managers to Soldier Diplomats: The Coming Revolution in Civil-Military Relations." *Small Wars Journal* 5 (6): 1–33.

Costa Vaz, Alcides. 2004. "Brazilian Foreign Policy under Lula: Change or Continuity?" Briefing Paper. Berlin: Friedrich Ebert Stiftung. www.fes.org.gt/documentos/Foreignpol-Brazil.PDF.

Cruz, Ademar Seabra de, Antonio Ricardo F. Cavalcante, and Luiz Pedone. 1993. "Brazil's Foreign Policy under Collor." *Journal of Interamerican Studies and World Affairs* 35 (1): 119–44.

Cruz Aguilar, Sérgio Luiz, ed. 2005. *Brasil em Missões de Paz*. São Paulo, Brazil: Usina do Livro.

Cunha Velloso, Ludovico. 2002. "Brazil and the United Nations Peacekeeping Operations in the 21st Century." MA diss., Marine Corps University, Quantico, VA.

Daniel, D. C. F., and Leigh C. Caraher. 2006. "Characteristics of Troop Contributors to Peace Operations and Implications for Global Capacity." *International Peacekeeping* 13 (3): 297–315.

Danziato Rego, Fernando. 1995. *A Desmobilização da Guerrilha Nicaragüense: Ensinamentos*. Rio de Janeiro: Escola de Comando e Estado Maior do Exército.

De León, Mauricio. 1996. *Primera mission de paz del ejército uruguayo al servicio de las Naciones Unidas en India y Pakistán*. Montevideo: Centro Militar.

Demurenko, Andrei, and Alexander Nikitin. 1997. "Concepts in International Peacekeeping." *Low Intensity Conflict and Law Enforcement* 6 (1): 6.

Desch, Michael. 1999. *Civilian Control of the Military: The Changing Security Environment*. Baltimore: Johns Hopkins University Press.

Diamint, Rut. 1992. "Cambios en la política de seguridad: Argentina en busca de un perfil no conflictivo." *Fuerzas Armadas y Sociedad* 7 (1): 1–17.

———. 1995. "Política exterior, seguridad regional y medidas para el fomento de la confianza." In *Defensa no ofensiva: Una propuesta de Reforma Militar para Argentina*, ed. Thomaz Sheetz and Gustavo Cáceres. Buenos Aires: Editorial Buenos Aires.

———. 1997. "Un producto de la posguerra fría: La cooperación en seguridad. El caso argentino." In *El MERCOSUR de la Defensa*, ed. Francisco Rojas and Claudio Fuentes, 31–41. Santiago: FLACSO.

———. 2001. *La OTAN y los desafíos en el MERCOSUR: Comunidades de seguridad y estabilidad democrática*. Buenos Aires: Nuevohacer-Grupo Editorial Latinoamericano.

———. 2007. "El 2x9 una incipiente comunidad de seguridad em América Latina?" Policy Paper 18. Friedrich Ebert Stiftung, Berlin. http://library.fes.de/pdf-files/bueros/la-seguridad/50501.pdf.

———. 2010. "Security Communities: Defense Policy Integration and Peace Operations in the Southern Cone, An Argentine Perspective." *International Peacekeeping* 17 (5): 662–77.

Diehl, Paul F. 1994. *International Peacekeeping*. Baltimore: Johns Hopkins University Press.

Diniz, Eugenio. 2005. "O Brasil e a MINUSTAH." *Security and Defense Studies Review* 5 (1): 90–108.

———. 2006. "O Brasil e as Operações de Paz." In *Relações Internacionais do Brasil*. Vol. 2, *Temas e Agendas*, ed. Henrique Altemani and Antônio Carlos Altemani, 303–37. São Paulo, Brazil: Saraiva.

———. 2007. "Brazil: Peacekeeping and the Evolution of Foreign Policy." In *Capacity Building for Peacekeeping: The Case of Haiti*, ed. John T. Fishel and Andrés Sáenz, 91–111. Washington, DC: National Defense University Press.

Doyle, Michael. 1998. "Introduction: Discovering the Limits and Potential of Peacekeeping." In *Peacemaking and Peacekeeping for the New Century*, ed. Olara A. Otuu and Michael W. Doyle, 1–18. New York: Rowman & Littlefield.

———. 2001. "War Making and Peace Making: The United Nations' Post–Cold War Record." In *Turbulent Peace: The Challenges of Managing International Conflict*, ed. Chester A. Crocker, Fen Osler Hampson, and Pamela Aall, 529–60. Washington, DC: U.S. Institute of Peace.

Doyle, Michael W., and Nicholas Sambanis. 2000. "International Peacebuilding: A Theoretical and Quantitative Analysis." *American Political Science Review* 94 (4): 779–801.

Eckstein, Harry. 1975. "Case Study and Theory in Political Science." In *Handbook of Political Science*, ed. Fred Greenstein and Nelson Polsby, 94–137. Reading, MA: Addison-Wesley.

EFE. 2003. "Argentina-ONU: Argentina puede perder su derecho a voto en la ONU por deudas." *Spanish Newswire Services*, August 3. http://www.emol.com/noticias /economia/2003/08/03/119180/argentina-puede-perder-su-derecho-a-voto-en-la -onu-por-deudas.html.

*Economist*. 2000. "The UN's Missions Impossible." August 5, 24–26.

———. 2004a. "Brazil's Foreign Policy: A Giant Stirs." June 10. www.economist.com /world/la/displaystory.cfm?story_id=2752700.

———. 2004b. "Football Diplomacy: Haitians Unite—for a Day." August 19. www .economist.com/node/3109441.

———. 2004c. "Brazil's Armed Forces: Resurrecting the Right to History." November 27, 55.

———. 2007a. "Uruguay: The Next Chile." February 1. www.economist.com/node /8636271.

———. 2007b. "Haiti: A Small Success for the UN." August 2. www.economist.com /node/9587689.

———. 2009a. "Brazil Takes Off." November 14. www.economist.com/node/14845197 ?story_id=E1_TQRQVTJS.

———. 2009b. "Brazil's Army: But What Is It for?" January 15. www.economist.com /node/12936593.

———. 2010a. "Brazil and Peacekeeping: Policy, Not Altruism." September 25, 52.

———. 2010b. "Haiti's Election: A Vote Rubbished." December 2. www.economist .com/node/17627945.

———. 2010c. "Organized Crime in Brazil: Conquering Complexo de Alemão." December 2. www.economist.com/node/17627963.

———. 2011. "Haiti and the UN: Mission Fatigue." October 15. www.economist.com /node/21532299.

Egnell, Robert. 2009. *Complex Peace Operations and Civil-Military Relations: Winning the Peace*. New York: Routledge.

Ejército Argentino. 1997. *Soldados Argentinos por la paz*. Buenos Aires: Servicio Histórico del Ejército Argentino.

Ejército de la República Uruguay. 1999. *El Ejército Uruguayo en Misiones de Paz*. Montevideo.

———. 2011. "Defensa Nacional." Website of the Uruguayan Army. www.ejercito.mil .uy/conozca.htm.

Ejército de la República Oriental del Uruguay. 1994. "Fuerzas de paz: La experiencia del Ejército de Uruguay." *Revista Seguridad Estratégica y Regional 2000* 5: 37–41.

*El Clarín*. 2003. "Acusan a cascos azules de Uruguay por torturas en África." September 21. http://old.clarin.com/diario/2003/09/21/i-02201.htm.

*El Observador*. 2011. "Tres informes descartan abuso sexual y hablan de mala conducta." September 9. http://www.elobservador.com.uy/noticia/208839/tres-informes-des cartan-abuso-sexual-y-hablan-de-mala-conducta/.

*El País*. 2006. "Haití: urnas vigiladas por cascos azules de Uruguay." February 7. http://historico.elpais.com.uy/06/02/07/pinter_199973.asp.

———. 2009a. "Un Avión militar uruguayo se estrelló en Haití: 11 muertos." October 20. http://www.elpais.com.uy/091010/pinter-447143/americalatina/un-avion-militar-uruguayo-se-estrello-en-haiti-11-muertos.

———. 2009b. "Rosadilla reiteró que no se fraguaron horas de vuelo." December 14. http://www.elpais.com.uy/101214/ultmo-535349/ultimomomento/Rosadilla-reitero-que-no-se-fraguaron-horas-de-vuelo/.

*Environment News Service*. 2009. "Deadly Hurricanes Devastate Impoverished Haiti." September 8. http://www.ens-newswire.com/ens/sep2008/2008-09-08-02.html.

Escudé, Carlos, and Andrés Fontana. 1998. "Argentina's Security Policies: Their Rationale and Regional Context." In *International Security and Democracy: Latin America and the Caribbean in the Post–Cold War Era*, ed. Jorge I. Domínguez, 51–79. Pittsburgh, PA: University of Pittsburgh.

Esteban, Carlos Daniel. 1994. "UNIIMOG: Irán-Irak. Observadores militares en Medio Oriente." *Revista del Suboficial* 75 (611): 12–14.

Etchehun, Adolfo. 1994. "Observadores militares en Medio Oriente." *Revista del Suboficial* 75 (611): 9–11.

Etchegaray, José. 2001. "Policy Paper: Operaciones Militares de Paz." Permanent Mission of Argentina to the United Nations, New York.

Farah, Douglas. 2000. "American Troops Arrive in Nigeria: Soldiers to Train UN Peacekeepers." *Washington Post*, August 25, A23.

Feaver, Peter D. 1998. " 'Crisis as Shirking': An Agency Theory Explanation of the Souring of American Civil-Military Relations." *Armed Forces and Society* 24 (3): 407–34.

———. 2003. *Armed Servants: Agency, Oversight, and Civil-Military Relations*. Cambridge, MA: Harvard University Press.

Findlay, Trevor. 1996. *Challenges for the New Peacekeepers*. Oxford: SIPRI-Oxford University Press.

Finer, S. E. 1962. *The Man on Horseback: The Role of the Military in Politics*. New York: Praeger.

Fitch, Samuel J. 1998. *The Armed Forces and Democracy in Latin America*. Baltimore: Johns Hopkins University Press.

Fleshman, Michael. 2005. "Tough UN Line on Peacekeeper Abuses: Action Initiated to End Sexual Misdeeds in Peacekeeping Missions." *Africa Renewal* 19 (1): 16. http://www.un.org/africarenewal/magazine/april-2005/tough-un-line-peacekeeper-abuses.

*Folha de São Paulo*. 2010a. "Livro narra experiencia do soldado brasileiro no Haiti; leia trecho." January 13. www1.folha.uol.com.br/folha/livrariadafolha/ult10082u678584.shtml.

———. 2010b. "Ministro Nelson Jobim discutiu agenda para visita a Washington; leia telegram." November 30. www1.folha.uol.com.br/mundo/838771-ministro-nelson-jobim-discutiu-agenda-para-visita-a-washington-leia-telegrama.shtml.

Follietti, Gilda. 2005. "La participación argentina en Haití: El papel del Congreso." *Revista Fuerzas Armadas y Sociedad* 19 (1): 37–56.

Fontana, Andrés. 1993. "Percepciones militares del rol de las fuerzas armadas en la Argentina." Cuadernos Simón Rodríguez. Buenos Aires, Argentina.

————. 1994. *Argentina-OTAN: Perspectivas sobre la Seguridad Global.* Buenos Aires: Consejo Argentino para las Relaciones Internacionales-Grupo Editorial Latinoamericano.

————. 1998. "La seguridad internacional y la Argentina en los años 90." In *Política Exterior Argentina, 1989–1999: Historia de un éxito,* ed. Andrés Cisneros, 275–340. Buenos Aires: Nuevohacer-Grupo Editorial Latinoamericano.

————. 2001. "Seguridad Internacional y Transición Democrática: La Experiencia Argentina, 1983–1999." Documentos de Trabajo de la Facultad de Estudios para Graduados de la Universidad de Belgrano, Buenos Aires.

Fortna, Virginia Page. 1993. "Regional Organizations and Peacekeeping: Experiences in Latin America and Africa." Occasional Paper 11. Henry L. Stimson Center, Washington, DC.

————. 2003. "Scraps of Paper? Agreements and the Durability of Peace." *International Organization* 57 (2): 337–72.

————. 2004a. *Peace Time: Cease Fire Agreements and the Durability of Peace.* Princeton, NJ: Princeton University Press.

————. 2004b. "Interstate Peacekeeping: Causal Mechanisms and Empirical Effects." *World Politics* 56 (4): 481–519.

————. 2004c. "Does Peacekeeping Keep the Peace? International Intervention and the Duration of Peace after Civil War." *International Studies Quarterly* 48 (2): 269–92.

————. 2008. *Does Peacekeeping Work? Shaping Belligerents' Choices after Civil War.* Princeton, NJ: Princeton University Press.

Fraga, Rosendo. 1988. *La cuestión militar: 1987–1989.* Buenos Aires: Editorial Centro de Estudios Unión para la Nueva Mayoría.

————. 1991. *Menem y la cuestión militar.* Buenos Aires: Editorial Centro de Estudios para la Nueva Mayoría.

————. 1994. "El financiamiento condiciona el desarrollo de las fuerzas multinacionales de paz." *Revista del suboficial* 75 (611): 49–50.

————. 1996a. "La política exterior y la política de defensa: Las fuerzas de paz." Centro de Estudios para la Nueva Mayoría, Buenos Aires.

————. 1996b. "La globalización y las fuerzas armadas." Centro de Estudios para la Nueva Mayoría, Buenos Aires.

————. 1999. "El concepto de las hipótesis de conflicto." In *Política Exterior Argentina, 1989–1999,* ed. Andrés Cisneros, 237–73. Buenos Aires: Nuevohacer-Grupo Editorial Latinoamericano.

————. 2000. "La política exterior y las relaciones cívico-militares." Centro de Estudios para la Nueva Mayoría, Buenos Aires.

————. 2001. "La interoperabilidad." Centro de Estudios para la Nueva Mayoría, Buenos Aires.

Fuentes, Claudio. 1997. "Fuerzas Armadas y Democracia en Uruguay: El Desafío de la Reingeniería de la Defensa." In *Relaciones Cívico-Militares Comparadas: Entendiendo los mecanismo de control civil en las pequeñas democracias,* ed. Kevin Casas Zamora, 227–60. San José, Costa Rica: Fundación Arias para la Paz y el Progreso Humano.

Fuerza Aérea. 1996. *La fuerza aérea y las operaciones de mantenimiento de la paz.* Buenos Aires: Fuerza Aérea Argentina.

Gallego Díaz, Soledad, and Juan Arias. 2009. "Brasil es el país más parecido del mundo a EE UU." *El País,* September 2. http://www.elpais.com/articulo/internacional /Brasil/pais/parecido/mundo/EE/UU/elpepuint/20090209elpepuint_2/Tes.

Gallo, Daniel. 2002. "El 63% de los uniformados del Ejército cobra menos de $716." *La Nación*, October 28. www.lanacion.com.ar/444720-el-63-de-los-uniformados-del -ejercito-cobra-menos-de-716.

Gargiulo, Gerardo R. 1988. "Gasto militar y política de defensa." *Desarrollo Económico* 28 (1): 107–19.

Gaubatz, Kurt Taylor. 1997. "Democratic States and Commitment in International Relations." In *Liberalization and Foreign Policy*, ed. Miles Kahler, 27–65. New York: Columbia University Press.

George, Alexander L. 1993. *Bridging the Gap: Theory and Practice in Foreign Policy.* Washington, DC: U.S. Institute of Peace.

George, Alexander L., and Andrew Bennett. 2004. *Case Studies and Theory Development in the Social Sciences.* Cambridge, MA: MIT Press.

Gerschenson, Ana. 2001. "Hay que hacer lo que nos pida Estados Unidos: El mundo que viene, entrevista con Guido di Tella, ex-canciller." *El Clarín*, September 16. http://edant.clarin.com/diario/2001/09/16/i-02602.htm.

Gheciu, Alexandra. 2005. "Security Institutions as Agents of Socialization? NATO and the 'New Europe.'"*International Organization* 59 (4): 973–1012.

Gillespie, Charles Guy. 1991. *Negotiating Democracy.* New York: Cambridge University Press.

Gomes de Sousa, Luiz Afonso. 1994. "Missões de Paz da ONU: Nicarágua, El Salvador e Iugoslávia. Experiencias e Ensinamentos." Escola de Comando e Estado Maior do Exercito, Rio de Janeiro.

Gonnet Ibarra, Diego, and Diego Hernández Nilson. 2007. "La participación uruguaya en las misiones de paz, una herramienta de inserción subestimada." *Cuadernos del CLAEH* 4 (94-95): 58–59. http://socialsciences.scielo.org/scielo.php?script=sci _arttext&pid=S0797-60622008000100003&lng=en&nrm=iso.

González, Julián. 2002. "Fuerzas Armadas en tiempos de escasez: El riesgo de la desnaturalización funcional." *Observatorio Político* 3: 101–3.

———. 2010. "The *Frente Amplio* in Government and the Military Situation: After Five Years, the Most Complex Challenges Arrive." In *A Comparative Atlas of Defense in Latin America and Caribbean*, 284–93. Buenos Aires: Resdal. www.resdal.org/atlas/atlas10 -ing-25-uruguay.pdf.

González, Luis. 1993. *Estructuras políticas y democracia en Uruguay.* Montevideo: Fundación de Cultura Universitaria.

Goodman, Amy. 2011. "As UN Mission Mandate Faces Renewal: UN Soldiers' Sexual Assault of Haitian Man Provokes Outrage and Protest." *Haïti Liberté*, September 6. http://www.haiti-liberte.com/archives/volume5-8/As%20UN%20Mission %20Mandate.asp.

Gourevitch, Peter. 1978. "The Second Image Reversed: The International Sources of Domestic Politics." *International Organization* 32 (4): 881–912.

Greig, Michael J., and Paul L. Diehl. 2005. "The Peacekeeping-Peacemaking Dilemma." *International Studies Quarterly* 49 (4): 621–45.

Grossi, Rafael Mariano. 1999. *Penúltima Alianza: El Proceso de Expansión de la OTAN y el Nuevo Mapa de la Seguridad Internacional.* Buenos Aires: Nuevohacer-Grupo Editorial Latinoamericano.

———. 2000. *Los límites del intervencionismo humanitario.* Buenos Aires: Instituto del Servicio Exterior de la Nación-Nuevohacer-Grupo Editorial Latinoamericano.

Guedes da Costa, Thomaz. 1998a. "Democratization and International Integration: The Role of the Armed Forces in Brazil's Grand Strategy." In *Civil-Military Relations: Building Democracy and Regional Security in Latin America, Southern Asia, and Central Europe*, ed. David Mares, 223–37. Boulder, CO: Westview Press.

———. 1998b. "Segurança Coletiva: Pensamento e Política do Brasil." *Caderno Premissas* 17–18: 16–35.

———. 2001. "Brazil's SIVAM: As It Monitors the Amazon, Will It Fulfill Its Human Security Promise?" Environmental Change and Security Project Report. Woodrow Wilson International Center for Scholars, Washington, DC.

Haggard, Stephan, and Robert R. Kaufman. 1995. *The Political Economy of Democratic Transitions*. Princeton, NJ: Princeton University Press.

Halling, Matt, and Blaine Bookey. 2008. "Peacekeeping in Name Alone: Accountability for the UN in Haiti." *Hastings International and Comparative Law Review* 31: 461–86. http://works.bepress.com/matt_halling/6.

Hampson, Françoise J., and Ai Kihara-Hunt. 2007. "The Accountability of Personnel Associated with Peacekeeping Operations." In *Unintended Consequences of Peacekeeping Operations*, ed. Cedric de Coning and Ramesh Thakur, 195–220. New York: United Nations University Press.

Harvard Human Rights Program. 2005. "Peace in Haiti? An Assessment of the United Nations Stabilization Mission in Haiti: Using Compliance with its Prescribed Mandate as a Barometer for Success." Harvard Law Student Advocates for Human Rights, Cambridge, MA. http://www.law.harvard.edu/programs/hrp/documents/haitireport.pdf.

Heine, Jorge, and Andrew S. Thompson, eds. 2011. *Fixing Haiti: MINUSTAH and Beyond*. New York: United Nations University Press.

Heller, Zoe. 2011. "The Accidental Activist." *New York Times Style Magazine*, March 25. http://tmagazine.blogs.nytimes.com/2011/03/25/the-accidental-activist/.

Herz, Mônica, and João Pontes Nogueira. 2002. *Ecuador vs. Peru*. New York: International Peace Academy.

Herz, Mônica, and Paulo S. Wrobel. 2002. "A Política de Segurança no Pós-Guerra Fria." In *Brasil e o Mundo: Novas Visôes*, ed. Clóvis Brigagâo and Domicio Proença Júnior, 255–318. Rio de Janeiro: Francisco Alves and Konrad Adenauer Stiftung.

Hirst, Monica, ed. 2009. "La intervención sudamericana en Haití." In *Crisis del Estado e intervención internacional: Una mirada desde el sur*, 338–57. Buenos Aires: Edhasa.

Howard, Lise Morjé. 2008. *UN Peacekeeping in Civil Wars*. New York: Cambridge University Press.

Hristoulas, Athanasios, and Monica Herz. 2005. "Brasil y México enfrentan a la seguridad regional e internacional después de la Guerra Fría." In *Brasil y México: Encuentros y Desencuentros*, ed. Antonio Ortiz Mena, Octavio Amorim Neto, and Rafael Fernández de Castro, 259–320. Mexico City: Instituto Matías Romero-SRE.

Hudson, Rex A., ed. 1997. "Foreign Policy Decision Making." In *Brazil: A Country Study*. Washington, DC: GPO for the Library of Congress. http://countrystudies.us/brazil/106.htm.

Human Rights Watch. 2009. "Brazil: Curb Police Violence in Rio, São Paulo." December 8. http://www.hrw.org/en/news/2009/12/08/brazil-curb-police-violence-rio-s-o-paolo.

Hunter, Wendy. 1994. "The Brazilian Military after the Cold War: In Search of a Mission." *Studies in Comparative International Development* 28 (4): 31–49.

———. 1997. *Eroding Military Influence in Brazil: Politicians against Soldiers.* Chapel Hill: University of North Carolina Press.

———. 1999. "State and Soldier in Latin America." Peaceworks 10. U.S. Institute of Peace, Washington, DC. http://www.usip.org/publications/state-and-soldier-latin -america.

Huntington, Samuel. 1957. *The Soldier and the State: The Theory and Politics of Civil-Military Relations.* Cambridge, MA: Belknap Press of the Harvard University Press.

———. 1961. "Interservice Competition and the Political Roles of the Armed Services." *American Political Science Review* 55 (1): 40–52.

Huser, Herbert C. 1998. "Democratic Argentina's Global Research: The Argentina Military in Peacekeeping Operations." *Naval War College Review* 51 (3): 55–69.

Informativo mensal do Batalhão Brasileiro. 2007. "Operaçã Cajado." *Informativo Haiti: Informativo mensal do Batalhão Brasileiro* 4 (88): 2.

Infodefensa. 2010. "Uruguay no participará en Misiones de Paz de la ONU por falta de pilotos militares." Revista Poder Militar, December 13. http://podermilitar. blogspot.com/2010/12/uruguay-no-participara-en-misiones-de.html.

Instituto de Ciencia Política de la Universidad de la República. 2003. "Del Observatorio Cono Sur de Defensa y Fuerzas Armadas." Informe Semanal No. 96. Montevideo.

*International Herald Tribune.* 1997. "Lauding Its Peacekeeping, Clinton Offers Special Ally Status to Argentina." October 17, 12.

International Institute for Strategic Studies. 1988–2001. *The Military Balance 1988–2001.* New York: Oxford University Press.

Isacson, Adam. 2011. "Rio de Janeiro's Pacification Program." Washington Office on Latin America, January 5. www.wola.org/rio_de_janeiro_s_pacification_program.

Jackson, Patrick. 2007. "How Peacekeeping Works." BBC News, April 17. http://news .bbc.co.uk/2/hi/6524867.stm.

Jaguaribe, Helio. 2005. *Urgências e Perspectivas do Brasil.* Brasilia: FUNAG.

Jakobsen, Peter Viggo. 2003. "The Danish Approach to UN Peace Operations after the Cold War: A New Model in the Making?" *International Peacekeeping* 5 (3): 106–23.

Jane's Sentinel Security Assessment–South America. 2003. "Executive Summary: Uruguay." IHS, Englewood, CO.

Janowitz, Morris. 1960. *The Professional Soldier: A Social and Political Portrait.* Glencoe, IL: Free Press.

Jaskoski, Maiah. 2012. "Civilian Control of the Armed Forces in Democratic Latin America: Military Prerogatives, Contestation, and Mission Performance in Peru." *Armed Forces and Society* 38 (1): 70–91.

Jervis, Robert. 1997. *System Effects: Complexity in Political and Social Life.* Princeton, NJ: Princeton University Press.

Jett, Dennis C. 1999. *Why Peacekeeping Fails.* New York: Palgrave.

Johnston, Alastair Iain. 2001. "Treating International Institutions as Social Environments." *International Studies Quarterly* 45 (4): 487–515.

Jomini, Antoine-Henri. 2009. "O apoio logístico no Haiti." *Verde Olivo* 37 (202): 29–32.

Kaufman, Stuart J. 1994. "Organizational Politics and Change in Soviet Military Policy." *World Politics* 46 (3): 355–82.

Kenkel, Kai Michael. 2010a. "Stepping out of the Shadow: South America and Peace Operations." *International Peacekeeping* 17 (5): 584–97.

———. 2010b. "South America's Emerging Power: Brazil as a Peacekeeper." *International Peacekeeping* 17 (5): 644–61.

Kent, Vanessa. 2007. "Protecting Civilians from UN Peacekeepers and Humanitarian Workers: Sexual Exploitation and Abuse." In *Unintended Consequences of Peacekeeping Operations*, ed. Cedric de Coning and Ramesh Thakur, 44–66. New York: United Nations University Press.

Keohane, Robert O. 1993. "Institutional Theory and the Realist Challenge after the Cold War." In *Neorealism and Neoliberalism: The Contemporary Debate*, ed. David Baldwin, 269–300. New York: Columbia University Press.

Keohane, Robert O., Stephen Macedo, and Andrew Moravcsik. 2009. "Democracy-Enhancing Multilateralism." *International Organization* 63 (1): 1–31.

Kipman, Igor. 2009. "MINUSTAH Go Home?" *Verde-Oliva: Exército Brasileiro* 37 (202): 58–59.

Koremenos, Barbara, Charles Lipson, and Duncan Snidal. 2001. "The Rational Design of International Institutions." *International Organization* 54 (4): 761–99.

Kowert, Paul, and Jeffrey Legro. 1996. "Norms, Identity, and Their Limit: A Theoretical Reprise." In *The Culture of National Security: Norms and Identity in World Politics*, ed. Peter J. Katzenstein, 485–86. New York: Columbia University Press.

Krauss, Clifford. 2001a. "World Briefing Americas: Argentina: Ex-President Due in Court." *New York Times*, June 6, A:14.

———. 2001b. "World Briefing Americas: Argentina: Arrest in Arms Case." *New York Times*, June 7, A:10.

Krebs, Ronald R. 2004. "A School for the Nation?" *International Security* 28 (4): 85–124.

Kretchik, Walter E. 2007. "Haiti's Quest for Democracy: Historical Overview." In *Capacity Building for Peacebuilding: The Case of Haiti*, ed. John T. Fishel and Andrés Sáenz, 8–34. Washington, DC: National Defense University Press.

Lagorio, Ricardo E. 1998. "Institutionalization, Cooperative Security, and Peacekeeping Operations: The Argentine Experience." In *International Security and Democracy: Latin America and the Caribbean in the Post–Cold War Era*, ed. Jorge I. Domínguez, 121–29. Pittsburgh, PA: University of Pittsburgh Press.

Lake, David. 2001. "Beyond Anarchy: The Importance of Security Institutions." *International Security* 26 (1): 129–30.

Lampreira, Luiz Felipe. 1995. "O Brasil e a reforma das Nações Unidas." *O Estado de São Paulo*, August 21, A:2.

———. 1998. "A política externa do governo FHC: Continuidade e renovação." *Revista Brasileira de Política Internacional* 41 (2): 5–17.

*La Nación*. 2003. "Controversia por fondos de cascos azules argentines." January 12. http://www.lanacion.com.ar/465630-controversia-por-fondos-para-cascos-azules -argentinos.

Lavopa, Jorge H., and Leonardo Hekimián, eds. 1993. *El Rol de las Fuerzas Armadas en el Mercosur.* Buenos Aires: CARI-Konrad Adenauer Foundation.

Leeds, Christopher. 2001. "Culture, Conflict Resolution, Peacekeeper Training and the D Mediator." *International Peacekeeping* 8 (4): 92–110.

León, Mauricio de. 1996. *Primera mission de paz del ejército uruguayo al servicio de las Naciones Unidas en India y Pakistán.* Montevideo: Centro Militar.

Leone Pepe, Leandro, and Suzeley Kalil Mathias. 2005. "Operaciones de paz de las Naciones Unidas: La perspective brasileña." *Revista Fuerzas Armadas y Sociedad* 19 (1): 57–71.

Lindley, Dan. 2006. *Promoting Peace with Information.* Princeton, NJ: Princeton University Press.

Linz, Juan, and Alfred Stepan. 1996. *Problems of Democratic Transition and Consolidation.* Baltimore: John Hopkins University Press.

Llenderrozas, Elsa E. 2006. "Argentina, Brasil y Chile en la reconstrucción de Haití: Intereses y motivaciones de la participación conjunta." Paper presented at the Meeting of the Latin American Studies Association, San Juan, Puerto Rico, March 15–16.

López, Ernesto. 1988. *El ultimo levantamiento.* Buenos Aires: Editorial Lagasa.

López Chirico, Selva. 1985. *El Estado y las fuerzas armadas en el Uruguay del Siglo XX.* Montevideo: Ediciones Banda Oriental.

———. 1999. "Las FF.AA Uruguayas en la democracia post-dictatorial: Notas sobre misión y estrategias política." In *Control civil y fuerzas armadas en las nuevas democracias latinoamericanas,* ed. Rut Diamint, 276–79. Buenos Aires: Grupo Editorial Latonoamericano.

Loveman, Brian. 1999. *For* la Patria: *Politics and the Armed Forces in Latin America.* New York: Rowman & Littlefield.

Maharaj, Davan, and Alexis Masciarelli. 2003. "Refugees Describe Massacres in Congo: Battle between Ethnic Militias Is Part of a Civil War Consuming the Mineral-Rich Country." *Los Angeles Times.* May 27, Foreign Desk:3.

Mansfield, Edward D., and Jon C. Pevehouse. 2006. "Democratization and International Organizations." *International Organization* 60 (1): 137–67.

Marcella, Gabriel. 1994. "Warriors in Peacetime: Future Missions of the Latin American Armed Forces." In *Warriors in Peacetime: The Military and Democracy in Latin America,* ed. Gabriel Marcella. Portland, OR: Frank Cass.

Marconedes de Souza Neto, Danilo. 2009. "A Participaçâo e a Cooperaçâo entre os Países de Cone Sul em Operaçôes de Paz: O Caso da MINUSTAH." In *Defesa, Segurança Internacional e Forças Armadas: II Encontro da Abed,* ed. Eduardo Svartman, Maria Celina D'Araujo, and Samuel Alves Soares, 169–96. Campinas, Brazil: Mercado Letras.

———. 2010. Operaçôes de Paz Cooperaçâo Regional: O Brasil e o Envolvimento Sulamericano na MINUSTAH." *Revista da Escola de Guerra Naval* 15 (June): 25–58.

Mares, David R. 1998. "Civil-Military Relations, Democracy, and the Regional Neighborhood." In *Civil-Military Relations: Building Democracy and Regional Security in Latin America, Southern Asia, and Central Europe,* ed. David R. Mares, 1–24. Boulder, CO: Westview Press.

Martin, Lisa L., and Beth Simmons. 1998. "Theories and Empirical Studies of International Institutions." *International Organization* 52 (4): 729–57.

Martins Filho, João Roberto. 2000. "O governo Fernando Henrique e as Forças Armadas: Um Passo à frente, dois passos atrás." *Revista Olhar* 2 (4): 104–20.

Martins Filho, João Roberto, and Daniel Zirker. 2000. "The Brazilian Military under Cardoso: Overcoming the Identity Crisis." *Journal of Interamerican Studies and World Affairs* 42 (3): 143–70.

Mattos, Irene Badaro. 1994. "O Poder da ONU: As Forças de Intervenção." Curso de Altos Estudos de Política e Estratégia, Rio de Janeiro.

Mearsheimer, John. 1994. "The False Promise of International Institutions." *International Security* 19 (3): 5–49.

Melgar, Pablo. 2010. "Haití: Batallón uruguayo no superó inspección de ONU; 70% inoperativo." *El País*, September 21. http://www.elpais.com.uy/100921/pnacio-516703 /sociedad/haiti-batallon-uruguayo-no-supero-inspeccion-de-onu-70-inoperativo/.

Mendelson Forman, Johanna. 2011. "Latin American Peacekeeping: A New Era of Regional Cooperation." In *Fixing Haiti: MINUSTAH and Beyond*, ed. Jorge Heine and Andrew S. Thompson, 138–56. New York: United Nations University Press.

Mendonça, Maria Luisa. 2008. "U.N. Troops Accused of Human Rights Violations in Haiti." Worldpress, January 29. http://www.worldpress.org/Americas/3056.cfm.

MercoPress. 2011a. "UN Secretary General Praises Uruguay's Contribution to Peace Keeping Worldwide." June 16. http://en.mercopress.com/2011/06/16/un-secretary -general-praises-uruguay-s-contribution-to-peace-keeping-worldwide.

———. 2011b. "Haiti UN Peacekeeping Force Led by Brazil Will Begin Gradual Pullout." September 9. http://en.mercopress.com/2011/09/09/haiti-un-peacekeeping -force-led-by-brazil-will-begin-gradual-pullout.

Mesquita Neto, Paulo de. 1999. "Fuerzas armadas, políticas y seguridad pública en Brasil: Instituciones y políticas gubernamentales." In *Control civil y fuerzas armadas en las nuevas democracies latinoamericanas*, ed. Rut Dimanit, 195–221. Buenos Aires: Grupo Editorial Lationamericano.

Micha, Luciana. 2005. "Una visión integrada de la participación argentina en MINUSTAH." *Security and Defense Studies Review* 5 (1): 109–29.

———. 2007. "Argentina: An Integrated View of Participation in Peacekeeping." In *Capacity Building for Peacekeeping: The Case of Haiti*, ed. John T. Fishel and Andrés Sáenz, 112–30. Washington, DC: National Defense University Press.

Miller, Laura L. 1997. "Do Soldiers Hate Peacekeeping? The Case of Preventive Diplomacy Operations in Macedonia." *Armed Forces and Society* 23 (3): 415–50.

Ministério de Defesa. 2008. "Estratégia Nacional de Defesa." Federal Government of Brazil, Brasilia. www.sae.gov.br/site/?p=210.

Ministerio de Defensa. 2009a. *Equidad Género y Defensa: Una Política en Marcha (III)*. Buenos Aires: Presidencia de la República y Ministerio de Defensa.

———. 2009b. *Argentine Model for the Defense System Modernization*. Policy Paper 32. Presidencia de la República y Ministerio de Defensa, Buenos Aires.

Mirodan, Seamus. 2003. "Judge Clears Menem of Arms Trafficking Charges." *Daily Telegraph London*, August 29, 18.

Miyamoto, Shiguenoli. 1988. "Escola Superior de Guerra: Mito e Realidade." *Politica e Estrategia* 2 (1): 3–29.

Moneta, C. J., and Ernesto López. 1985. *La Reforma Militar*. Buenos Aires: Editorial Legasa.

Moravcsik, Andrew. 2000. "The Origins of Human Rights Regimes: Liberal Democracy and Political Uncertainty in Postwar Europe." *International Organization* 54 (2): 217–52.

Moreno, Miguel Angel. 2002. "General argentino comanda en Iran-Irak." *Soldados* 7 (74): 2–3.

Moritán, García. 1993. "Las operaciones de mantenimiento de la paz en un mundo cambiante." *Revista del Ministerio de Relaciones Exteriores, Comercio Internacional y Culto* 1 (3): 79–88.

Morrow, James. 1999. "The Strategic Setting of Choices: Signaling, Commitment, and Negotiation in International Politics." In *Strategic Choice and International Relations*, ed. David A. Lake and Robert Powell, 77–114. Princeton, NJ: Princeton University Press.

Moskos, Charles C., Jr. 1976. *Peace Soldiers: The Sociology of a United Nations Military Force*. Chicago: University of Chicago Press.

———. 2000. "Toward a Postmodern Military: The United States as a Paradigm." In *The Postmodern Military: Armed Forces after the Cold War*, ed. Charles C. Moskos, John Allen Williams, and David R. Segal, 14–31. New York: Oxford University Press.

Moskos, Charles C., John Allen Williams, and David R. Segal, eds. 2000. *The Postmodern Military: Armed Forces after the Cold War*. New York: Oxford University Press.

Neack, Laura. 1995. "UN Peace-Keeping: In the Interest of Community or Self?" *Journal of Peace Research* 32 (2): 181–96.

Neves, Juan Carlos. 1995. "Interoperability in Multinational Coalitions: Lessons from the Persian Gulf War." *Naval War College Review* 48 (1): 50–62.

*New York Times*. 2011. "Editorial: Haiti's Continuing Cholera Outbreak." May 10. http://www.nytimes.com/2011/05/11/opinion/11wed3.html.

Norden, Deborah. 1995. "Keeping the Peace, Outside and In: Argentina's UN Missions." *International Peacekeeping* 2 (3): 330–49.

———. 1996a. *Military Rebellion in Argentina: Between Coups and Consolidation*. Lincoln: University of Nebraska Press.

———. 1996b. "The Transformation of Argentine Security." In *Beyond Praetorianism: The Latin American Military in Transition*, ed. Richard L. Millet and Michael Gold Biss, 241–60. Miami, FL: North-South Center Press.

Norden, Deborah, and Roberto Russell. 2002. *The United States and Argentina: Changing Relations in a Changing World*. New York: Routledge.

Novarese, Carina. 2005. "Cascos azules lidian con corrupción, violentos enfrentamientos y narco-pandillas." *El País*, June 10. http://www.elpais.com.uy/Suple/LaSemanaEnElPais/05/06/10/lasem_delo_157156.asp.

O'Donnell, Guillermo, and Philippe C. Schmitter. 1986. *Transitions from Authoritarian Rule: Tentative Conclusions about Uncertain Democracies*. Baltimore: Johns Hopkins University Press.

Orlando, Lionel, and José L. Viggiano. 1989. "Participación del Ejército uruguayo en el grupo de observadores militares de las Naciones Unidas en India y Pakistán (UNMOGIP)." *Soldado* 3 (6): 49.

Pairone, Alejandro. 2004. "Devela Argentina centro de torturas." *Reforma*, January 14. http://busquedas.gruporeforma.com/reforma/Documentos/DocumentoImpresa.aspx.

Palá, Antonio. 1998. "Peacekeeping and Its Effects on Civil-Military Relations." In *International Security and Democracy: Latin America and the Caribbean in the Post–Cold War Era*, ed. Jorge I. Domínguez, 130–50. Pittsburgh, PA: University of Pittsburgh Press.

Peláez, Amíclar Andrés. 2007. "Country Survey XX: Spending and Peacekeeping in Uruguay." *Defense and Peace Economics* 18 (3): 281–301.

Penna Filho, Pio. 2004. "Segurança seletiva no pós-Guerra Fria: Uma análise da política e dos instrumentos de segurança das Nações Unidas para os países periféricos—O caso africano." *Revista Brasileira de Política Internacional* 47 (1): 31–50.

Pereira, Arthur, and Oliveira Filho. 1998. "O Brasil e o Conselho de Segurança da ONU: Revelaçôes Vinte Anos Depois." *Parceiras Estratégicas* 5 (September): 94–120.

Perelli, Carina. 1990. "The Legacies of Transitions to Democracy in Argentina and Uruguay." In *The Military and Democracy: The Future of Civil-Military Relations in Latin America*, ed. Louis W. Goodman, Johanna S. R. Mendelson, and Juan Rial, 39–54. Lexington, MA: Lexington Books.

Pérez Aquino, Carlos. 2001. *Operaciones de paz en la posguerra fría: Una nueva relación entre la ONU y las Organizaciones Regionales*. Buenos Aires: Círculo Militar.

Perito, Robert, and Greg Maly. 2007. "Haiti's Drug Problem." US Institute of Peace, Washington, DC. http://www.usip.org/publications/haitis-drug-problem.

Pevehouse, Jon C. 2002a. "Democracy from the Outside-In? International Organizations and Democratization." *International Organization* 56 (3): 515–49.

———. 2002b. "With a Little Help from My Friends? Regional Organizations and the Consolidation of Democracy." *American Journal of Political Science* 46 (3): 611–26.

Piarroux, Renaud, Robert Barrais, Benoît Faucher, Rachel Haus, Martine Piarroux, Jean Gaudart, Roc Magloire, and Didier Raoult. 2011. "Understanding the Cholera Epidemic, Haiti." *Emerging Infectious Diseases* 17 (7): 1161–68.

Pierson, Paul. 2003. "Big, Slow-Moving, and . . . Invisible: Macrosocial Processes in the Study of Comparative Politics." In *Comparative Historical Analysis in the Social Sciences*, ed. James Mahoney and Dietrich Rueschemeyer, 177–207. New York: Cambridge University Press.

Pion-Berlin, David. 1997. *Through Corridors of Power: Institutions and Civil-Military Relations in Argentina*. University Park: Pennsylvania State University Press.

———. 1998. "From Confrontation to Cooperation: Democratic Governance and Argentine Foreign Relations." In *Civil-Military Relations: Building Democracy and Regional Security in Latin America, Southern Asia, and Central Europe*, ed. David R. Mares, 79–100. Boulder, CO: Westview Press.

———. 2001. "Civil-Military Circumvention: How Argentine State Institutions Compensate for a Weakened Chain of Command." In *Civil-Military Relations in Latin America: New Analytical Perspectives*, ed. David Pion-Berlin, 154–55. Chapel Hill: University of North Carolina Press.

———. 2005. "Political Management of the Military in Latin America." *Military Review* 85 (1): 19–31.

Pion-Berlin, David, and Craig Arceneaux. 2000. "Decision-Makers or Decision-Takers? Military Missions and Civilian Control in Democratic South America." *Armed Forces and Society* 26 (3): 413–36.

Pion-Berlin, David, and Erenesto López. 1992. "A House Divided: Crisis, Cleavage, and Conflict in the Argentine Army." In *The New Argentine Democracy: The Search for a Successful Formula*, ed. Edward C. Epstein, 84–85. New York: Praeger.

Pion-Berlin, David, and Harold Trinkunas. 2007. "Attention Deficits: Why Politicians Ignore Defense Policy in Latin America." *Latin American Research Review* 42 (3): 76–100.

Pirnie, Bruce R., and William E. Simons. 1996. *Soldiers for Peace: An Operational Typology.* Santa Monica, CA: Rand.

Poladura, Fernando. 1998. "Peligro, Minas." *El Soldado* 22 (149): 31–36.

Posen, Barry R. 1984. *The Sources of Military Doctrine: France, Britain, and Germany between the World Wars.* Ithaca, NY: Cornell University Press.

Pridham, Geoffrey. 1995. "The International Context of Democratic Consolidation: Southern Europe in Comparative Perspective." In *The Politics of Democratic Consolidation: Southern Europe in Comparative Perspective,* ed. Richard Gunther, P. Diamandouros, and Hans-Jurgen Phule, 166–203. Baltimore: Johns Hopkins University Press.

Proença, Domício, Jr. 2002. "O enquadramento das Missões de Paz (PKO) nas teorias da guerra e de polícia." *Revista Brasileira de Política Internacional* 45 (2): 146–97.

Pugh, Michael C., ed. 1994. *Maritime Security and Peacekeeping: A Framework for United Nations Operations.* New York: St. Martin's Press.

Redick, John R., Julio C. Carasales, and Paulo S. Wrobel. 1995. "Nuclear *Rapprochement*: Argentina, Brazil, and the Nonproliferation Regime." *Washington Quarterly* 18 (1): 107–22.

Regan, Patrick M. 1998. "Choosing to Intervene: Outside Interventions in Internal Conflicts." *Journal of Politics* 60 (3): 754–79.

Rego, Fernando Danziato. 1995. *A Desmobilização da Guerrilha Nicaragüense: Ensinamentos.* Rio de Janeiro: Escola de Comando e Estado Maior do Exército.

Reiter, Dan. 2001. "Why NATO Enlargement Does Not Spread Democracy." *International Security* 25 (4): 41–67.

Republic of Argentina. 1999. *White Book of National Defense.* Buenos Aires: Ministry of Defense.

Resdal. 2010. *Comparative Atlas of Defence in Latin America and Caribbean.* Buenos Aires. http://www.resdal.org/atlas/atlas-libro-10-ingles.html.

Resende-Santos, João. 2002. "The Origins of the Security Cooperation in the Southern Cone." *Latin American Politics and Society* 44 (4): 89–126.

———. 2007. *Neorealism, States, and the Modern Mass Army.* New York: Cambridge University Press.

Reuters. 2011. "Uruguay Open to Rights Cases of Dictator Era." *New York Times,* July 1, A6. http://www.nytimes.com/2011/07/01/world/americas/01uruguay.html.

Rial, Juan. 1986. *Las Fuerzas Armadas: ¿Soldados-Políticos Garantes de la Democracia?* Montevideo: Ediciones Banda Oriental.

Risse-Kappen, Thomas. 1996. "Collective Identity in a Democratic Community: The Case of NATO." In *The Culture of National Security: Norms and Identities in World Politics,* ed. Peter K. Katzenstein, 357–99. New York: Columbia University Press.

———. 2001. "Let's Argue: Communicative Action in World Politics." *International Organization* 54 (1): 1–39.

Rizzo de Oliveira, Eliézer. 1994. *De Geisel a Collor: Forças Armadas, Transição e Democracia.* São Paulo, Brazil: Papirus.

———. 1998. "Brazilian National Defense Policy and Civil-Military Relations in the Government of President Fernando Henrique Cardoso." In *The Role of the Armed Forces in the Americas: Civil-Military Relations for the 21st Century,* ed. Donald E. Schulz, 31–169. Carlisle, PA: U.S. Army War College. www.strategicstudiesinstitute.army.mil/pdffiles/pub35.pdf.

Rizzo de Oliveira, Eliézer, and Samuel Alves Soares. 2000. "Brasil: Forças armadas, direção política e formato institucional." In *Democracia e Forças Armadas no Cone Sul*, ed. Maria Celina D'Araujo and Celso Castro, 98–124. Rio de Janeiro: Editora FGV.

Rohter, Larry. 2004. "Brazil Is Leading a Largely South American Mission to Haiti." *New York Times*, August 1. http://www.nytimes.com/2004/08/01/world/brazil-is-leading-a-largely-south-american-mission-to-haiti.html.

Römer and Associates. 2001. "Militares y sociedad en Argentina: Siglo XXI, El Ejército actual y su proyección." Graciela Römer & Asociados Consultoría en Opinión Pública y comunicación, Buenos Aires.

Romero, Carlos A. 1998. "Exporting Peace by Other Means: Venezuela." In *International Security and Democracy: Latin America and the Caribbean in the Post–Cold War Era*, ed. Jorge I. Domínguez, 151–66. Pittsburgh, PA: University of Pittsburgh Press.

Romo, Rafael. 2011. "Uruguayan Peacekeepers in Haiti Investigated for Alleged Assault." CNN World, September 4. http://articles.cnn.com/2011-09-04/world/haiti.peacekeepers..assault_1_haiti-cell-phone-video-investigation?_s=PM:WORLD.

Rosales, Jorge W. 2007. "Uruguay: Meeting the Challenges of Modern Peacekeeping Operations." In *Capacity Building for Peacebuilding: The Case of Haiti*, ed. John T. Fishel and Andrés Sáenz, 131–49. Washington, DC: National Defense University Press.

Rosenberg, Joel. 2003. "Uruguayos en el infierno. Misión imposible: Mantener la paz en el Congo." *El País*, July 5. http://www.elpais.com.uy/Especiales/uruguayos_congo/1.asp.

Rouquié, Alain. 1978. *The Military and the State in Latin America*, transl. Paul E. Sigmund. Berkeley: University of California Press.

Ruppenthal, Tailon. 2007. *Um Soldado Brasileiro no Haiti*. São Paulo, Brazil: Globo.

Saín, Marcelo Fabián. 1999. "Seguridad regional, defensa nacional y relaciones cívico-militares en Argentina." In *Argentina, Brasil y Chile: Integración y seguridad*, ed. Francisco Rojas Aravena, 125–62. Santiago: FLACSO.

Sambanis, Nicholas. 1999. "The UN Operation in Cyprus: A New Look at the Peacekeeping-Peacemaking Relationship." *International Peacekeeping* 6 (1): 79–108.

Sánchez, Alex. 2008. "The South American Defense Council, UNASUR, the Latin American Military and the Region's Political Process." Council of Hemispheric Affairs, Washington, DC. http://www.coha.org/the-south-american-defense-council-unasur-the-latin-american-military-and-the-region%E2%80%99s-political-process/.

Sancinetti, Marcelo A. 1988. *Derechos humanos en la Argentina posdictatorial*. Buenos Aires: Lerner Editores Asociados.

Santos Cruz, Lt. Gen. Carlos Alberto dos. 2009. "Cooperation between Civilians and the Military–UN Level." Brief presented at the Workshop on Revisiting Borders Between Civilians and Military: Security and Development in Post-Conflict Situations in United Nations Peace Operations, Viva Rio, Rio de Janeiro, August 3.

Segal, David, and Mady Wechsler Segal. 1993. *Peacekeepers and Their Wives: American Participation in the Multinational Force of Observers*. Westport, CT: Greenwood Press.

Segal, David, and Ronald B. Tiggle. 1997. "Attitudes of Citizen-Soldier toward Military Missions in the Post–Cold War World." *Armed Forces and Society* 23 (3): 373–90.

Seitenfus, Ricardo. 2008. "De Suez ao Haiti: A Participação Brasileira nas Operações de Paz." In *Brazil e a ONU*, 39–58. Brasilia: Fundação Alexandre de Gusmã e Ministério das Relações Exteriores.

Sena Cardoso, Alfonso José. 1998. *O Brasil nas Operações de Paz das Nações* Unidas. Brasilia: Instituto Rio Branco-Fundação Alexandre de Gusmão-Centro de Estudos Estratégicos.

Serbin, Andrés, ed. 2007. *Paz, conflict y sociedad civil en América Latina y el Caribe.* Buenos Aires: CRIES.

Simmons, Beth A., and Zachary Elkins. 2003. "Globalization and Policy Diffusion: Explaining Three Decades of Liberalization." In *Governance in a Global Economy: Political Authority in Transition*, ed. Miles Kahler and David A. Lake, 275–304. Princeton, NJ: Princeton University Press.

Sims, Calvin. 1997. "U.S. Alliance Brings Prestige to Argentines." *New York Times*, October 20, A9.

Soares, Marcelo, and Chris Kraul. 2010. "Brazil Troops to Stay in Rio Slum after Backing Anti-gang Assault." *Los Angeles Times*, December 1. http://articles.latimes .com/2010/dec/01/world/la-fg-brazil-riots-20101201.

Soares Alsina, João Paulo, Jr. 2009. "O poder militar como instrumento da política externa brasileira contemporãnea." *Revista Brasileira de Política Internacional* 52 (2): 173–91.

Soares de Lima, Maria Regina. 1996. "Brazil's Response to the New Regionalism." In *Foreign Policy and Regionalism in the Americas*, ed. Gordon Mace and Jean-Philippe Thérien, 137–58. Boulder, CO: Lynne Rienner.

———. 2000. "Instituiçôes Democráticas e Política Exterior." *Contexto Internacional* 22 (2): 265–303.

Socín, Carlos, and Alaciel Campos Dugone. 1999. "El corazón del entrenamiento para participar en operaciones para el mantenimiento de la paz." *Military Review Hispano-American* 79 (6): 55–61.

Solingen, Etel. 1998. *Regional Orders at Century's Dawn: Global and Domestic Influences on Grand Strategy.* Princeton, NJ: Princeton University Press.

———. 2008. *Nuclear Logics: Contrasting Paths in East Asia and the Middle East.* Princeton, NJ: Princeton University Press.

Sorensen, David. 1992. "Soldiers, States, and Systems: Civil-Military Relations in the Post–Cold War World." Paper presented at the Mershon Center Conference on Civil-Military Relations, Ohio State University, Columbus, December 4–5.

Sotomayor, Arturo C. 2004. "Civil-Military Affairs and Security Institutions in the Southern Cone: The Sources of Argentine-Brazilian Nuclear Cooperation." *Latin American Politics and Society* 46 (4): 29–61.

———. 2010a. "Why Some States Participate in UN Peace Missions while Others Do Not." *Security Studies* 19 (1): 160–95.

———. 2010b. "Peacekeeping Effects in South America: Common Experiences and Divergent Effects on Civil-Military Relations." *International Peacekeeping* 17 (5) 629–43.

———. 2013. "Militarization in Mexico and Its Implications." In *The State and Security in Mexico: Transformation and Crisis in Regional Perspective*, ed. Brian Bow and Arturo Santa-Cruz, 42–60. New York: Routledge.

Souza, Amaury de. 2009. *A Agenda Internacional do Brasil.* Rio de Janeiro: Campus Elsevier.

Stepan, Alfred. 1971. *The Military in Politics: Changing Patterns in Brazil*. Princeton, NJ: Princeton University Press.

———. 1973. "The New Professionalism of Internal Warfare and Military Role Expansion." In *Authoritarian Brazil: Origins, Policies, and Futur*, ed. Alfred Stepan, 47–65. New Haven, CT: Yale University Press.

———. 1988a. *Rethinking Military Politics: Brazil and the Southern Cone*. Princeton, NJ: Princeton University Press.

———. 1988b. "State Power and the Strength of Civil Society in the Southern Cone of Latin America." In *Bringing the State Back In*, ed. Peter Evans, Dietrich Rueschemeyer, and Theda Skocpol, 317–43. Cambridge: Cambridge University Press.

Stryker, Sheldon, and Anne Statham. 1985. "Symbolic Interaction and Role Theory." In *The Handbook of Social Psychology*, vol. 1, ed. G. Lindzey and E. Aronson, 311–78. New York: Random House.

Sucena do Carmo, Antonio Eleuterio. 1998. "CIGS: Centro de Instrução de Guerra na Selva." *Revista do Exercito Brasileiro* 135 (3): 29–35.

Sussumu Fujita, Edmundo. 1996. "O Brasil e o Conselho de Segurança: Notas Sobre Uma Década de Transição, 1985–1995." *Parcerias Estratégicas* 2 (December): 95–119.

Taylor, Paul. 1997. "The British Compared with Brazilian Policies Regarding the Reform of the International Political System, with Particular Reference to the United Nations." Paper presented at the Seminario Brasil-Reino Unido, Rio de Janeiro, September 18–19.

Thakur, Ramesh, and Albrecht Schnabel. 2001. "Cascading Generations of Peacekeeping: Across the Mogadishu Line to Kosovo and Timor." In *United Nations Peacekeeping Operations: Ad Hoc Missions, Permanent Engagement*, ed. Ramesh Thakur and Albrecht Schnabel, 3–25. New York: United Nations University Press.

Thucydides. 2005. "The Melian Dialogue." In *Conflict after the Cold War: Arguments on Causes of War and Peace*, ed. Richard K. Betts, 55–59. New York: Pearson-Longman.

Tibiletti, Luis. 2004. "Haití en diez aciertos." Página 12, June 16. http://www.lpp -buenosaires.net/internacional/documentos/Politica/El%20conflicto%20en %20Hait%C3%AD/Hait%C3%AD%20en%20diez%20aciertos.htm.

Tokatlian, Juan Gabriel. 2004. "El desacierto de enviar tropas a Haití." Página 12, June 13. http://www.lpp-buenosaires.net/internacional/documentos/Politica/El%20con flicto%20en%20Hait%C3%AD/El%20desacierto%20de%20enviar%20tropas%20a %20Hait%C3%AD.htm.

Trenchard, Tommy. 2009. "UN Guns Impose Uneasy Peace at Haiti-Dominican Border." *Dominican Today*, December 4. http://www.dominicantoday.com/dr/local/2009 /12/4/34093/UN-guns-impose-uneasy-peace-at-Haiti-Dominican-border.

Trinkunas, Harold A. 2005. *Crafting Civilian Control of the Military in Venezuela: A Comparative Perspective*. Chapel Hill: University of North Carolina Press.

Tulchin, Joseph S. 1988. "Continuity and Change in Argentine Foreign Policy." In *Argentina: The Challenges of Modernization*, ed. Joseph S. Tulchin and Allison M. Garland, 163–97. Wilmington, DE: Scholarly Resources.

Ubiraci, Sennes Ricardo. 2000. "Intermediate Countries and the Multilateral Arenas: Brazil in the General Assembly and UN Security Council between 1980–1995." In *Paths to Power: Foreign Policy Strategies of Intermediate States, Working Paper 224*, ed. Andrew Hurrell, 82–117. Washington, DC: Woodrow Wilson International Center for Scholars.

Ulery, Eduardo. 2005. "The Uruguayan Armed Forces and the Challenge of 21st Century Peacekeeping." MA diss., Department of National Security Affairs, Naval Postgraduate School, Monterey, CA.

UN. United Nations. 1945. *Charter of the United Nations and Stature of the International Court of Justice.* New York: Department of Public Information.

UNDPKO. UN Department of Peacekeeping Operations. 2000. *Angola: UNAVEM II, Background Conditions.* New York: United Nations. http://www.un.org/Depts/DPKO /Missions/Unavem2/UnavemIIB.htm.

———. 2003. *Iraq/Kuwait: UNIKOM, Facts and Figures.* New York: United Nations. http://www.un.org/en/peacekeeping/missions/past/unikom/facts.html.

———. 2008. *United Nations Peacekeeping Operations: Principles and Guidelines.* New York: United Nations. http://pbpu.unlb.org/pbps/Library/Capstone_Doctrine _ENG.pdf.

———. 2010a. "Peacekeeping Fact Sheet Archives 2004–2010." United Nations, New York. http://www.un.org/en/peacekeeping/resources/statistics/factsheet _archive.shtml.

———. 2010b. "Troop and Police Contributions Archive: Missions Detailed by Country." United Nations, New York. http://www.un.org/en/peacekeeping/resources /statistics/contributors_archive.shtml.

———. 2010c. "Troop and Police Contributions Archive: Contributions by Country." United Nations, New York. http://www.un.org/en/peacekeeping/resources/stati stics/contributors_archive.shtml.

———. 2010d. "Cholera Outbreak in Haiti." United Nations, New York. http://www .un.org/en/peacekeeping/missions/minustah/emergency.shtml.

———. 2011. "Contributors to United Nations Peacekeeping Operations: Monthly Summary of Contributions (Police, UN Military Experts on Mission and Troops." United Nations, New York. http://www.un.org/en/peacekeeping/contributors/2011 /dec11_1.pdf.

———. 2012a. "Haiti: Background." United Nations, New York. http://www.un.org/en /peacekeeping/missions/past/unmihbackgr2.html.

———. 2012b. "MINUSTAH Background." United Nations, New York. http://www .un.org/en/peacekeeping/missions/minustah/background.shtml.

UN Department of Safety and Security. 2011. "Sexual Abuse Allegations Decline against UN Peacekeepers in DR Congo and Liberia." UN News Centre, July 27. www.un.org/apps/news/story.asp?NewsID=39164#.UPtIcfLzjTo.

UNGA. UN General Assembly. 2009. "UNGA Adopts Peacekeeping Budget of Nearly $7.8 Billion for Period 1 Jul 2009 to 20 Jun 2010." Reliefweb, June 30. www.reliefweb .int/rw/rwb.nsf/db900SID/MINE-7TJ4YC?OpenDocument.

UN Integrated Regional Information Network. 2003. "Seven UN Uruguayan Peacekeepers Probed for Stealing Sacred Objects in Democratic Republic of Congo." United Nations, New York. September 12. http://www.lexisnexis.com.libproxy.nps .edu/lnacui2api/api/version1/getDocCui?oc=00240&hl=t&hns=t&hnsd=f& perma=true&lni=49HN-0K70-00KJ-D4XJ&hv=t&csi=10962&hgn=t& secondRedirectIndicator=true.

Urgente 24. 2011. "Inseguridad: Uruguay pone militares en funciones policíacas." February 16. http://www.urgente24.com/4266-uruguay-pone-militares-en-funciones -policiacas.

U.S. Arms Control and Disarmament Agency. 2000. *World Military Expenditures and Arms Transfers, 1999–2000.* Washington, DC: U.S. Department of State, Bureau of Verification and Compliance. www.fas.org/asmp/profiles/wmeat/WMEAT99-00/WMEAT99-00.pdf.

U.S. State Department. 2009. "Haiti 2009 International Narcotic Strategic Report." Washington, DC. http://haitipolicy.org/content/4148.htm.

Vargas Garcia, Eugênio. 1994. "A candidatura do Brasil a um assento permanente no Conselho da Liga das Nações." *Revista Brasileira de Política Internacional* 37 (1): 5–23.

Vassoler-Froelich, Ivani. 2007. "A Self-Centered or an Altruistic International Conflict Mediator: The Determinants of Brazil's Decision to Participate in the United Nations Peacekeeping Mission in Haiti." Paper presented at the International Studies Association Conference, Chicago, IL, February 28 to March 3.

Walter, Barbara. 2002. *Committing to Peace: The Successful Settlement of Civil Wars.* Princeton, NJ: Princeton University Press.

*Washington Post.* 2003. "Menem Cleared of Arms Smuggling." *Washington Post,* August 29, A17.

Watson, Cynthia A. 2005. "Argentina." In *The Politics of Peacekeeping in the Post–Cold War Era,* ed. David S. Sorenson and Pia Christina Wood, 52–67. London: Frank Cass.

Weinberger, Naomi. 2002. "Civil-Military Coordination in Peacebuilding: The Challenge in Afghanistan." *Journal of International Affairs* 55 (2): 245–74.

Weiner, Tim, and Lydia Polgree. 2004. "The Aristide Resignation: The Turmoil; Haitian Rebels Enter Capital; Aristide Bitter." *New York Times,* March 2. http://www.nytimes.com/2004/03/02/world/aristide-resignation-turmoil-haitian-rebels-enter-capital-aristide-bitter.html?pagewanted=all&src=pm%20www.nytimes.com/2004/08/01/world/brazil-is-leading-a-largely-south-american-mission-to-haiti.html.

Welch, Claude E., Jr., ed. 1976. *Civilian Control of the Military: Theory and Cases from Developing Countries.* Albany: State University of New York.

Werner, Suzanne, and Amy Yuen. 2005. "Making and Keeping the Peace." *International Organization* 59 (2): 261–92.

Whitehead, Laurence, ed. 1996. *The International Dimensions of Democratization: Europe and the Americas.* New York: Oxford University Press.

Williams, Michael C. 1998. "Civil-Military Relations and Peacekeeping." Adelphi Paper 321. International Institute of Strategic Studies, London.

Worboys, Katherine J. 2007. "The Traumatic Journey from Dictatorship to Democracy: Peacekeeping Operations and Civil-Military Relations in Argentina, 1989–1999." *Armed Forces and Society* 33 (2): 158–59.

Yapp, Robin. 2011. "Uruguayan Peacekeepers Investigated over Haiti Sexual Assault." *Telegraph,* September 5. http://www.telegraph.co.uk/news/worldnews/centralamericaandthecaribbean/haiti/8742878/Uruguayan-peacekeepers-investigated-over-Haiti-sexual-assault.html.

Zagorcheva, Dessie. 2001/2002. "Correspondence: NATO and Democracy." *International Security* 26 (3): 227–30.

Zagorski, Paul W. 1994. "Civil-Military Relations and Argentine Democracy: The Armed Forces under the Menem Administration." *Armed Forces and Society* 20 (3): 423–37.

Zavarucha, Jorge. 1988. "The 1988 Brazilian Constitution and Its Authoritarian Legacy: Formalizing Democracy." *Journal of Third World Studies* 15 (1): 105–24.

———. 2000. "Fragile Democracy and the Militarization of Public Safety in Brazil." *Latin American Perspectives* 27 (3): 8–31.

———. 2003. "The 'Guaranteeing Law and Order Doctrine' and the Increased Role of the Brazilian Army in Activities of Public Security." *Nueva Sociedad* 213 (1): 1–31.

———. 2006. "La Fragilidad del Ministerio de Defensa Brasileño." In *Operaciones Conjuntas: Civiles y Militares en la Política de Defensa*, ed. José Huerta et al., 51–80. Lima: Serie Democracia y Fuerza Armada.

Zawels, Estanislao. 1998. "Medio Siglo de las Operaciones de Mantenimiento de la Paz de las Naciones Unidas, 1948–1998." *Boletín del Instituto de Seguridad Internacional y Asuntos Estratégicos* 1 (3): 1–2.

———. 1999. "Lecciones aprendidas de la participación Argentina en las misiones de paz." *Boletín del Instituto de Seguridad Internacional y Asuntos Estratégicos* 1 (2): 8–9.

———. 2000. *Hacia un sistema de seguridad colectiva para el siglo XX: El Consejo de Seguridad de la ONU en la década de los 90.* Buenos Aires: Nuevohacer-Grupo Editorial Lationamericano.

Zisk, Kimberly Marten. 1993. *Engaging the Enemy: Organization Theory and the Soviet Military Innovation, 1955–1991.* Princeton, NJ: Princeton University Press.

Zurbriggen, Cristina. 2005. "Política exterior, defensa y las operaciones de paz: Una estrategia coherente? El caso de Uruguay." *Revista Fuerzas Armadas y Sociedad* 19 (1): 85–109.

# Index

Note: Page numbers in *italics* indicate figures and tables.